DEVELOPMENT
of
INSURANCE
in
MOZAMBIQUE

T0275019

DEVELOPMENT
of
INSURANCE
in
MOZAMBIQUE

ISRAEL MUCHENA

TATE PUBLISHING
AND ENTERPRISES, LLC

Published by Tate Publishing & Enterprises, LLC
127 E. Trade Center Terrace | Mustang, Oklahoma 73064 USA
1.888.361.9473 | www.tatepublishing.com

Tate Publishing is committed to excellence in the publishing industry. The company reflects the philosophy established by the founders, based on Psalm 68:11,
"The Lord gave the word and great was the company of those who published it."

Book design copyright © 2016 by Tate Publishing, LLC. All rights reserved.
Cover design by Bill Francis Peralta
Interior design by Jomar Ouano

Published in the United States of America

ISBN: 978-1-68207-251-6
Business & Economics / Insurance
15.11.26

ACKNOWLEDGMENTS

First and foremost, I would like to thank Firda, Ishmael, Nyasha, Chenai, Simba, Shona and other members of the Muchena family, relatives and friends for their inspiration and support during the period of research and writing of this book. I would like to also acknowledge the guidance that I received from Simão Nhambi, the Managing Editor of the African Journal of Governance & Development. I would like to also acknowledge the contribution of Mr. Simon Cartwright that assisted with a review of the final proof.

Furthermore, I would like to thank Henri Mittermayer and all members of staff at Hollard Moçambique Companhia de Seguros for sharing insights with me during the period that I was working and living in Maputo. I would like to also thank the African Management Services Company (AMSCO) for facilitating my accreditation in Mozambique. I would like to also acknowledge all the people in the insurance market and the insurance regulatory authority with whom I was able to share ideas on the development of the insurance market of Mozambique.

In addition, I would like to thank Professor Richard Haines and members of staff in the Development Studies Group at the Nelson Mandela Metropolitan University in

South Africa. They gave me an opportunity to learn about theories, policies and practice of development. I have used some of the knowledge and research tools gained from these studies to connect our concerns in the insurance sector to the broad questions about human and economic development.

I also had opportunities to present some of the ideas covered in this book in conferences on insurance and microinsurance in Abuja, Colombo, Harare, Khartoum, Lagos, Lusaka, Kigali, Maputo and Mauritius. I would like to thank the following organisations that facilitated my participation in these events: the African Insurance Organisation (AIO); the German Development Agency GIZ; the International Labour Organisation (ILO); the International Finance Corporation (IFC); FinMark Trust; Enhancing Financial Innovation & Access (EFInA); the Centre for Financial Regulation and Inclusion (Cenfri); the Microinsurance Network and the Organisation for Eastern and Southern Africa Insurers (OESAI).

Finally, I would like to thank the most important person in this book. You the reader. You and I, WE are going to look at a number of new and old ideas covered in this book. We can also continue our discussions beyond the boundary of this book and, if we agree on the essence of any of the issues that we shall discuss, we could also take the next steps of starting to explore our options for addressing our situation.

LIST OF TABLES

LIST OF FIGURES

LIST OF APPENDICES

CONTENTS

FOREWORD

When my special friend and colleague, Israel Muchena, asked me to write a foreword for this book, I was naturally honored and humbled. Our relationship goes back to 1997. At the time, Israel was with the Munich Re and I was struggling to establish what was arguably the first private insurance licence in Mozambique, following the opening up of the 'free' market in the early 1990's.

I asked Israel to join me and he took up the challenge, without hesitation. A challenge that at the time was viewed by most industry colleagues with reserved scepticism. How was this the right career move? Most at the time would describe the move from the dynamic South African market to Mozambique as 'unreasonable'. Essentially it was a decision that challenged convention. But herein lies Israel's spirit of innovation and vision. The ability to imagine what others cannot and the willingness to challenge preconceptions.

The playwright George Bernard Shaw aptly wrote: 'The reasonable man adapts himself to the world: the unreasonable one persists in trying to adapt the world to himself. Therefore all progress depends on the unreasonable man.'

In 2000, circumstance allowed Israel and I, to start Hollard Mozambique. Enabled by another of the industry's most renowned innovators – Miles Japhet. At the time Miles was Vice Chairman of Hollard Insurance Company of South Africa. It was a time when an African Strategy was not even on the horizon for Hollard. Because Miles believed in what he saw of our pioneering initiatives in Mozambique, he went against conventional wisdom at that time and convinced the shareholders of Hollard to invest in Mozambique. As chairman of Hollard Mozambique, Miles became an important, mentor and friend to both Israel and I.

I recall that our start up financial capacity was immediately tested soon after commencement of the company in 2001, following the occurrence of a severe tropical storm which, ironically, was named Cyclone Japhet. You can imagine the jokes from some colleagues given the co-incidence of the name.

Following Cyclone Japhet, there have been other events of severe tropical storms and flooding seriously affecting people, infrastructure and the economy of Mozambique, like in the past. The key question that is posed in this book is should society continue to wait until occurrence of other major catastrophic risks and then pray for divine intervention and launch urgent pleas for relief and assistance after the events, as we have witnessed in the past? Is that all we can do? Placing aside such reactive tactics, the science of risk management proposes a more systematic approach to the treatment of risks that threaten our welfare.

Insurance is one of the options for dealing with certain types of risks. In this book Israel presents introductory information on risk management and the different types of insurance that can be arranged in certain situations. In writing this book, Israel is attempting to realign where and how the Insurance Industry in Mozambique is evolving. The book specifically challenges the practitioners in the Mozambican industry to look beyond market practices and challenge convention.

We did not hesitate to support and sponsor the publication of this book given the valuable contribution that we believe it could make in the development of insurance in Mozambique.

As part of our corporate goals of supporting local development initiatives, we are also concerned about training and development of local skills in our sector. Up to now, our market has been relying mainly on course material from training institutes in South Africa and Zimbabwe. The tuition material of the courses from these institutions provides useful knowledge on principles and practice of insurance, in general. However, such courses tend to provide virtually no insights on the local insurance market, our regulatory framework and the context within which we are operating. We believe that this book is a key preliminary step in the process of publication of material that speaks about the local market situation.

Furthermore, Israel did not limit himself to only describing the past and present situation of the insurance market. He has also identified some of the key development trends that are likely to affect our sector in the future. In the final chapter of the book, there is an extensive range of recommendations drawn from observations throughout the book. We earnestly hope that these insights will be used to stimulate debate on the development policy of our insurance sector going forward.

The content of this book displays genuine 'Israel style' of consistent growth and research for academic and technical excellence.

It goes without saying that Israel holds a very special place in all of our hearts, the 'pocket rocket professor' of the Mozambican insurance industry who has made a significant contribution to both our business and the market in general.

Congratulations Israel! We are very proud to be associated with you, and to be sponsoring the publication of your 1st Edition of '*The Development of Insurance in Mozambique*'.

Henri Mittermayer
Managing Director
Hollard Moçambique

PREFACE

I started the process of writing of this book when I prepared an article on the '*The Mozambican insurance market*' for a publication of the African Reinsurance Corporation called The African Reinsurer (pages 32 to 35 of volume number 26 of 2012). Following the numerous inquiries that I received about our market, I saw an opportunity to expand this first article into some form of basic reference book that is aimed at presenting and discussing as broadly as possible the development of the insurance market of Mozambique. I was able to expand material covered in that first article into the 15 chapters in this book.

Furthermore, I had also observed that there is a very limited range of current publications on insurance in Mozambique. For purposes of formal training and development of insurance personnel, the market relies on manuals and courses from training institutions in neighbouring countries. As a key consequence of this lack of local insurance training facilities and manuals, only a few people have at least the basic professional qualification in insurance known as the **Certificate of Proficiency** (**COP**). This certificate can be attained through a correspondence course with either the **Insurance Institute of South Africa**

(IISA) or the **Insurance Institute of Zimbabwe (IIZ)**. The material covered in their training manuals focuses on the local situation of the insurance markets in the countries where they are located. The courses are also conducted in English, the official language in those territories.

Besides the two courses noted above, there are also optional courses in Portugal that are conducted in Portuguese, which is also the official language in Mozambique. However, while the different courses in the region and overseas may provide useful knowledge on universal concepts of insurance, their manuals do not contain any references to local conditions of doing insurance business here. I believe that, by relying only on such foreign courses, local candidates are deprived of an opportunity to learn about many of the interesting developments in this insurance market in the last four decades since independence. I have tried to reflect some of these developments in this book.

Furthermore, I had observed that most insurance manuals from the professional insurance training institutions have tended to focus dogmatically on traditional concepts of insurance. In my research in preparation for the writing of this book, I found that there is little or no reference to emerging concepts such as **Plain Language**, **Financial Inclusion**, **Microinsurance**, **Takaful**, **Treating Customers Fairly**, **Weather Index Insurance**, **Digital Marketing** and **Bancassurance**. In this book, I have provided introductory information on some of these new concepts besides traditional principles and practice of insurance.

Finally, I also had plans to have this book published in both Portuguese and English. I believe that it is vital for local practitioners of insurance to learn about basic fundamentals of insurance in Portuguese, as the official language in Mozambique. I believe that language is one of the key factors contributing to low enrolments, poor pass rates and a high number of drop-outs of local candidates in the courses of the IISA and IIZ. However, I also intend to publish an English version of the book because this language has become a useful alternative for doing business here. Mozambique is completely surrounded by countries that use English as the principal language for business. Furthermore, English also plays a critical role in insurance worldwide as the main language for handling transactions with key international financial markets.

CHAPTER 1

History of Development of Insurance

We shall begin our review of the history of development of insurance by looking at ancient origins of insurance-related practices among traders in China. Then, we shall look at the earliest references of written rules relating to insurance in ancient Iranian kingdoms followed by developments of insurance through guilds in Mesopotamia and then the development of early markets in Europe. Thereafter, we shall discuss the introduction of insurance in African countries including Mozambique during the period of colonisation and identify key stages of development of the local insurance market.

1. ANCIENT ORIGINS OF INSURANCE

1.1. Risk sharing systems in China

The first recorded history of basic insurance practice can be traced back to customs of Chinese merchants from as far back as 3000 B.C. (Vaughan, 1992: 63 and Irukwu, 1998:7). According to these records, these merchants developed an arrangement which allowed them to share burdens of misfortunes in their business. The main business activity of these merchants was transportation of merchandise by boats. During the course of shipment of their cargo from one point to another, the merchants faced the danger of losing their cargo as a result of accidents in 'treacherous rapids' along the rivers that were part of their means of transportation.

In order to protect themselves from financial ruin that could be caused by loss of their merchandise, the traders adopted a practice of sharing risk. They would distribute commodities of each merchant in many boats in order to limit the amount that could be lost by any one of them in case any one of the boats would be lost during the journey. In such an arrangement, you could look at what they were doing as a practical application of the proverb—'not putting all your eggs in one basket'. This mechanism of sharing risk created a situation where, if one of their boats was lost, all the members of the group would suffer only a small loss for part of their cargo on that boat affected by the misfortune. The principal underlying concept in this ancient practice of spreading of costs of losses of a few among many people remains one of the key pillars of universal insurance business models up to now.

1.2. Earliest recording of an insurance agreement

Then, the next key milestone in the history of the development of insurance occurred in 2000 B.C. There was the first formal recording of an insurance agreement as part of an ancient merchant law. This law, which is viewed as one of the oldest forms of written law, is known as the '**Hammurabi Code**' (Vaughan, 1992: 63). This ancient law was followed by Mediterranean merchants of the Babylonian kingdom in ancient Mesopotamia. As part of key business practices of the period, businessmen would hire hawkers or traders to sell their commodities on their behalf in the kingdom and neighbouring territories. In order to secure loans to do their business, these hawkers, known as '**darmatha**', would 'pledge' their belongings including 'property, wife and children.' Unfortunately, many of the traders would lose their possessions as a result of a growing problem of robberies in their trade routes. Following a revolt of traders that had suffered many losses, the businessmen agreed to have what can be viewed as the first form of an 'insurance contract', as part of the ancient legal system of the Code (Mehr and Cammack, 1972: 744).

1.3. Ancient forms of risk transfer

As part of the agreements covered under the ancient law described above, it was agreed that, if traders borrowed money for their commodities, the lender could charge the concerned traders an additional amount in exchange for an agreement that the loan would be cancelled if any of the covered shipments did not reach their destination due to some catastrophe (Irukwu 1998: 6). As a result of this rule of the code, risk could be transferred from a trader to a money-lender. This arrangement was further developed by Phoenician and Greek traders into agreements where ships or cargo were pledged as security for loans from money-lenders. These are part of what are known as **bottomry contracts** (Mehr and Cammack, 1972: 744).

Please note that the process discussed above where risks are transferred from one party to another has continued to be one of the key defining features of modern insurance business. In this case, by risk we are referring to the prospect that something of interest could be damaged or lost as a result of causes beyond our control. We shall define and discuss further the concept of risk and how we can try to handle it later in this book.

1.4. Early forms of mutual fund arrangements

The next key milestone was achieved through practices of insurance-related activities in guild systems of the dark and middle ages. In that period, young men would join societies or guilds through which they would be trained by a master in order to become craftsmen. In exchange for regular contributions, the members of the guild would enjoy benefits such as a form of funeral coverage. In the same period, rulers of ancient Iranian kingdoms, known as the '**Achaemenian monarchs**' were practicing basic types of **mutual fund arrangements**. In this tradition, at the beginning of each year, the subjects would make donations to the rulers who would assist them in case of misfortunes. We should note that in the earliest forms of insurance described above, the activity of assuming risk was not an autonomous business (Waty, 2007: 8).

Before moving to the next stage of development, we should note that the concept of a mutual fund described above has continued to co-exist along with insurers set up in the form of for-profit type of business entities. Contrary to the model of a typical for-profit business entity which is owned by a certain set of shareholders, in a mutual insurance company, the insured members are the owners of the business entity. As we shall discuss later, the insurance legislation in Mozambique also permits formation of mutual insurers. At this stage, we do not yet have any mutual insurance company operating in our market.

2. MEDIEVAL AND EARLY MODERN DEVELOPMENTS

2.1. Separate insurance agreements

As part of the next stage of development of insurance, there emerged in Genoa in the fourteenth century the first form of insurance contracts as separate agreements not combined together with other business. This development of separate insurance agreements has also remained a key feature of insurance as we practice it nowadays. There have been recent innovations where entities such as banks try to combine insurance contracts with other types of agreements such as lending agreements. This is part of a process known as **bundling**. However, as part of key emerging trends that we shall discuss later, there is growing pressure on financial institutions in some insurance markets to keep separate types of transactions as separate agreements that are transparently disclosed to the client. Part of the reason for this emerging rule is to prevent a process called **conditional selling**. This is a situation where consumers might be forced to also accept certain types of services like insurance that might not be from preferred insurers or at acceptable costs that are presented as a package deal combined together with what they might desperately need such as a loan.

2.2. Roots of Probability Theory

Then, in the seventeenth century there was a development of a key mathematical concept which would be of benefit to society, in general, and insurance business, in particular. According to Bernstein (1996: 3), Blaise Pascal and Pierre de Fermat developed the concept of probability from the ancient pastime of gambling. Risk, which is a key element of insurance, is calculated on the mathematical basis of probability (IISA, 2011A: 127 and Hafeman, 2009: 2). If we look at some of the technical terms used today in insurance, we can identify a few keys words that originated from gambling, the basis on which probability was developed. For instance, the word 'risk', which is used extensively in insurance business, was derived from the early Italian word *riscare*, which means 'to dare'. Hazard, which is the other word used to refer to situations of risk covered by insurance, came from the Arabic word for dice— *al zahr* (Bernstein, 1996: 3).

Furthermore, on the basis of development of the theory of probability, another key milestone was achieved in the same period with the construction of the first '**Mortality Table**' (Ferreira, 1966: 123). This was a result of preliminary work from a study of demography of London by John Graunt and of the German town of Breslau by Caspar Neumann. Edmond Halley used this material to produce a Mortality Table which became a key reference for purposes of calculating premium for life insurance (Ciecka, 2008: 65). As we shall discuss later in this book, this practice of using mortality tables has been maintained in life insurance business up to today. Our key challenge in Mozambique is that we have not yet found an equivalent of Edmond Halley to help us construct our own tables that are based on local mortality statistics.

2.3. Lloyd's of London

Following the developments outlined above, the next stage of development in insurance business was the emergence of a marine insurance market in London. Towards the end of the seventeenth century, with growing trade between European empires and the New World that they were exploring, there was an increase of demand for marine insurance. Then, there was the beginning of what is now universally defined by insurance practitioners as the first insurance market. This started from the late 1680s, in a coffee shop in London owned by a Mr. Edward Lloyd. The shop became a popular meeting place for, on one hand, people wanting to insure ships and cargo, and on the other hand, those that wanted to provide such insurance. From that period up to today, this place has grown into the principal international market for financial and technical capacity to support insurance business worldwide. It is now formally known as the **Lloyd's of London**[1].

2.4. Emergence of the Practice of Underwriting

Before looking at the following key milestone of emergence of other types of insurance, we should briefly review something else which had started with the emergence of the marine insurance market as described above. In order to provide the service of insurance, the people involved in this type of activity would, at first, negotiate and agree on terms and conditions of insurance with the merchants. After drafting the respective written agreement, the person representing the insurer that would be assuming the responsibilities to 'make good' losses suffered by the merchants would sign underneath the written contract as part of the process of proof of insurance cover. This process of signing underneath the agreement would mark the beginning of the profession in insurance business known as **underwriting**. The person signing would be referred to as the **underwriter**. On most insurance policies there can be more than one underwriter assuming risk.

---

1. You may find more information on this market on their website: http://www.lloyds.com/

2.5. The Insurance Institute of London

Furthermore, the activity described above has developed from that period into a well-established formal profession, as we see it today. As one of the ways of gaining appropriate qualifications in this profession, nowadays, one can enrol for training to become a Chartered Insurance Practitioner. The principal institution responsible for development of this area, the **Insurance Institute of London**[2], was formed in 1907. There are also affiliated or associated institutes in many countries worldwide including Malawi, South Africa, Zambia and Zimbabwe, in southern Africa. We do not yet have an equivalent entity in Mozambique and in other countries in our region including Angola, Botswana, Lesotho, Namibia and Swaziland.

2.6. The Great Fire of London

Then, the next area of development after marine was that of property insurance. This became a key area of focus following the **Great Fire of London** of September 1666 (Mehr and Cammack, 1972: 748). The fire destroyed most of the city and left many people without homes (Borscheid, 2013: 43). Following this tragic event, Dr. Nicolas Barbon formed in 1680 the **Fire Office**, the first fire insurance company in the world (Vivian & Morgan, 2001: 21). There were three fire

---

2. You may obtain more information on their website: http://www.iilondon.co.uk/

offices in London by the end of the seventeenth century. Following this development of Fire insurance, the next key area of development was that of Life and Accidents insurance. We should now discuss key developments in Portugal, a country that would influence developments in Mozambique, amongst other countries in Africa.

2.7. Development of the Insurance Market in Portugal

Besides the developments in insurance business in England, as discussed above, we should also now look at some of the key historical milestones in Portugal. It is vital to look at this history because Portugal played a significant role in the expansion of insurance and other business activities to Mozambique and other territories in the era of the Portuguese colonial empire up to the time of the 'Carnation Revolution'[3] in Portugal in Abril 1975. Portugal has continued to influence development of insurance and other economic activities in Mozambique and other former colonies.

According to Luís Portugal (2007: 13), the first Portuguese insurance company, *Companhia Permanente de Seguros*, was formed in 1791. Following this development, eight other insurers were setup in the same decade followed

---

3. Known in Portuguese as 'Revolução dos Cravos'. The reference to carnations is due to the fact that it was a revolution with almost no violence against the uprising civilian population, as described on the following website: http://en.wikipedia.org/wiki/Carnation_Revolution#Decolonisation

by *Companhia de Seguros Bonança* at the beginning of the nineteenth century. From this period, only Bonança would survive the longest in some form following acquisition by another insurance company. By the end of the nineteenth century, this emerging Portuguese insurance market would play a key role with other European markets in the process of expansion of business into new overseas markets including Mozambique.

2.8. Global Expansion of Insurance

Following, the key stages of development of insurance noted above, we should now focus on emergence of formal insurance business in Africa, in general, and in Mozambique, in particular. At this stage, we have looked at the first two principal types of insurance. These policies were intended to cover the two 'most feared' perils of fire and marine, besides war (Borscheid, 2013: 23). The development of these two types of insurance would be followed by the emergence of many other types of insurance available today. We should now discuss how this Western model of insurance expanded to other territories including Africa during the following period of growth of global trade.

3. EARLY AFRICAN INSURANCE MARKETS

We should now look at the introduction of formal insurance business in Africa. We shall begin by looking at pre-existing traditional mechanisms that were used to cope with risk prior to the emergence of the formal insurance market. This traditional system has actually continued to exist and remains a viable option for the majority of local communities that are not covered by formal insurance markets. Then, we shall look at the first forms of entities that started doing insurance business in Africa.

3.1. Traditional Risk Sharing Systems

The history of the development of the insurance market of Mozambique is very similar to that of most countries in Africa. According to Irukwu (1998: 7), most African societies had basic forms of **traditional social risk sharing mechanisms** which had been in existence before the formation of the contemporary insurance sector. They include things such as basic forms of **burial societies** and traditional forms of savings and credit clubs. Examples of such traditional practices in Mozambique include 'Xitique', 'Tsima', 'Nssongo-nssongo', 'Kuphezana', 'Odjyana Ossókela' and 'Thôthôtho' (Quive: 2009). They may have different names in the different communities where they are practiced, but, they share many common characteristics. In general, they mainly serve the purpose of providing some form of traditional social protection mechanism.

From the traditional risk-sharing practices outlined above, we should briefly review **Xitique**, which is a more widely practiced activity especially in the southern parts of Mozambique. It is an informal scheme where members of a community agree to make certain contributions to a form of rotating fund for the benefit of that community. The system is based on trust and does not involve charging of interest rate like in the banking system. Besides systems similar to Xitique, other types of such traditional practices may be in the form of solidarity schemes where members of the community will assist each other if there is occurrence of key events such as funerals, births and ceremonies of marriage.

We should also note that, sadly, there has been very little research and development of financial products based on these traditional practices. However, it appears that some of the communities have continued to rely more on these traditional systems than the supposedly modern equivalent services of insurance and banking. This continued reliance on informal traditional systems instead of emerging financial systems is part of what our policy-makers are trying to address today through interventions like the **Financial Inclusion** development initiatives which we shall discuss further in this book.

3.2. Expansion of Formal Insurance to Africa

Following the development of insurance in Europe, as described in the previous section, there was an expansion of insurance to other territories during the period of growth of world trade in the middle of the nineteenth century. Given this background, early insurers in Africa depended on traders as both clients of insurance and agents through which insurance could be arranged with other interested parties (Borscheid, 2013: 33). Insurers preferred to nominate trading firms as agents because they were well acquainted with the risks of shipment and storage of cargo. Fire and Marine were the most critical types of insurance in these new territories.

The first agents to do business in southern Africa from 1806 were John Houghton and Alexander MacDonald who represented Phoenix Assurance Company of London through a 'power of attorney' (Vivian & Morgan, 2001: 21). According to this same reference, the first insurance company in South Africa was set up in 1831.

CONCLUSION

In this chapter we have looked at the origins of insurance and have identified some of the key milestones in the development of insurance business. We started our historical review in 3 000 B.C. with risk sharing systems among Chinese traders. Then, we looked at earliest recording of insurance and ancient forms of risk transfer in 2 000 B.C. Following this, we discussed key developments in the medieval and early modern period. There was the emergence of insurance contracts as separate agreements and the first development of the mathematical concept of probability. In this period we also witnessed the birth of key institutions—Lloyds of London insurance market and the Insurance Institute of London.

Furthermore, we have looked at how key insurance markets emerged in Europe and how insurance expanded to other parts of the world with increasing global trade in the nineteenth century. We have also discussed pre-existing risk sharing traditions in Mozambique, like other African countries. We have seen how general trading agents were the first types of entities that handled insurance business in Africa. We should now look at key milestones in the history of development of the formal insurance market in Mozambique.

REFERENCES

- Bernstein, P. L. (1996). *Against the gods: the remarkable story of risk*. New York: John Wiley.

- Borsheid, Peter (2013). Global insurance networks. in James, Harold (ed.). The value of risk: Swiss Re and the History of Reinsurance. New York: Oxford University Press. Pp. 23-105.

- Ciecka, James, E. (2008). *Edmond's Life Table and Its uses* in the Journal of Legal Economics. Volume 15, Number 1: pp. 65-74.

- Ferreira, Monteiro, Rolando (1966). *Como e seguro nasceu*. Seguros: Série Técnica. No. 114, December 1966. Pp. 121-123. Lisboa: Largo do Intendente Pina Manique.

- Hafeman, Michael (2009). *The Role of the Actuary in Insurance*. Primer Series on Insurance, Issue 4, May 2009. Washington: The World Bank.

- Irukwu, J.O. (1998). *Insurance Management in Africa*. Lagos: BIMA Publications

- IISA, 2011A: 127). *Principles of Short Term Insurance.* Insurance Institute of South Africa

- Mehr, Robet, I. and Cammack, Emerson (1972). Principles of Insurance. 5th Edition. Illinois: Richard D. Irwin, Inc.

- Portugal, Luís (2007). *Gestão de Seguros Não-Vida*. Lisboa: Instituto de Formação Actuarial

- Quive, Samuel (2009). *Sistemas formais e informais de protecção social e desenvolvimento em Moçambique*. Maputo: IESE—Instituto de Estudos Sociais e Económicos.

- Vaughan, Emmet, J. (1992) *Fundamentals of risk and insurance*. 6th Edition. New York: John Wiley & Sons Inc.

- Vivian, Robert, W. and Morgan, Jim (2001). *Morgan's History of the Insurance Institute Movement in South Africa*. Cape Town: Francolin Publishers.

- Waty, Teodoro, A. (2007). *Direito de Seguros*. Maputo: W&W Editora Lda

CHAPTER 2

EMERGENCE OF INSURANCE IN MOZAMBIQUE

Following the review of the history of development of early forms of insurance in Asia, Europe and other parts of the World, we shall now look at the emergence of insurance in Mozambique. We shall see how the development of the formal commercial insurance market that we have today started in the period of colonisation. Then we shall look at key shifts in the post-independence period from a monopoly insurance market starting in 1975 to the time of liberalization of the insurance market in the early 1990s. We shall discuss some of the key developments in the political-economy of Mozambique that paved the way for the key shifts in the development policy of the local insurance market.

1. KEY STAGES OF DEVELOPMENT OF INSURANCE IN MOZAMBIQUE

The underwriting of insurance business in Mozambique started in the beginning of the twentieth century as part of business connected to the colonial economy set up by the Portuguese. The development of a local formal insurance market was marked by the following three key historical epochs:

- 1943 to 1975—Private sector operators from mainly Portugal, Britain and other emerging international markets.

- 1977 to 1990—Centralized insurance **monopoly** in the post-independence period.

- 1992 to date—**Economic liberalisation** and opening up of the market.

The three phases defined above also marked critical turning-points in the development of the insurance market of Mozambique and the legislative environment. We should now discuss these three stages of development of insurance business in Mozambique.

2. EARLY DEVELOPMENT PHASE

Like in the rest of Africa, insurance agencies were the first forms of providers of insurance in Mozambique. Insurers from Portugal, South Africa and Britain saw opportunities of setting up insurance agencies in Mozambique following the construction in the 1890s of railway lines linking Transvaal to Lourenco Marques (now Maputo), in the south and Rhodesia (now Zimbabwe) to Beira, in the central parts of the country (Borscheid, 2013: 64). Like in other emerging African insurance markets, insurance was not the primary business of these agencies. They were mainly general trading companies that would also have insurance agency agreements with insurers domiciled abroad (Mucusse[1]). According to Irukwu (1998: 240), **Nauticus**, the first insurer in Mozambique was set up in 1943. During this period of the emergence of the Western model of insurance business in Mozambique, the local market relied on the regulatory framework of Portugal for legislation of insurance business.

2.1. First Forms of Supervision of insurance

From 1969 to the period of independence, the insurance regulatory authority was the **Inspecção de Crédito e Seguros** (Sigaúke, 2013: 3). This body had been formed as part of the colonial administration of Angola and Mozambique, which were considered then as overseas provinces of the Portuguese colonial regime. We can assess the development of the insurance market in this period through fairly informative insurance market reports that were published by this regulatory body. It appears to us that this exercise of compilation of market reports was one of the critical functions that was not maintained in the following transition phase after independence and has only recently been resumed. We have started seeing again in the last few years some market reports from the regulator albeit not yet formally published, as was the case in the past.

---

1. As noted in the website page: http://mucusse.no.comunidades.net/index.php?pagina=1731356382

2.2. Make-up of the early insurance market

According to the annual insurance regulator's report of 1971, the following were the companies operating in this market at its peak period:

Table 1–Insurance market in 1971
(Source IPCS Relatório Anual de 1971)

DOMICILE	OPERATORS
Mozambique	4 insurance companies • Lusitana • Mundial e Confiança de Moçambique • Nauticus • Tranquilidade
Portugal	14 insurance companies 1 reinsurer (Equidade)
Other territories	7 insurance companies: • African Life • Alliance Assurance • Assicurazioni Generali • Commercial Union of South Africa • Guardian Assurance • Sourh British • L'Urbaine

From the same report, it also appears that the operators were in the process of building extensive branch networks across the country. Like in other emerging economic activities, the insurance sector consisted mainly of privately owned companies that were supposed to compete for business in the market. This situation of private capital and an environment of competition were key aspects of what can be classified as a form of **capitalist economy**.

2.3. Early global connections

Furthermore, as can be noted from the profile of operators listed in Table 1, the market was fairly cosmopolitan. It appears that, from its early stages of development, our market had the unique characteristic of dual language practice of insurance in Portuguese as well as in English. This has remained a key distinguishing feature of Mozambique up to today compared to other Portuguese-speaking markets in Africa like Angola, Cape Verde and São Tomé that tend to rely a lot more on Portuguese for doing business. Part of the reason for this situation might have to do with the proximity of Mozambique to South Africa, which was, even in those early days, the largest economy by far in the region.

2.4. Exclusion of the indigenous population

Furthermore, we should also note that the insurance market from the early days, like all other economic activities, was focused on the new formal economy and not the majority indigenous population (Francisco, 2002: 27). In our opinion, it appears that this legacy of excluding the majority indigenous population has continued in some ways up to today. While in the past the exclusion might have been connected with the colonial orientation of the regimes then; today it is mainly an issue of a lack of access for the majority low-income population. We shall discuss later in this book current efforts to address this issue.

2.5. 'Wind of change'

The emergence of the colonial capitalist economy in Mozambique was part of a broader historical development following the contentious partitioning of Africa by European super-powers at the Berlin Conference of 1884. However, in the 1960s, the colonial empires emerging from this process began to fall apart as one of the key consequences of the Second World War. Harold Macmillan, a British Prime Minister at that time, noted looming changes as a consequence of a growing spirit of African nationalism. In a speech that he made during a tour of Africa in early 1960, it is reported that he described this movement as a 'wind of change' that was sweeping across the continent (Arnold, 2005: 48).

According to Shillington (2005: 383), 14 Francophone states attained their independence in 1960. This same year would become 'annus mirabilis' for Africa as, in addition to these developments in Francophone Africa, independence would also be achieved at the same time in the Belgian Congo, Somalia and Nigeria (Arnold, 2005: 45). As the stories of African countries gaining independence spread, there was an intensification of nationalism in countries that had not yet gained independence. As part of the outcome of the growing spirit of nationalism, wars of independence broke out in the 1960's in other African countries such as the Portuguese colonies—Angola, Guinea-Bissau and Mozambique.

The wars of independence in Portuguese colonies in Africa came to an end following the revolution in Portugal which was triggered by a military coup against a dictatorship of Portuguese rulers of that time. Following the collapse of the authoritarian Portuguese regime which was known as 'Estado Novo', the new revolutionary government decided to grant all the African colonies of Portugal their independence at the same time in 1975.

3. POST-INDEPENDENCE PHASE

Following the attainment of independence in Mozambique in 1975, the new government decided to apply Marxist-Leninist principles of a centrally planned economy. (Lalá and Ostheimer, 2003: 4) This new approach to the economy had a direct impact on the insurance sector. As part of the efforts to transform the existing capitalist economy, there were major changes in the regulatory framework of insurance. The policy-makers passed a new piece of Insurance Law number 3 of 13 January 1977[2]. As one of the key outcomes of the new legislation, a new state-owned insurer was formed following **nationalization** of infrastructure of the insurance companies that had continued doing business at that time: *Nauticus*, *Lusitana* and *Tranquilidade*. The word nationalization is used to describe a situation where a government passes laws in order to legitimize a process of seizure of privately-owned companies and changing ownership to the state. Besides the 3 companies that were fused, *Mundial e Confiança*

---

2. Referred to in Portuguese as *Decreto-Lei nº. 3/77 de 13 de Janeiro*

de Moçambique, the fourth company which had stopped operating, was put into liquidation.

3.1. Formation of a monopoly

Following the developments described above, the new state-owned national insurer, *Empresa Moçambicana de Seguros* (EMOSE) had a **monopoly** of all insurance and reinsurance business in Mozambique. As a monopoly it means that it was the only permitted operator in the insurance market. Please note that the approach of establishing a state-owned monopoly, was also implemented in various other countries in Africa in the post-independence period. Companies that enjoyed a similar status included *Empresa Nacional de Seguros de Angola* (ENSA), Ethiopian Insurance Corporation, *Société Nacionale d'Assurance du Congo*, *Société Nacionale d'Assurance et Réassurance de la République de Guinée*, Swaziland Royal Insurance Corporation, State Insurance Corporation of Ghana and Zambia State Insurance Company. The model of a state-owned monopoly insurer was one of the key characteristics in countries that followed models of socialism or communism such as Angola and Mozambique. However, the same statist approach to the insurance market was also implemented in some of the countries that tended to maintain some forms of capitalism such as Swaziland and Zaire (which is now known as the Democratic Republic of Congo).

3.2. State interventions

Besides the approaches of direct state-ownership of a monopoly insurance operator, as per the examples above, there are other ways a government or state can influence or be involved in the insurance sector. According to Professor Irukwu (1981:174), '**state intervention**' or involvement by the state can be in the form of complete nationalization or '**partial state ownership**' or only regulatory control and supervision without taking ownership of the businesses. Examples of some forms of partial state ownership include cases such as Malawi and Zimbabwe, where there exist national insurers partially owned by the state and operating in **competition** with privately owned insurers. In other markets, there were also some forms of controls at a higher level through reinsurance, which is one of the key tools for financial and technical support of insurance markets.

Coming back to Mozambique, following the creation of the monopoly insurer as described above, the same entity also had the responsibilities of the regulatory authority for insurance business, according to the Insurance Law of 1977 (Sigaúke, 2013: 4). This was consistent with the approach to regulation in socialist or centrally planned economies. At the same time, insurance brokerage, amongst other commercial services, was banned. It is partly as a result of this historical legacy that all insurance companies in our market have continued to maintain **direct insurance**[3] placements besides the business from intermediaries, as we shall discuss further in Chapter 8.

Unfortunately for the new nation, the war of independence was immediately followed by a protracted, brutal and highly destructive civil war. It is estimated that more than 1 million people died in this war which only ended in October 1992, after the signing of a General Peace Agreement in Rome (Lalá and Ostheimer, 2003: 6). We shall now look at the next stage of development of the economy and insurance sector of Mozambique.

4. MARKET LIBERALISATION PHASE

Prior to the signing of the peace agreement, as described above, the government of Mozambique had initiated a process of political and economic reforms. This was started as early as 1985 as part of the strategy to end the civil war and to start a process of economic recovery (Francisco, 2002: 31). In the political sphere, there was a shift from the socialist one-party system to a policy of a multi-party electoral democracy. In terms of the economy, the policy-makers initiated a process of economic restructuring and market liberalization. For the insurance sector, this would lead to the termination of the

---

3. Direct insurance is a placement of insurance directly by covered persons without the involvement of any intermediary. We shall discuss further in Chapter 8 the concept of Financial Intermediary Services.

state monopoly, re-emergence of private sector insurance companies and the unbanning of insurance brokerage services. The principal piece of legislation that paved the way for this reform process was Insurance Law number 24/91 of 31 December 1991[4] (Firmino et al. 2011: 3).

Following the reform process outlined above, private sector insurance companies started re-emerging in Mozambique from 1992. The first two new entrants were *IMPAR Companhia de Seguros de Moçambique* and *Companhia Geral de Seguros de Moçambique* (CGSM). They were followed by *Moçambique Companhia de Seguros* (MCS) formed in 2000. Then, in 2001, Hollard, an emerging global insurer from South Africa, started operating in Mozambique. As such, in the period leading up to the next key reforms of insurance legislation in 2003, the insurance market had a total of 5 insurance companies including the state-owned insurance company which had been changed into a public limited company.

4.1. Expansion of the national insurance market

In the next phase of development and expansion of the insurance market from 2003 to the time of writing of this book, there have been 11 other new registered insurance companies. As we shall discuss later in this book, the changes of the Insurance Law of 2003 also marked the beginning of a

---

4. This law is referred to in Portuguese as *Lei n°. 24/91 de 31 de Dezembro*

separation of licenses of life and non-life insurance business. We should also note that this change has only been applied for new license applications from this period going forward. Despite this change of rules regarding nature of insurance licenses, the first three insurance companies have continued to operate as composite insurance businesses, combining both types of business under one license. Starting from the oldest to the most recently established, the list of insurance companies currently operating in Mozambique as at the end of 2014 is as outlined in Appendix I.

4.2. Insurance law reforms

Furthermore, we would like to also note that, besides the liberalization processes of the 1990s and further changes in the Insurance Law of 2003, there were further reforms in the Insurance Law in 2010. However, the changes of 2003 and 2010 have been more of refinements of the key policy shift in the 1990s following the phase of opening up of the market. According to Firmino et al (2011: 3), the reforms of 2003 and 2010 were useful for purposes of closing certain gaps in the existing regulatory framework.

In fact, some of the key processes connected to the shifts from the 1990s are still work-in-progress up to today. There are also a number of other aspects of the current Insurance Law that require further review. Furthermore, at the time of writing of this book, the project of changing EMOSE from a state-owned insurer to a public company with minimal state ownership was also an ongoing initiative. It appears that, as part of its broader strategy of reducing direct interference in the market, the state is aiming to further reduce its shareholding in this company and other public companies in other economic sectors.

Moreover, we should note that the major changes in the nature and direction of development of our insurance market were significantly influenced by critical shifts in the political economy and related reform policies. It appears to us that there is a certain pattern where all significant changes in law and development policies of the insurance sector were implemented following and in alignment with changes in certain key areas including the constitutional order and the national development policies. This can be illustrated as per the outline in Table 2.

Table 2–Key Historical Epochs and Major Developments

Key Historical Epochs		Constitutional Order	Key Economic Policies	Insurance Sector Policy
1st	Up to 1975	Portuguese colonial constitutional order	Imperialist capitalism	Portuguese regulatory framework: • Private sector • Competition
2nd	1977 to 1990	Constitution of 1975 • Equal rights for all • One-party political system	Socialism	Insurance Law of 1977 • State-owned insurer • Monopoly

3rd	1991 to 2014	Constitutions of 1990 & Amendments of 2004 • Multi-party political system • Electoral democracy	Economic liberalisation	Insurance Laws of 1991, 2003 & 2010 • Private sector operators • Competition

Besides the refinements in 2003 and 2010, there has not been a major change of thrust or direction of legal, political and economic policy to trigger any key shifts in the insurance market amongst other economic activities, as has tended to be the case in the past four decades. There has not been the kind of radical transition such as that which was experienced in the period after independence in 1975 and in the time of major political and economic changes in the 1990s. The policy reforms in the two periods outlined above also marked key turning points that set in motion processes leading to fundamental changes in the development policy of the insurance sector amongst other economic activities. We should now look at the current formal insurance market emerging from this process.

5. EMERGING INSURANCE MARKET

5.1. Commercial insurance vs. Social Insurance

Before presenting the structure of the emerging insurance market in Mozambique, it is vital to understand the distinction between types of insurance that are compulsory by force of law and those that are not. The compulsory types of insurance are referred to as **social insurance** and those that are not compulsory are referred to as **private insurance** or **commercial insurance** (Irukwu, 1998: 196). In countries in southern Africa like Namibia and South Africa as well as in most developed economies, there is a clear separation of markets for compulsory insurance covered by public funds and private insurance covered by the private commercial insurance market.

However, in Mozambique and most other developing countries, the private insurance market tries to cover both voluntary types of commercial insurance as well as some of the compulsory types of insurance. In Mozambique, social security and bank deposit guarantees are the only areas where there is a public fund to provide some form of social protection. As illustrated in Figure 1, there is an element of overlap in the sense that, in the area of social or obligatory insurance, cover is provided in some areas by public funds and in others by the private commercial insurance market. We shall discuss further in Chapter 9 the issues concerning the handling of social insurance.

Figure 1—Commercial vs. Social Insurance

Uninsured by the Commercial Market	Commercial Insurance Market		Key Unprotected Basic Fundamental Risks
* Public infrastructure	* Very low penetration: 1.5% of GDP		* Natural disasters (public property & uninsured people)
		Obligatory Insurance in the Commercial Insurance Market / Social Protection covered by Public Funds	* War & political risks (100% exposure)
			* Public health
* 95% of adult population not covered	* Very low coverage: only 5% of adult		
	* Complimentary pensions	* Workmen's Compensation / * Contributory social security (+/-3% of total employed population)	* Social security for informal labour, Unemployed & others
		* Deposit Guarantee	* No depositors insurance for 90% of population which is unbanked
* +/-90% vehicles on public roads uninsureed	* Only +/-10% of vehicles insured	* Motor Liability & other obligatory	

5.2. Commercial insurance market structure

Following the transition process described above, we are seeing the emergence of a fairly vibrant commercial insurance market and a rapid expansion of the number of operators especially at the level of insurance companies and insurance intermediaries. We shall discuss further in this book the roles of the different elements in our insurance market including key supporting services. The structure of the emerging commercial insurance market we have today following the historical developments outlined above is as per Figure 2.

Figure 2—Structure of Emerging Commercial Insurance Market

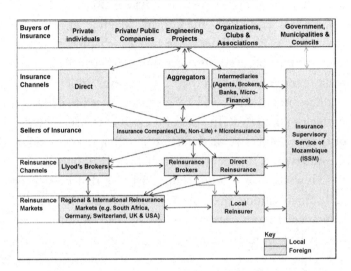

From the representation of the market in Figure 2, we can see that our insurance market involves a broad range of operators. It is also a type of business where, like banking, the national insurance market is directly linked to international markets. It is partly as a result of this direct interaction with the international market that insurance is one of very few sectors that are permitted to transact directly in international currencies and handle placements with international markets, as we shall discuss later in this book.

5.3. Buyers of Insurance

We should complete our discussion on the emerging commercial insurance market by looking at buyers of insurance. As we shall discuss in the next chapter, insurance is a unique type of service that is required by virtually all people and organisations. Given that risk is an ever present threat in our lives, in principle, we have a constant need to address the problems posed by it. In view of the fact that insurance is one of the most effective methods for handling risk, it should be the one type of service that everyone needs all the time.

However, the reality of our market is that most people and organisations that need insurance do not purchase insurance. In our experience of our market, insurance is mainly bought by medium and large commercial enterprises. The bulk of small enterprises and the majority of people rarely buy any insurance. This situation was highlighted in a research on financial services that showed that only 5% of the adult population has some form of formal insurance (FinMark, 2009: 7). We have also observed that in relation to other economic activities, insurance represents only 1.5% of Gross Domestic Product of Mozambique as per the statistical research from the Swiss Reinsurance Company. Mozambique is part of a group of countries at the bottom of the log in Africa, which itself has poor performance compared to other zones in the world, as you may see in Appendix II.

CONCLUSION

In this chapter we have looked at the key stages of development of our commercial insurance market up to now. In many respects, the market went through a full circle starting with a market based on concepts of competition (capitalism), through a transitional period of a closed monopoly market and then back to an open market of competition. We discussed how these major changes were connected to key shifts in the political economy of Mozambique and connected reforms of the constitutional order and regulatory framework. We have also noted that, notwithstanding the expansion of the number of operators in the emerging market, insurance remains with a very low penetration in the economy and covers a tiny portion of the population. In the following Chapter, we shall examine one more key historical aspect of the development of insurance business. We shall examine the foundational principles of insurance that were established in the early period of development of insurance in order to resolve key preoccupations of this economic activity.

REFERENCES

- Arnold, G., 2005. Africa—A Modern History. London: Atlantic Books.

- Borsheid, Peter (2013). Global insurance networks. in James, Harold (ed.). The value of risk: Swiss Re and the History of Reinsurance. New York: Oxford University Press. Pp. 23-105.

- FinMark, 2009: 7 FinScope Mozambique 2009. Cape Town: FinMark Trust

- Firmino, Luisa; Saturnino, Eduardo; Neves, Alexandre and Chongo, Angelina (2011). *Colectânea de Legislação Sobre Seguros*. Maputo: Centro de Formação Jurídica e Judiciária—Ministério da Justiça

- Francisco, António, A. Da Silva (2002). Evolução da Economia de Moçambique da Colónia à Transição para a Economia de Mercado in Rolim, Cássio; Franco, S. António; Bolnick, Bruce and Andersson, Per-Ake (eds) A Economia Moçambicana Contemporânea—Ensaios. Maputo: Ministério do Plano e Finanças. Pages 15-41.

- Inspecção Provincial de Crédito e Seguros, 1971, *Relatório Anual*. Maputo: Inspecção Provincial de Crédito e Seguros

- Irukwu, J.O. (1998). *Insurance Management in Africa.* Lagos: Bima Africa Ltd

- Lalá, Anícia and Ostheimer, Andrea, E. (2003) *How to remove the stains on Mozambique's democratic track record: Challenges for the democratisation process between 1990 and 2003.* Maputo: Konrad-Adenauer-Stiftung[1]

- Quive, Samuel (2009). *Sistemas formais e informais de protecção social e desenvolvimento em Moçambique.* Maputo: IESE—Instituto de Estudos Sociais e Económicos.

- Shillington, K. 2005, History of Africa, 2nd Edition, Palgrave Macmillan: New York.

- Sigaúke, Abílio, Feliciano (2013). *Evolução histórica e papel da entidade de supervisão de seguros em Moçambique.* Paper presented at the Insurance Seminar of the ISSM.

---

1. There is a Portuguese version of this book where this title is translated as: '*Como limpar as nódoas do processo democrático? Os desafios da transição e democratização em Moçambique (1990-2003)*'.

CHAPTER 3

TRADITIONAL PRINCIPLES OF INSURANCE

Insurance is a fairly conservative profession steeped in traditions that not many people outside the field understand. In this chapter, we are going to review the key foundational concepts of insurance. We shall begin by providing a definition of insurance and explaining unique features of this business activity. We shall look at fundamental preoccupations of insurance arising from the nature of service that it tries to provide. Then, we shall review the key historical principles of insurance and how they are intended to address some of these concerns. This discussion of the traditional principles is also a useful way for one to have a more grounded understanding of insurance and how it is supposed to work.

1. DEFINING INSURANCE

Insurance can be defined in simple terms as essentially a 'promise' by one party named the 'Insurer' that undertakes to pay a certain sum of money to another party known as the 'Insured' on the occurrence of an 'uncertain' future event (Silva, 2000: 85). The insurance cover is subject to payment by the insured of an agreed price (Cadilhe & Pinto: 2007:

18). Furthermore, the 'promise' to pay if an 'uncertain' event where to occur is premised on a number of assumptions by the insurer about the state of affairs of the insured item at the time of placement of insurance. For instance, it is not the intention of insurance to cover loss or injury that has already happened before insurance is placed. It is also a key condition of insurance that, after placing cover, the insured entity does not wilfully cause injury or damage to insured people and property. From this definition of insurance and some of the key assumptions about the subject of insurance, we can already see some of the unique characteristics of insurance that make it different from all other types of business activities.

In most economic transactions, in general, before you pay the agreed price for purchase of an item, you could find out a certain range of information on what you are buying. You could establish what, how, when and where it should be delivered. The situation of a potential buyer is even better in the case of purchase of tangible items. The buyer is able to see them and assess the quality of what is on offer before paying the agreed price. Furthermore, even in cases of something that is not tangible like services, one can request for a detailed description of the exact service that should be delivered. The person paying for the service is able to know beforehand when and how the required service should be provided in order to be satisfied about delivery of the agreed service. As we shall discuss in the following section, the situation of the parties in an insurance agreement is fundamentally different from the scenarios that we have described above.

Moreover, insurance has a unique vocabulary that can be very confusing even for practitioners in the business. As part of the unique features of insurance, there is a preference to use expressions such as **policy wording** or **insurance policy** in order to refer to what can be described appropriately in legal terms as an **insurance contract**. The price for insurance is known as **premium**. The request for settlement for a loss is referred to as a **claim**. The settlement of claims involving property insurance is known as **indemnity** while that involving bodily injury is described as **compensation**. The party in whose name the policy is issued is referred to as the **Policyholder**. The person or business entity that is covered by the policy is referred to as the **Insured**. The value of the insured item is called **sum insured**. We shall provide definitions of many other relevant technical expressions as we shall discuss the different themes covered in this book.

Furthermore, we should also note that although the use of unique technical expressions remains the predominant practice in insurance, there is now an emerging global initiative aimed at reducing the opaque nature of insurance contracts. As part of this process, we are seeing some of the more sophisticated insurance markets now passing legislation to force insurers and other service providers with similar problems to use a language which is clear, simple and concise. This is part of what is known as **Plain Language,** as we shall discuss later in this book. We should now look at the key foundational principles of insurance.

2. TRADITIONAL PRINCIPLES OF INSURANCE

In order for an insurance agreement to be effective, it should conform to certain critical conditions consisting of a set of traditional rules as well as standard legal elements. The application of such traditional principles and legal elements is part of accepted practice in insurance business worldwide. In the Insurance Law of Mozambique, the same rules and conditions are also specifically defined as essential elements of insurance. We shall start our review of the traditional principles by looking at the question about who has the right to insure and why this needs to be defined.

2.1. Insurable interest

Given that the principal goal of an insurance agreement is to 'make good' losses suffered following a misfortune, it is vital to have rules aimed at preventing harmful practices. Without such rules, one could take a gamble to win something in the event of injury to other people or damage of property belonging to others (Mehr and Lammack, 1972: 107). The specific principle which has been developed to address this concern is known as 'insurable interest'. Insurable interest, like all the other key principles of insurance, has origins in the legal system of England.

Furthermore, insurable interest is also defined as one of the key guiding principles of insurance in Article 88 of the current Insurance Law of Mozambique of 31 December

2010[2]. In order to understand what this principle means, we should look at the Marine Law of the United Kingdom which offers a classic definition as follows:

'In particular, a person is interested in a marine adventure where he stands in any legal or equitable relation to the adventure or to any insurable property at risk therein, in consequence of which he may benefit by the safety or due arrival of insurable property, or may be prejudiced by its loss, or by damage thereto, or by the detention thereof, or may incur liability in respect thereof.'

In simple terms, the rule covered in the principle is that the person proposing to insure something must be someone who wants the insured item to continue to exist and who would suffer some financial loss if the item in question is lost or damaged. Therefore, an owner of property is said to have insurable interest as long as he/she is the owner. It is on the basis of this interest that one has a legal right to insure. As a result of this principle, insurers always require proof of ownership of insured items or relationship to insured person.

However, there is a different application of the rule regarding insurable interest for marine, life and pensions (Sadler, 2012: 7/1). For life and pensions business there is a need to prove insurable interest at inception of the policy. For insurance of transportation of goods, the insured might not have insurable interest at inception, but must be able to prove its existence at the time of a loss. In a situation

---

2. Referred to in Portuguese as *Decreto-Lei nº. 1/2010 de 31 de Dezembro*

where, for instance, someone wants to import certain goods to Mozambique, that person could place insurance here in Mozambique even though the goods would still be in the possession of the entity at point of origin. In such cases, if the insurance is placed by the entity receiving the goods at the destination, then, it is sufficient for the insured to prove insurable interest at the time of occurrence of a loss. For insurance of other property, insurable interest must exist at both the time of placing of insurance and of occurrence of a loss.

Furthermore, it should be noted that financial institutions such as banks and micro-finance institutions (MFIs) also rely on their financial interest on financed property to exercise certain rights in insurance contracts. They try to protect their interests by making it a condition of their agreements for the financed items to be fully insured during the full period of the loan. They may also try to ensure that the insurers note in the insurance policy their financial interest and may require the insertion into the insurance contract of certain conditions designed to protect them. The conditions may require the insurers to treat the financial institutions as being jointly insured with their client. They may also require insurers to inform them if the debtor acts in any way that may affect the effectiveness of the insurance such as not paying respective premium. Then, there are also conditions such as the '**loss payee clause**', where a financial institution is able to secure its interests by reserving the right to, amongst other things, first priority in the event of a claim.

2.2. Utmost Good Faith

The next key preoccupation for insurance is that an insurer is agreeing to 'make good' any covered events that may affect at any time any of the insured entities. We should note that an insurer is not some form of a supreme entity existing in all places at the same time (omnipresent) and that can see and know everything (omniscient). Therefore, an insurer is not in a position to know the true nature of everything that is insured and to decide fairly on what is a genuine claim and the correct amount of indemnification. The insured persons or entities also face another set of ambiguities. They do not know for certain what may or may not happen and so what is the basis for a fair price on a service where there are no guarantees upfront when, how and if they will be indemnified or not.

In order to address the critical questions noted above, the traditional solution of insurance business has been to rely not merely on 'good faith'[3] like most other types of contracts, but on the principle of 'utmost good faith'[4] (Mehr and Lammack, 1972: 148). Although this is also one of the key traditional principles, it also remains one of the more contentions ones.

---

3. Known in Latin as *Bona Fide*
4. From the Latin expression *Uberrimae Fidei*

According to Madge (1990: 13), this principle was defined in a legal case over 200 years ago when Lord Mansfield stated that:

Insurance is a contract upon speculation. The special facts upon which the contingent chance is to be computed lie more commonly in the knowledge of the insured only. The underwriter trusts to his representation and proceeds upon confidence that he does not keep back any circumstance in his knowledge to mislead the underwriter into a belief that the circumstance does not exist and to induce him to estimate the risk as if it did not exist. The keeping back of such a circumstance is a fraud and therefore the policy is void. Although the suppression should happen through mistake without any fraudulent intention yet still the underwriter is deceived and the policy is void because the risk run is really different from the risk understood and intended to be run at the time of the agreement.

With the exception of mainly insurance, contracts for most other business activities are based on the legal principle of '**caveat emptor**' or '**let the buyer beware**' (IISA, 2011 B: 86). This means that, in a transaction such as a sales contract, the buyer could inspect and assess the item being sold before buying it. In an insurance contract, the insurer relies on the client disclosing truthfully all material information on the subject of insurance (Sadler, 2012: 1/1). The insurer would then decide on whether to insure or not based on the information presented by the insured. There is a risk that the client could refrain from disclosing any information that could cause the insurer not to cover them or to apply onerous conditions.

It should be noted that the definition of this concept has been reviewed and refined in subsequent legal cases. In the classic reference, there is more emphasis on the duty of the insured to disclose material information. In emerging views of this principle, there is a more balanced approach to the question of the duties of both the insurer and the insured. Both parties are supposed to act in trust towards each other. There are mutual obligations and duties on the part of both the entity selling insurance and the party buying it. The party proposing to place insurance should declare full, correct and clear information on the subject matter to be insured. The insurer should, in turn, inform the prospective client of full, correct and clear information on the terms and conditions of the proposed insurance contract.

Furthermore, we should also note that courts in countries such as South Africa have started moving away from the extreme version of utmost good faith to simply good faith (Price, 2008: viii). There is a growing concern that the extreme version of the concept is not sustainable given that there are no degrees of honesty (IISA, 2011B: 86). Either one is honest or not honest. The Insurance Law of Mozambique already reflects this shift. In the law, Article 86, which defines key guiding principles of insurance, refers to '**good faith**' and not '**utmost good faith**'. The next principle touches on a problem that tends to put further pressure on the concept of trust as the foundational basis for insurance. We shall now look at the principle of indemnity and connected concepts of average, contribution and subrogation.

2.3. Indemnity

The next concern for insurance is to address the problem of appropriately settling the claim after occurrence of an insured event. The insurer needs to ensure that the client does not receive more or less than a fair payout. The misfortune leading the insured to require a payout or settlement may have already left the clients injured and stressed. They would now be expecting the insurer to perform as promised in the insurance contract. This is part of what makes the principle of indemnity one of the most critical conditions especially for property insurance. In accordance with this principle, the insured may not receive more than the actual loss in the event of a covered claim (Vaughan, 2009: 163). The main purpose of insurance is for the insured persons to be put back in the same position in which they were immediately before the loss or damage of the insured item. In other words, the insurer promises to 'make good the loss.' According to Cannar (1979: 17), the classical reference for the definition of the principle of indemnity is based on the legal decision in the case of Castelain v. Preston, 1883, 11 QBD 380, Brett L.J.:

> 'The very foundation, in my opinion, of every rule which has been applied to insurance law is this, namely, that the contract of insurance contained in a marine or fire

policy is a contract of indemnity, and an indemnity only, and that this contract means that the insured, in a case of loss against which the policy has been made, shall be fully indemnified but shall never be more than fully indemnified. That is the fundamental principle of insurance, and if ever a proposition is brought forward which is at variance with it, that is to say, which either will prevent the insured from obtaining a full indemnity or which will give the insured more than full indemnity, that proposition must certainly be wrong'

In accordance with this principle, the purpose of insurance is not for one to gain or make a profit from an insurance contract. Through the principle of indemnity, insurance tries to return the insured to the same financial position that he/she enjoyed before the loss (Waty, 2007: 30). Given that insurance is intended to restore the situation which exists prior to a loss, it also tries to achieve the critical purpose of reducing the **moral hazard** of intentional losses that would exist if one could profit from an insured claim.

Furthermore, in order to fulfil the principle of indemnity, insurance policies for property have conditions intended to prevent the insured from being indemnified on more than one insurance policy. The principle of indemnity can be applied without difficulty in general insurance where the losses are quantifiable. However, due to the fact that it is not possible to fix a specific monetary value for a life or a limb, the rules relating to the principle of indemnity are not applicable for life and personal accident insurance. Such types of policies, which cannot be based on the rules of indemnity, are treated as compensation types of insurance. There is also a limited application of this principle for certain types of insurance policies that may have an agreed basis of valuation, such as insurance of transportation of cargo.

Furthermore, it is also vital to note that, in the case of contracts of indemnity, the insurer tends to reserve the right to choose the method of reimbursement. The options that are available to the insurer are as follows:

- Cash settlement
- Replacement
- Reinstatement

This right of the insurer is often not appropriately explained to insured clients. From our experience of working in insurance business, we have noted that, when claims occur, some clients tend to expect to receive a cash payment of exactly the value noted in their policy. After an event such as a car accident, many people tend to want to start all over again. They do not expect to be forced back to their original property and having to accept repairs which are often not going to give them exactly what they had before the accident. It is part of human nature to want to move forward and leave behind damaged goods. However, the business model of insurance would have limited economic viability if everyone could just throw away any insured item that is damaged in an accident even if it can be repaired.

We believe that, although the options of repairs may be grudgingly accepted by some clients, they also make a positive contribution to global efforts of promoting environmentally sustainable practices. When we refer to environmental sustainability, we are talking about being aware that our planet has limited natural resources which are being gradually depleted and about taking appropriate measures to ensure preservation of what we have for future generations. We should now look at an even more contentious principle which is intended to help uphold the principle of indemnity as we have discussed above.

2.4. Average Condition

The average condition is one of the key principles of insurance that causes a lot of conflict in insurance at the time of settlement of claims. It operates in a manner that is contrary to expectations of most customers that have a limited understanding of the rules of insurance. After suffering from an insured event on a valid insurance policy, the insured expects to be paid exactly the amount of cover stated in the policy. However, there is a technical reason why an insurer might not pay the amount stated in the policy even though the claim may be valid and the customers imagine that they have not done anything 'wrong'. This technical rule is called Average. It is one of the rules which is often not adequately explained by insurers or not properly understood by the customers.

Furthermore, we should also note that the average condition is found in most property policies. In addition to being part of traditional principles of insurance, our Insurance Law also specifically provides for the operation of this concept in Article 187. The average condition in standard property insurance policy documents in our market is expressed basically as follows:

> *If, at the time of any loss, the value of the property insured is greater than the sum insured thereon, the insured shall be deemed to be his own insurer for the difference and shall bear a rateable portion of the loss.*

In accordance with the rules of the principle of average, the insured should always receive a settlement that is proportional to the ratio of sum insured to the total value of the risk covered. The application of average assists to uphold the principle of indemnity, according to which the insured persons should be put back in the same position they were in before the occurrence of a loss. It is applied in order to prevent two principal problems arising from insuring for more or less than the actual value of the insured item, as described below.

a.   Over-insurance

Over-insurance refers to cases where the sum insured on a policy is higher than the value of the covered property. The first problem in such cases is that the insured would pay premium calculated on the wrong basis. The second problem is that, in the event of a claim on such a policy, the insurers would only indemnify up to the value of the insured item and not the over-inflated sum insured. Settling more than the actual value of the insured item would be some form of '**unjust enrichment**'. Insurance is not gambling and, as we have established when we looked at the principle of indemnity, it is not intended to put the insured in a better position than before the occurrence of a covered claim.

b.   Under-insurance

Under-insurance is a situation where the sum insured is lower than the value of the insured property. In such a case, there is also the problem that the client would have paid premium calculated on the wrong basis of a lower sum insured. In the event of a claim, the insurer would apply average. The impact of average has two possible scenarios depending on the size of claims as follows:

-   In the case of a **Partial Loss,** the insurer would apply average in order to calculate indemnity due to the insured. Let us look at an example of a policy with a vehicle worth Mt 1,500,000 that has been insured at an incorrect sum insured of Mt 750,000. By dividing the correct value of the property by the sum insured and expressing it as a percentage, we can see that we have 50% under-insurance. The formula is as follows: 750,000 ÷ 1,500,000 × 100. Let us now say the same client has a covered claim from an accident with repairs quoted at Mt 100,000. Following the rules of average, the appropriate indemnity would only be Mt 50,000. This is the result of applying the average factor into the claim amount. The insured would be responsible for the balance of the partial claim as well as the appropriate excess, as per the terms and conditions of the policy.

- In the case of a **Total Loss** the insurer would settle only the under-insured value, as per the policy in question. The insured would be responsible for the excess as well as the shortfall between under declared value and true value of the insured item.

As we can see from the above cases, it is crucial for the insured to ensure that their property is insured for the correct value. The insured client is prejudiced if the sum insured noted in their policy is too low or too high in relation to the actual value of the property. We should now discuss the methods that are used for determining sum insured for different types of property.

c. Determination of sum insured

Determination of value of an insured item is one of the key issues connected to most conflicts regarding insurance indemnity. The problem is caused by the fact that in many insurance transactions not enough attention is paid to ensuring that an adequate sum insured is defined. Why is it crucial to define an adequate sum insured? The most critical reasons for this requirement are as follows:

i.   It is a key determining factor of cost of insurance since pricing tools for most classes of insurance use this as a basis to apply defined premium rates.

ii. It represents the maximum financial exposure for the insurer for that specific policy and for which the insurer needs to verify availability of appropriate financial capacity in the event of a claim.

iii. It is the basis for defining indemnity to the insured in the event of a claim.

Given the effects of average discussed above, it is crucial to ensure that an adequate sum insured is calculated and specified in the insurance policy. The key approaches for defining sum insured of insured property are as outlined in Table 3.:

Table 3–Basis of Valuation

BASIS OF VALUATION	DEFINITION	SUITABLE CIRCUMSTANCES
Original Cost	The historical cost of acquisition or construction.	Buildings in first year of acquisition.
Book Value	Value of property after deducting depreciation[1] and inflation[2] as per processes of accounting for value.	This is useful for buildings after first year of acquisition.
Market Value	Value as defined by the price at which the item could be sold or bought in the local market in its current condition. The value calculated on this basis also takes into account the age of the item and inflation.	Most suitable for plant and machinery that are widely available in the market such as motor vehicles.
Reinstatement Value (also known as **"New for Old"**).	This is the value of replacing the insured property with similar new property. It does not take into account depreciation.	Suitable for any property after first year of acquisition and in particular electronic equipment.
"Agreed Value" basis.	This is for items which might have operated beyond warranty period of manufacturers and could technically have reached a value of zero but are still functioning appropriately due to good maintenance. Basis of insurance could be an agreed amount or percentage of value (usually in the range of 20% to 50% of original cost).	For old plant and machinery. This valuation method also usually requires a review of conditions such as Average so that appropriate approaches are followed in the event of a claim.

---

1   Depreciation is the process of taking into account the age.

2   Inflation represents the impact of rising of costs of things.

2.5. Contribution

Let us now look at an interesting scenario of a customer that appreciates the benefits of insurance who has placed cover for the same property on two different policies. If the client has arranged appropriate covers and paid the correct premium on the two policies, does he/she have the right to claim on both policies in the event of a covered loss situation? No. According to the principle of contribution, the insurers should not each pay the full amount of the claim as per their policies. The main reason for the application of this rule is that, if the two insurers were to pay the full claim each, the client would end up with more than what he/she had before the claim. That would be contrary to the principle of indemnity, as we discussed above.

Furthermore, the principle of *contribution* is intended to ensure a fair distribution of losses between insurers that may be covering the same subject matter. The Insured can claim a proportion of the claim from the two insurers or the insured could collect the full claim from one of the insurers that would then recover a portion from the other insurer. We should note that, in order for the procedure of contribution to be applied, all insurers affected on the same claim have to be aware of this overlap of coverage. It is crucial for the insurance association to consider setting up mechanisms for sharing of appropriate claims information in order to identify cases where contribution may be applicable.

2.6. Subrogation

The principle of subrogation is complementary to the principle of indemnity (Chiejina, 2004: 77). The name of the principle was developed from a Latin word which means 'substituting one creditor for another'. As an insurance principle, the rules of subrogation function exactly as per the definition of the name. As such, in insurance, subrogation refers to a process where, after settling claims of their insured clients, insurers are entitled to any remedy or right to any recoveries either from the insured property or from third parties that may be at fault for the loss or damage (Vaughan, 2009: 168). It prevents the Insured from being compensated for the same loss from two sources: the insurers and any third parties that may have caused the loss. According to Cannar (1979: 19), the classic reference which sets the basic rules of subrogation is the judgement of Lord Blackburn in the case Burnand v. Rodocanachi, 1882, 7 App. Cas. 333:

> 'The general rule of law is that when there is a contract of indemnity and a loss happens, anything which reduces or diminishes that loss reduces or diminishes the amount which the indemnifier is bound to pay, and, if the indemnifier has already paid it, then if anything which diminishes the loss comes into the hands of the person to whom he has paid it, it becomes an equity that the person who has already paid the full indemnity is entitled to be recouped by having that amount paid back'

In general, the rights of the insurers through subrogation are limited to the amounts that they may have paid to the insured as indemnity. The Insurance Law of Mozambique supports this rule and the operation of the principle of subrogation in Article 191. It should also be noted that this is one of the principles that some global industrial companies try to bypass. There are policies where the insurer may agree to forego its rights of subrogation. This process of foregoing of its rights is known as a **waiver**.

Up to now, we have been approaching claims in a very simplistic manner where there is a clear and direct link between the cause and effect of an insured event. However, the real life situations which insurers face in claims is that there is often no clear link between a loss event or accident and the effects of different factors that may already exist, trigger or worsen an event leading to loss or damage of insured property. We shall see how insurance tries to address this issue with the legal concept of proximate cause, as discussed below.

2.7. Proximate cause

The principle of proximate cause is intended to address one of the key challenges for insurance of making sure that a claim under review has been caused by an insured event, as defined in the insurance policy under consideration. The principle of proximate cause was developed from the Latin expression 'Causa Proxima' which means the 'nearest cause'.

The definition of this insurance principle, as provided by Mehr and Cammack (1972: 180), is as follows:

> *'In the event of the occurrence of several causes, the loss will be deemed to have been caused by the dominating peril so long as there exists an unbroken chain of cause and effect between the peril and the loss, whether or not the peril is active at the consummation of the loss. Proximate cause means the immediate, efficient cause without which the results could not or would not have happened.'*

A proximate cause is not necessarily the first or the last or the sole cause of the loss. It is the dominant or effective or operative cause. After the occurrence of a loss event which is covered by an insurance contract, the Insured can lodge a claim with the Insurer. In order for the insurer to settle the claim, the insured has the duty to prove that the loss was caused by an 'insured peril'. The peril in question should be the most effective, dominant or real cause of the loss. That is to say, the peril insured against must be the direct, dominant, efficient or material cause of the insured's loss. The loss would not be covered if it is caused by an 'independent, intervening and uninsured peril' (Sadler, 2012: 1/2).

In order to determine if the proximate cause of a loss is as a result of an insured event, it is vital to consider types of situation as outlined in Table 4.

Table 4–Category of Perils

NATURE OF PERIL	DESCRIPTION	EXAMPLES FROM A STANDARD POLICY FOR A HOUSE
Insured Peril	Perils or hazards that are stated in the policy as insured	Loss or damage as a result of Fire, Lightning or thunderbolt, Explosion and other perils specified in the policy
Excluded Peril	Perils noted on the policy as exclusions	Loss or damage as a result of perils such as political events, war and others as noted on the policy
Uninsured Peril	Perils not referred to in the policy and that are not subject of insurance	Failure by authorities to supply electricity and water to the house

In this way, depending on the type of peril that is the proximate cause of the loss, it should be possible to define for each loss if it is covered or not. In practice, it can be complex to make such a determination because a loss may be a result of two or more causes and it can become a major challenge to decide with certainty the proximate cause of the loss. In such a case, it becomes imperative to define what was the nearest, most powerful and most effective cause of the loss.

2.8. Principle of loss mitigation

Complacency of insured persons is the next challenge for insurance after achieving the often not so easy task of convincing someone to insure and after satisfying all conditions for the issuing of the insurance contract. Given a perception that insurance allows insured clients to 'transfer' their problems elsewhere, there is a grave danger that people overlook the fact that they still have the full responsibility to actually protect themselves and their property (Thomas and Reed, 1977: 69). The principle of loss mitigation serves to remind the insured persons of this responsibility.

The principle of loss mitigation states that when an unforeseen loss event occurs, the Insured must always take all measures to control and reduce the loss of insured property. The insured must '**act as if uninsured**'. This means that if a house were to catch fire, the owner must take all possible measures to put out the fire and to reduce the amount of property damaged with the same level of dedication that he/she would apply if that property was not insured.

Furthermore, loss mitigation is also one of the key principles that supports business practices aimed at ensuring safety of people as well as protecting and preserving our environment (Assoumana, 2012: 20). Major disasters such as the fire on the oil rig **Piper Alpha** in the North Sea in 1988 did not only generate one of the largest claims (more than $1.8 billion) from man-made disasters, but also caused massive irreparable damage to the environment.

The key lesson to note is that, even if the disaster described above and any others had some form of insurance; settlement of a financial amount does not heal all the human suffering and does not reverse the wastage of natural and economic resources caused by such events. That is why it is crucial to always look at, first and foremost, what we can do to mitigate risk. Following the above discussions, we have now covered the traditional principles of insurance as practiced worldwide today. We should discuss one more key legal principle, as defined in the Insurance Law of Mozambique. We should note that it is not part of the foundational principles of insurance and in some respects does not completely complement the traditional perspectives of insurance.

3. RIGHT OF RECOVERY

Besides the principles of insurance that we have discussed up to now, our Insurance Law also makes specific provision for an additional legal principle that we should also review. In Article 199, it is stated that an insurer has the right to recover[5] from the insured after settling a third party liability claim for injury or damage caused by the insured. This legal principle is applied in obligatory motor liability insurance (Associação Portuguesa de Seguradores, 2001: 12). This is supposed to happen in the case where the insured may have intentionally caused the claim or deliberately prejudiced the insurer. This principle is also stated in Article 5 of Law number 2/2003 of 21 January 2003 relating to the compulsory Motor third party liability insurance. For motor liability insurance, the basis for this recovery is expanded to include claims such as those caused by driving under the influence of alcohol or drugs.

It appears that the main goal of this principle is to protect innocent third party victims of events such as road

---

3. Referred to in Portuguese as *'direito de regresso'*

accidents. Although there are good intentions behind the formulation of this principle, there are issues that will need to be addressed in the future. The standard practice of insurance in our market and worldwide is not to allow insured persons to benefit from protection of insurance for any illegal acts or for failing to follow conditions of their insurance contract. If any insured person has committed a crime or not observed the conditions of his/her insurance contract, the standard approach of the insurer is to reject respective claims on such an insurance policy.

In the event that an insurer has rejected a claim or cancelled a policy, then, the insured is supposed to face the consequences of his/her actions. In my experience of underwriting insurance business in Mozambique, if an insurer settles a third party claim caused by such persons that would have failed to observe the law, it is next to impossible to actually recover any funds from the culprits that may have caused loss or injuries to third parties. In most cases the insurer is forced to abandon their right to recovery or write-off the debt.

In addition to the question of individuals unwilling or unable to honour their debts, there is also the fact that there are also many cases of pedestrians that are injured or killed in accidents where the concerned motorist flee from the scene of the accident. This type of accident is known as 'hit-and-run'. In order to address this major challenge, some countries in Southern Africa have taken the approach of setting up of road accident public funds which are intended to compensate third parties from road accidents. We shall discuss further this question and the broader subject of social protection mechanisms in Chapter 9.

CONCLUSION

In this chapter we have discussed the key principles of insurance. We have noted that the foundational principles of insurance provide rules and conditions that enable insurance to function appropriately. They address key moral and legal challenges that insurance would face if they are not applied. On the basis of the rules covered in these principles, it is clear that insurance is not intended to be some form of gambling. The principles help to ensure that insurance is only serving to make good losses suffered by the insured without offering any unjust enrichment. They also provide clarity on who is entitled to insure any item and how to define if a loss has been caused by a covered event or not. They also guide insurers on how to proceed if there is more than one policy covering the same item or if an incorrect value is applied. After reviewing the traditional principles of insurance, we should now look at the concept of risk and the ways it can be handled using a number of options including insurance.

REFERENCES

- Associação Portuguesa de Seguradores (2001). Seguro Automóvel. Lisboa: Associação Portuguesa de Seguradores

- Assoumana, Hassan (2012). *Industrial Enterprise: Role of Risk Surveys in Loss Prevention* in the African Reinsurer. Lagos: African Reinsurance Corporation.

- Cadilhe, Carla and Pinto, Mário, Santos (2007). *Do Regime Jurídico do Pagamento dos Prémios de Seguro.* Lisbon: DisLivro

- Cannar, Kenneth (1979). *Motor Insurance Theory and Practice.* London: Witherby & Co. Ltd

- Chiejina, Ezekiel, O. (2004). *Foundations of Insurance: Law, Agency and Salesmanship.* Lagos: Mbeyi & Associates Ltd.

- IISA (2001 B). Legal Framework of Short Term Insurance.

- Kirkham, Sharon. (2008). Going for Broke(r). in RiskSA, February 2008, Vol. 05 Issue 04. Pages 20-24.

- Madge, Peter (1990). *Indemnity and insurance: a guide to the aspects of building contracts.* London: RIBA Publications.

- Mehr, Robet, I. and Cammack, Emerson (1972). Principles of Insurance. 5th Edition. Illinois: Richard D. Irwin, Inc.

- Plural Editores and KPMG (2009). Código Civil. 3rd Edition.Maputo: Plural Editores

- Price, H. 2008. 'The review of insurance contract law' in the Insurance Research and Practice, a research paper insert of the Journal of the Chartered Insurance Institute, London. February 2008. pp. i—viii.

- Sadler, John (ed.) (2012). The Insurance Manual. West Midlands: Insurance Publishing & Printing Co.

- Silva, Carlos, Pereira (2000). *Da economia e da gestão nas empresas de seguros.* Porto: Vida Económica (Grupo Editorial Peixoto de Sousa

- Thomas, Paul, I. and Reed, Prentice, Sr. (1977). Adjustment of Property Losses. 4th Edition. New York: McGraw-Hill, Inc.

- Vaughan, Emmet, J. (1992) *Fundamentals of risk and insurance.* 6th Edition. New York: John Wiley & Sons Inc.

- Vivian, Robert, W. and Morgan, Jim (2001). *Morgan's History of the Insurance Institute Movement in South Africa.* Cape Town: Francolin Publishers.

- Waty, Teodoro, A. (2007). *Direito de Seguros.* M Maputo: W&W Editora Lda

CHAPTER 4

CONCEPT OF RISK

We have been referring to handling of risk as being part of the business activity of insurance in the previous chapters. We have presented risk as one of the principal concerns leading people and business to arrange insurance. Before moving any further, we should discuss the concept of risk and try to explain how insurance is only one of many solutions that can be used to address problems caused by risk. Then, we shall review some of the key elements of risks that can be insured. Insurance does not claim to be able to treat all types of risks. We shall also identify types of risks that cannot be transferred to traditional insurance markets and explain some of the key reasons why this is the case.

The word *Risk* is commonly used to refer to a number of different situations. Some people may use it to simply refer to a dangerous situation. Others could use it to refer to the state of affairs in a country in relation to political stability (political risk), ability to continue to honour debts (credit risk) and stability of the rate of exchange (foreign exchange risk). Furthermore, in a business situation, an entrepreneur is said to run risks when he/she chooses to start a company and is facing the prospect of losing or making money from the venture.

In insurance, the word risk tends also to be used loosely to refer to a number of different things depending on the context in which the word is used. Risk may be used to refer to a cause of misfortune such as the risk of burglary. It is also used to refer to a likelihood of something occurring. Insurance practitioners also tend to use the word to refer to an insured object (the insured risk is a car). Risk is also used to describe a loss situation in the event of an insurance claim. We should now try to provide a clear definition of risk, as we shall use it in this book .

1. DEFINITION OF RISK

Risk is an abstract concept (Crouhy, Galai and Mark: 2006: 4). This means that it is not something that we can touch, see or hear with our senses. If we were to look at it from the point of view of some of the theories of Physics like the **Big Bang** theory[1], risk probably marked the beginning of our universe. Some scholars of risk management see the biblical story of Noah, the Ark and the Flood as a clear presentation of a problem of risk and the planning and handling of risk.

---

1. According to this scientific theory, which was first developed by George Lemaître, in very simple terms, the universe was formed as a result of a random accident which sparked a certain chain of events leading to expansion from certain single point. You may obtain more information on the following website: http://en.wikipedia.org/wiki/Big_Bang

In this story, they see Noah as a perfect illustration of a risk manager that invested in a plan to save lives in anticipation of the flooding that was going to destroy the world. This case could also be seen as one of the best examples of a systematic approach to an identified risk similar to what we call today risk management. We shall discuss later in this chapter this approach of proactively handling risk.

As can be noted in some of the illustrations of risk described above, the quest to overcome challenges posed by risk is as ancient as the history of humanity. Peter Bernstein, one of the key writers on the question of risk, also connects development of society with the ability of handling of risk. He asserts that 'the boundary between modern times and the past was the mastery of risk: the notion that the future is more than a whim of the gods and that men and women are not passive before nature' (Bernstein, 1996: 1).

Furthermore, it has also been argued that risk is a 'pervasive condition of human existence' (Vaughn, 1992:3). This means that while people tend to refer to risk after the occurrence of an accident or disaster; in fact, risk actually always exists in all our social and business activities. There is always the possibility that the future we are going to experience tomorrow is not going to be in accordance with our expectations from today. There is always a chance that something will not go according to our plans. It is in accordance with this viewpoint that one could assert that nobody 'can escape risk' (Holmes, 2004:

1). The following are some of the definitions of **risk** (IISA, 2011C: 4; Vaughn, 2009: 4 and Swiss Re, 1999: 13):

- *'The possibility of an unfortunate occurrence'*
- *'combination of hazards'*
- *'unpredictability—the tendency that actual results may differ from predicted results'*
- *'uncertainty' or 'possibility of loss'*
- *'a condition in which there is a possibility of an adverse deviation from a desired outcome that is expected or hoped for'*
- *'threat of a possible future event and its financial impact'*

The definitions given above can probably be best summarised by the definition from Holton (2004: 22) who defines risk as 'exposure to a proposition of which one is uncertain.' In providing this definition, Holton also further defines 'exposure' and 'uncertainty', which are critical elements of risk. To be *'exposed'* is to be in a situation that has 'material consequences' for us. *Uncertainty* is a state where we do not know what will happen. The mathematical concept of probability is used as one of the tools for measuring levels of uncertainty.

The different ways of defining risk and its key elements, as outlined above, are helpful for the purposes of understanding the full scope of the concept of risk. The common expression which is used to describe the groups of solutions that can be used to deal with risks is called risk management. Insurance is part of this process.

2. RISK MANAGEMENT

As we have already noted above, risk management is a process that seeks to treat risks and the adverse impact that they may cause on people, society and the environment (Assoumana, 2012: 20). The key activities in a risk management process as presented in the introductory manual of the Insurance Institute of South Africa on risk management (2011d: 21 -24), can be illustrated as per Figure 3 below.

Figure 3–The Risk Management Process

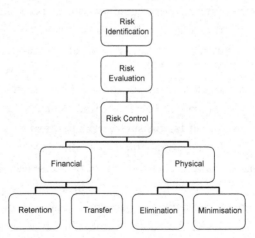

Before discussing the different steps illustrated above, we should note that there are other theories of risk that do not support some of the key assumptions underpinning this model. For instance, one of the key arguments from **Chaos theory** is that, in general, randomness of certain events and their effects in nature is such that it is virtually impossible to anticipate what may happen in the future. Notwithstanding the challenges posed by unpredictability of things such as nature, we should aim to be prepared for unexpected events. The principal motivation in such an exercise is to understand how we could try to mitigate or reduce the impact of risk despite the realisation that we do not have perfect and complete knowledge about the future.

2.1. Identification of risk

The first step in a risk management process is to identify the risks which threaten our property and well-being (Young, 2006: 33). For a more effective risk identification exercise, it is important to look at both the processes within the specific business under review and the environment in which it is located. A review of the environment of the business includes looking at factors such as the political situation, the economy and geography which may affect the business. As an example, properties located close to the sea-shore in the central parts of Mozambique tend to have a high exposure to cyclone and storm damages. Mozambique is classified as one of the countries in Africa that is most highly exposed to the weather-related hazards of **cyclones, flooding** and **droughts** (Schmuck, 2013: 3).

Furthermore, we should note that these same risks have been the principal factors which have caused major shocks to the otherwise excellent track record of growth of the Mozambican economy since the period of economic transition in the 1990s. As was observed by Lalá and Ostheimer (2003: 44), the major floods of 2000 in central and southern Mozambique caused 'economic stagnation'. The risks of flooding and storms have also probably been the most challenging perils on most insured properties. This same peril is also closely associated to that of flooding which affects most of the vast low-lying areas. Please look at Appendix III which has a map of the exposure of flooding per district in Mozambique.

Furthermore, it is important to understand the impact of the natural hazards described above in relation to the nature of business under review. Most of the properties located in exactly the area described above tend to be holiday homes with thatch roofing. While such types of construction may be ideal for creating the right exotic feel and comfort for holiday-makers, the same types also significantly increase chances of damage. Thatch and other types of construction that are not of solid brick and mortar are more likely to be damaged extensively in storms, which tend to also have a higher frequency in that same area. As part of a broad exercise of identifying and understanding the risks to which we are exposed, we could consider the following techniques:

a. Legal review

Given the low levels of placement of insurance in Mozambique, it is useful to start the exercise of risk identification from the point of view of legal obligations. Whether we see the risks involved or not, when there is a specific *legal obligation* to insure, it becomes imperative for us to be aware of our responsibilities and to comply. The legal obligation maybe as a result of requirements stipulated by law or may arise from contractual agreements. The requirement in our current labour law for all employers to arrange certain types of insurance for their employees is an example of a legal obligation by law.

Besides the obligatory insurance as required by the labour law, there are also other pieces of legislation that impose additional types of compulsory insurance. For instance, insurance intermediaries are required to have Professional Indemnity insurance, as specified in the Insurance Law. There are also compulsory types of insurance for travel agents, marine business, security firms, aviation operators, public road transporters and sports organisations, as we shall discuss later in this book. When identifying risks applicable for any type of entity, it is essential to also identify which laws may affect them depending on the sector where they operate. For types of business such as aviation and marine, it is also vital to identify international conventions that may be applicable as such activities are not only governed by national laws.

b. Physical inspection

Physical inspection is a process which involves, in general, walking through the property under review and checking how the business in question is operating and identifying what may fail to function as intended. The professional that may be hired to do such types of exercises is known as a **risk surveyor**. The surveyor should try to literally walk through the property under review from the beginning to the end gathering information on the risk first-hand. The surveyor should also aim to test all safety equipment in order to make sure that it is working as required. In order to systematically identify all possible hazards to which a business is exposed, risk surveyors may use risk inspection forms, flow charts and organisational charts (Valsamakis et al, 2010: 109)

c. Check-lists

Check-lists or risk inspection forms are an essential tool for effective risk surveying. They are usually prepared in such a way that the person doing the exercise is able to effectively review all possible areas of exposure of the given business activity. It is essential for the forms to be customised appropriately for each type of business activity. It is also crucial to continuously update the forms. With progress, there comes new technology and new ways of doing business which may bring about fundamental changes in the scope and nature of risks to which a business is exposed.

d. Flow charts

In industrial activities involving many processes, it is crucial to have diagrams which show all the activities involved. A surveyor can use such charts to identify what may fail to work as expected and affect the business under review. Depending on the technical detail contained in the charts, they can also be a useful tool for the process of evaluation of potential impact of identified risks.

e. Organisational charts

An organisational chart is a presentation of the structure of a company which shows the relationship between different functions in an organisation. In a review of financial risks, for instance, one may check adequacy of mechanisms to detect risks of fraud. It is also possible to identify in such a chart key individuals on which the organisation may be over-dependent. Furthermore, as part of best practices, it is also possible to check if certain critical activities such as risk management and auditing are reporting to the right people at the right level so that any critical findings are not easily swept under the carpet.

There are many other ways of identifying risks besides the ones reviewed above. According to Vaughan, 2009: 34-35, the other approaches may include exercises such as insurance policy checklist, analysis of financial statements and other internal reports, interviews as well as a combination of the different tools outlined above. After the process of identification of risks, the next step is that of risk evaluation.

2.2. Evaluation of Risk

Risk evaluation involves analysis of possible frequency or severity of losses or damage that may occur as a result of identified risks (Young, 2006: 33). By frequency, we are referring to the number of times that an unexpected event may occur. Severity is a measure of the impact of the event, if it occurs. An effective risk evaluation exercise will have both quantitative measurement and qualitative analysis.

In quantitative assessments, one tries to measure the impact or severity of harm or damage that may be caused by identified risks. If there is a reliable recording of all incidents and accidents suffered by a business in the past, that can be a very useful basis for calculating past trends of certain loss occurrence events. This process of measuring risk can be a complex exercise and the approach depends on the business activity under review. Furthermore, we should note that risk evaluations are vital exercises even if the numbers or prices (premium) calculated may appear like arbitrary figures. They create some form of scale for grading risks and enable concerned parties to make more 'rational economic' choices on whether to accept, absorb, handle or transfer identified risks (Crouhy, Galai and Mark, 2006: 17).

Besides the processes of measurement described above, it is also essential to do qualitative type of assessments. This type of analysis involves non-measurable aspects of risk such as root causes and categorisation of risks. Arranging risks into categories is useful for purposes of devising appropriate guidelines on how to handle risks in question. Please note in Table 5 below an illustration of types of risks which is based on risk categories as presented by KPMG (2008: 14-15).

Table 5–Categories of Risk

CATEGORY	DESCRIPTION
Business risk	The uncertainty about whether certain business ideas, models or products will be economically viable.
Operational risk	Potential of loss resulting from inadequate or failed internal processes, people and systems or from external events.
Legal & regulatory risk	This is a risk connected with failure to comply with laws, regulations and rules in the area of operation.
Reputational risk	The potential problem of a loss of confidence in the business by key stakeholders.
Credit risk	Problems that may be caused by change of the quality of things such as debtors of the business.
Liquidity risk	The danger of failing to raise cash to cover needs or capital withdrawal.

| Market risk | Potential losses from changes in prices and rates of financial markets. |
| Strategic risk | The problem of high uncertainty of success and profitability of major investment decisions. |

From the broad categories of risks outlined above, we should note that insurance tends to be very effective for transfer of mainly operational risks (Valsamakis et al, 2010: 45). Insurers tend to avoid types of risk that a business may be able to control through different processes. For instance, business risk should be controlled by the owner of the business by ensuring that they have chosen the correct approach and that the business has the right structures to operate effectively. For strategic risks, the concerned entrepreneurs need to ensure that they have correctly assessed the business environment and are appropriately planning for the execution of the defined business model (Crouhy, Galai and Mark, 2006: 33

After identifying and evaluating the risks to which a business is exposed, the next step is to decide how to 'reduce the probability of loss' (Young, 2006: 33). The principal aim of risk control is to 'eliminate or minimise the potential effect of the identified risk exposure.' There are a number of different approaches to risk control. We shall focus mainly on the two basic approaches: **physical risk control** and **financial risk control**.

2.3. Physical Risk Control

Physical risk control consists of practical measures that one can plan and implement in order to mitigate risk. The principal measures of physical risk control are elimination and minimization. Whenever possible, risk managers try to eliminate risk as an ultimate measure to avoid unwanted losses. However, it is not always feasible to completely eliminate all risks. By trying to avoid risk, one could end up not being able to do anything. In some instances, the government could pass laws to prevent certain activities that may be too hazardous. A good example of a legislative change in order to eliminate a certain type of risk is the specification of asbestos as a prohibited substance which businesses are not permitted to handle in most countries worldwide.

Minimisation is a measure where steps are taken to reduce frequency or severity of risk (Valsamakis, 2010: 16). **Loss minimisation** actions can be subdivided into the following:

- **Pre-loss minimization**—This is a situation where we take measures to prevent certain risk situations that we know may occur. A good example of such measures is putting of burglar bars on windows and doors of a building in order to prevent burglaries. When we ask a business to store money and other valuables in an appropriate safe; that is also a pre-loss minimisation measure.

- **Post-loss minimization**—This is when steps are taken in order to reduce the severity of risk situations that we might not be able to prevent. Air-bags in a car can be viewed as an example of a post-loss minimization measure. They are not designed to prevent an accident but are intended to reduce the impact of accidents that might occur.

2.4. Financial Risk Control

Risk financing involves the exercise of setting up of the most efficient means of accessing funds intended to cover loss situations caused by risk (Young, 2006: 34). There are a number of internal and external sources of risk financing that can be considered. For the purpose of this study, we shall focus on two basic methods of Financial Retention and Financial Risk Transfer, as described below.

2.5. Financial Retention

This is a risk control mechanism where a business may elect to use internal financial resources to cover partially or in full the losses that may affect it. Depending on the '**risk appetite**' of the business, there are a number of ways of funding the portion of risks that the business may choose to retain. Risk appetite is the expression used to describe the 'total impact of risk an organization is prepared to accept in the pursuit of its strategic objectives' (KPMG, 2008: 3).

After understanding the balance between risk and reward that an organisation would want to achieve, one would need to consider the methods to be employed to execute the defined strategy. There are a number of options that a business can consider to cover retained risks including the following:

- **Unplanned retention**—If one does not create specific financial provisions to cover potential loss situations of retained risks, then that can be viewed as some form of unplanned financial retention. It essentially means that if the retained risk were to occur, then the client would need to find funds to cover its losses.

- **Funded retention**—If a business makes a plan to cover financial impact of retained risks, then that is treated as funded or planned risk retention. This funding can be in the form of pre-loss or post-loss funding. A good example in our market of a pre-loss funding mechanism is the case of self-funded health schemes used by some large public companies. In such schemes, the companies setup budgets to pay for health claims by employees. Post-loss funding may involve financial agreements such as **contingency funds** and debt facilities that can be accessed in case of claims.

- **Self-insurance** or **captive insurance**—A company or group of companies may set up an entity to insure their own risks and handle the risks in a way similar to a conventional insurance company (Sharp, 2009: 34). Such an entity is known as a captive. It may be set up in the same territory as its beneficiaries (onshore) or it could be in a different domicile (offshore). Some of the key international companies that have recently invested in the new oil and gas extractive industry tend to use offshore captive insurance models to cover insurance requirements of their investments world-wide (Chambeze, 2014: 8).

2.6. Financial Risk Transfer

This is a situation where a business may transfer parts of risk to financial markets in exchange for a certain cost (premium). Besides traditional insurance markets, there are other options for financial risk transfer including captive or self-insurance programmes, financial capital markets and other financial facilities (Valsamakis, 2010: 223). In this book, we shall focus on insurance, as the predominant mechanism for risk transfer in our market. Concepts such as captives and alternative risk transfer markets are still virtually non-existent in Mozambique. The few multi-national companies in our market that use such tools rely mainly on entities setup in international financial markets that are able to take the risks from the local market structured as reinsurance placed offshore.

While this would all not be illegal in terms of the local Insurance Law, this could become a key area of interest with planned new legislation on **transfer pricing**[2], which is currently being debated in Mozambique. Tax authorities are concerned about how these processes may be used to inflate costs in one area and transfer profits to territories with more favourable tax regimes.

3. PLANNING FOR AN UNCERTAIN FUTURE

The final question we should discuss before closing this section on management of risk is how do we plan and prepare today for a future that we do not know? What actions should we execute today in order to make sure that, if any unexpected events were to happen, our business would continue to survive and operate effectively? There are a number of business tools that have been developed on how to handle future uncertainty. We would like to briefly discuss two concepts that are part of solutions to the questions outlined above.

3.1. Scenario Planning

The technique of **scenario planning** is used for purposes of long range planning notwithstanding the uncertainty of the future. It is used to facilitate decision-making on issues relating to risk management and other business decisions

2. Transfer price is 'the price at which one part of an entity sells a product or service to another part of the same entity', as defined on the website www.accountingtools.com

(Swiss Re, 2009: 3). The concept of scenarios can also be used for purposes checking and testing capacity of an insurance company to withstand a range of adverse financial situations. This is part of an exercise known as '**stress testing**'. In such an activity, 'adverse scenarios' are used to make projections on possible impact on the financial capacity of insurers to meet its current and future commitments (Hafeman, 2009: 14).

3.2. Business Continuity Planning

Business Continuity Planning (BCP) is a form of planning designed to enable an organisation to effectively manage the risks which threaten its existence. It is aimed at ensuring the survival of an organisation following occurrence of any disaster which disrupts its operations (Sadler, 2012: 8/11.2. The process involves defining of action to be executed after occurrence of a crisis to protect people and property, measures to be adopted to ensure continuation of activities, recovery of operations and return to normal.

4. INSURABLE RISKS

From the exercises of risk management identified above, we have defined a model for identifying risks, assessing their impact and determination of how to handle them. We have noted that insurance is one of the financial solutions for handling risks. While prospective clients may want to transfer all critical risks identified, it is vital to be aware that insurance markets are not able to underwrite all the risks which threaten the property and livelihood of prospective buyers of insurance. We shall now discuss the key features of insurable risks in the following section

4.1. Particular or fundamental risks

One of the key determinants of insurable risks is whether they are particular or fundamental. Particular risks are those types of risks which may expose us to loss situations affecting a person or a business entity as a result of identifiable 'individual causes' (IISA, 2011A: 46). Such individual loss events can involve situations such as road accidents, theft, fire, fraud, accidental breakage, etc. The impact of a loss or injury is also usually limited to a specific location or to a small number of people. It is also believed that it is possible for the people likely to be affected to take measures to prevent or minimise frequency of occurrence of such types of risks (Silva, 2000: 90). In general, particular risks tend to be insurable in traditional insurance policies.

As for fundamental risks, they usually involve broad political or socio-economic phenomena or natural events that affect many people and businesses at the same time (Vaughan, 2009: 8). The loss situations arising from fundamental risks can potentially be of a catastrophic nature and are not within the control of an individual (Silva, 2000: 90). Examples of fundamental risks include war, inflation, unemployment, drought, depreciation and economic recession. Some of the fundamental risks such as the natural phenomenon of earthquakes, tsunamis, storms and floods can be insured on property insurance policies. However, our insurance market does not cover fundamental risks such as war, terrorism and economic risks. This situation where the insurance market is unable to cover risks that society may expect to be covered can be viewed as part of what economists classify as a '**market failure**'.

Following the identification of cases where markets may fail to provide certain items as discussed above, classical economic theories suggest that the government could try to provide some form of service to make up for the lack of a market solution. This approach of some form of state intervention is applied even in developed countries that follow philosophies of market-led economic policies. It is on this basis that most developed countries have government funds to cover principal fundamental risks such as war, terrorism and sabotage, which are not insured on standard insurance policies (Silva, 2000: 90). In countries that are described as '**welfare states**' such as Finland, Sweden and the United Kingdom, even complex fundamental risks like unemployment have some form of public protection.

Furthermore, these types of mechanisms for protection of society against such fundamental risk are part of what is known as **social insurance**. Some of the social insurance funds such as the national pension fund in Mozambique are **contributory funds.** They are classified as such because they only provide cover to people who have contributed premium for a defined period of time. For **non-contributory funds** such as the social grant in South Africa, you may apply for support if you meet the criteria of people that are supposed to be covered by the fund. Most countries in Africa do not have public funds to cover most of the principal fundamental risks that are not covered by conventional insurance markets. We shall discuss later in this book the key social protection systems in Mozambique.

4.2. Pure or speculative risks

The second aspect we shall review which determines insurability of risks is whether they are pure or speculative risks. Insurance is not intended to cover speculative risks, as defined in Article 182 of Insurance Law in Mozambique. The understanding in the legal framework is that there should not be 'unjust enrichment' through insurance. This standpoint is also supported by the insurance traditional principle of indemnity.

According to the Risk Management manual of the IISA (2011D: 4), a pure risk is when we face a situation of only two possible outcomes of either making a loss or remaining in the same position (no loss). Pure risks, which are also known as '**downside risks**', do not hold a prospect of making a profit. The loss events connected to pure risks may be caused by factors within or outside of direct control and influence of entities affected by them. Factors outside control and influence of affected entities include events such as burglaries, flooding, droughts and others. An entity may also face the prospects of losses as a result of factors which are within their 'direct control and influence'. Such events, which are also known as '**operational risks**', may be caused by incorrect or inappropriate operation of employees, systems and structures within a company. Within a business environment, the exposure to speculative risks can be sub-divided into the following two groups:

- **Inherent business risks** or **core business risks** which consist of the economic activities in which an entrepreneur may invest with the expectation to gain something. Depending on the nature of decisions made on how to do the business in question and/or the environment where it is located, the business venture faces the prospects of making an economic loss, breaking-even or making a profit.

- **Incidental risks** are not risks involved in the deliberate activities or choices of the business but are associated with the situation of the business and also affect performance of the business. Examples of typical incidental risks include problems of fluctuations of the costs of borrowing money (interest rate) or problems of valuation of currencies in international markets.

A speculative risk involves an outcome of a possible gain or profit from the concerned undertaking (Vaughan, 2009:

8). It usually involves a risk that one chooses to accept. For instance, when one chooses to gamble, there is a deliberate assumption of risk of losing or remaining in the same situation or winning. The economic activity of starting a business is also one of the best examples of a speculative risk situation.

In general, it is not the intention of insurance to cover speculative risk situations. However, in certain speculative activities, it may be possible to distinguish elements of pure risk that could be insurable. For instance, when a bank gives credit–that is a speculative undertaking in the sense that the bank is aiming to gain more than what it lends through interest rates charged. However, besides the credit risk, it is possible to cover the life of the debtor in case of death where the bank may be at risk of losing capital amount extended to the debtor. The distinction between pure and speculative risks, as described above, can be illustrated as shown in Table 6.

Table 6–Pure vs Speculative Risks

DESCRIPTION	PURE RISK	SPECULATIVE RISK
Possible outcomes	- Loss (negative) - No loss (neutral)	- Loss (negative) - Break-even (neutral) - Gain (profit).
Principal motivation	- Not lose	- Make profits
Source of exposure in a Business Activity	- Operational risks - External factors	- Inherent business risk - Incidental risks.

4.3. Certain or uncertain

The degree of certainty of a defined risk situation is also a crucial aspect for defining whether it is insurable or not. On one hand, as defined in the Oxford Dictionary, to be certain is to have no doubts. On the other hand, to be uncertain is not to know what will happen in the future. This lack of knowledge or 'doubt' is as a result of the fact that we have 'imperfect information' about what will happen in the future (IISA, 2011C: 5). It is this element of uncertainty which is one of the key elements of insurable risks. In cases where there is a high degree of certainty of a loss, it is usually not the objective of insurance to cover such losses. This is part of the reason why insurers either exclude from cover or apply what are known as excesses or deductibles to avoid small minor damages such as dents and scratches on standard insurance policies covering damages of property such as vehicles.

Furthermore, standard insurance policies tend to be designed to avoid covering types of incidents with a high likelihood of repetitive losses. These types of minor losses with a high frequency are also referred to as **attritional losses**. By applying excesses or deductibles, insurers define a limit below which the insured client should pay for his/her own losses. We shall discuss later in this book the insurance concepts of excesses, deductibles and franchises.

4.4. Lawful or unlawful

It is also imperative to note that insurance should not provide protection 'against public policy' (IISA, 2011A: 47). Insurance is not supposed to operate contrary to laws, rules and regulations of society. This is a fundamental requirement for all business activities. Compared to other markets in our region such as South Africa, there are still fairly few regulatory and compliance requirements in the insurance market of Mozambique, at this stage. This situation is likely to change in the future as more conditions are likely to be imposed by appropriate authorities in alignment with some of the key emerging global trends on refined regulation models of insurance markets, as we shall discuss later in this book.

5. FUNCTION OF INSURANCE

Firstly, it should be noted that risk is the principal area of focus of insurance (Swiss Re, 1999: 14). According to Casanova (1964: 140) 'there is no insurance without risk.'[3] As we discussed at the beginning of this chapter, risk is something that is always present and can happen to any one of us at any time. Insurance, as one of the key tools for financial protection against certain types of risks, can be utilised by all types of businesses, organisations and people at all times. Like other financial services, it is a type of economic activity which

---

3. This is a translation of the original text in Portuguese which reads: 'Não há seguro sem risco'

supports all other social and economic activities. Here is an outline of some of the key functions of the insurance market:

5.1. Risk transfer

As already discussed, insurance is one of the key options in the process of managing of risks that threaten the livelihood of society. Instead of having to deal with the consequences of an 'uncertain' future, one can pay a defined price (premium) and transfer the financial risk to an insurer (IISA, 2011C: 165). Although the premium payable to the insurer represents a certain financial cost; it is invariably a much smaller proportion of the value of the covered item and of the respective impact if the item is lost or damaged. As a result of this function, the insured entities and people are able to focus and invest more of their time and resources on their core activities instead of worrying about making financial provisions for unexpected events. In this way, the function of risk transfer to insurance supports the economic processes of efficient allocation of scarce resources.

5.2. Pooling of risks

The insurance market plays a critical role of creating a shared fund for the financing of losses that may affect insured people and business (Vaughan, 1992: 20). Through the charging of premium from many insured clients across a given geographic area, insurance contributes to the building up of a fund that can be used to settle claims of the unfortunate entities that may be affected by the perils covered through their insurance policies. In this way, insurance attempts to take advantage of what is known as the '**Law of Large Numbers**' (Mehr and Cammack, 1972: 33). This is a concept from **Probability Theory.** In accordance with this theory, the financial model of insurance works if an insurer is able to cover a large number of similar types of risks over a broad area so that there is a large enough fund of premium to cover the costs of the few clients that may suffer any unexpected losses. The critical condition regarding existence of a group of similar risks is what is referred to as **homogenous risks** and their existence over a broad area is what is known as a **spread of risk** (Silva, 2000: 115).

5.3. Equitable contributions

In practice, insured risks are not all lumped together in one portfolio without taking into account the nature and scope of risk that each insured person or item represents. In insurance, risks are pooled in different categories depending on the types of covered items, on values at risk and on the nature of hazards that may affect the subject of insurance (IISA, 2011C: 165). Ideally, each pool should have homogenous or fairly similar types of risks (Silva, 2000: 115). In this way, the underwriters are able to apply appropriate pricing for each group of risks. Even within each specific risk pool, premium rates will vary depending on, amongst other things, the key characteristics of each insured item, performance of the client in the past and measures taken to control the risk of loss or damage, as per the risk management process described above.

5.4. Mobilising of savings

Insurance also plays a critical role of mobilisation of domestic long term savings (Silva, 2000: 21 and Das et al, 2003:3). As we shall discuss in this book, some of the products of insurance such as life insurance policies and pension funds are designed to promote savings for the future. Such savings can be a key source of investments in the national economy as insurers try to grow the value of the contributions of covered persons.

5.5. Financial security

Insurance also serves as a mechanism for providing financial security in case of a misfortune. Through insurance, it is possible to protect a family from financial ruin in case a bread-winner fails to work as a result of illness or injury. This is a very critical social role which ensures that at least the financial interest of the insured person is protected. It is also possible for partnerships and other forms of business entities to secure some form of financial security through types of life insurance policies intended to provide compensation in case of death or permanent disability of key personnel who affect performance of the business.

CONCLUSION

We have discussed different aspects of risk in this chapter. We started with a review of definitions of risk. Then we explored the concept of risk management. The key steps involved in this process are identification, evaluation and control of risk. The main purpose of the process is to mitigate the impact of risk. We have noted that insurance is one of the possible options for handling risk. It is vital to note that even after transferring risks to an insurer, the insured remains with full control of their property. They should continue to protect it as if it is not covered by insurance.

We also discussed in this chapter the key functions of insurance. We have identified how insurance offers a mechanism for transfer of risk, pooling of risk and ensuring equitable contributions from all insured entities. Some of the types of insurance such as life and pensions are also useful mechanisms for mobilising long term domestic savings. Finally, insurance also provides financial security that enables people, other business and organisations to focus on their activities with confidence knowing that their insurance policies provide cover for certain identified risks that they face. For the next chapter, we shall look at current laws applicable to insurance business activities and the respective insurance regulatory authorities in Mozambique.

REFERENCES

- Assoumana, Hassan (2012). *Industrial Enterprise: Role of Risk Surveys in Loss Prevention* in the African Reinsurer. Lagos: African Reinsurance Corporation

- Bernstein, P. L. (1996). Against the gods: the remarkable story of risk. New York: John Wiley

- Casanova, Manuel, (1964) *Princípios Básicos de Seguros* in Seguros, Série Técnica. No. 106. Sindicatos de Seguros de Lisboa e Porto. Pages 140-152

- Chambeze, Isaias (2014) in a Conference Paper presented at the ISSM Insurance Seminar with title– *Colocação de Seguro no Exterior e Desafios para as Seguradoras Nacionais*

- Crouhy, Michael; Galai, Dan and Mark, Robert (2006). *The Essentials of Risk Management*. New York: McGraw-Hill

- Das, U.S., Davies, N., and Podpiera, R. (2003). *Insurance and Issues in Financial Soundness*: IMF Working Paper, WP/03/138, IMF: Washington.

- Hafeman, Michael (2009). *The Role of the Actuary in Insurance*. Primer Series on Insurance, Issue 4, May 2009. Washington: The World Bank.

- Holmes, Andrew (2004) *Smart risk*. West Sussex: Capstone Publishing Limited.

- Insurance Institute of South Africa (2011 C). *Risk and Insurance*. Insurance Institute of South Africa.

- Holton, Glyn, A. (2004) Defining Risk. Financial Analysts Journal, Volume 60, Number 6. CFA Institute.

- KPMG (2005). *Risk and Capital Management: A new perspective for insurers*. Netherlands: KPMG

- Lalá, Anícia and Ostheimer, Andrea, E. (2003) How to remove the stains on Mozambique's democratic track record: Challenges for the democratisation process between 1990 and 2003. Maputo: Konrad-Adenauer-Stiftung

- KPMG (2008). *Understanding and articulating risk appetite*. Sydney: KPMG

- Mehr, Robert, I. and Cammack, Emerson (1972). Principles of Insurance. 5th Edition. Illinois: Richard D. Irwin, Inc.

- Sadler, John (ed.) (2012). The Insurance Manual. West Midlands: Insurance Publishing & Printing Co.

- Holton, Glyn, A. (2004) Defining Risk. Financial Analysts Journal, Volume 60, Number 6. CFA Institute.

- Sharp, David (2009). *Upstream and Offshore Energy Insurance*. Livingston: Witherbys Insurance

- Silva, Carlos, Pereira (2000). *Da economia e da gestão nas empresas de seguros.* Porto: Vida Económica (Grupo Editorial Peixoto de Sousa

- Schmuck, Hanna (2013). The Economics of Early Response and Resilience: Mozambique Country Study

- Swiss Re (2009). Sigma: Scenario analysis in insurance. No. 1/2009. Zurich: Swiss Reinsurance Company Ltd

- Swiss Re (1999). *From risk to capital: an insurance perspective.* Zurich: Swiss Reinsurance Company

- Valsamakis, Anthony, C.; Vivian, Robert, W. and du Toit, Gawie, S. (2010) *Risk management.* 4th edition. Sandton: Heinemann Publishers (Pty) Ltd

- Vaughan, Emmet, J. (1992) *Fundamentals of risk and insurance.* 6th Edition. New York: John Wiley & Sons Inc.

- Young, Jackie (2006). *Operational Risk Management.* Pretoria: Van Schaik Publishers.

CHAPTER 5

LEGAL FRAMEWORK OF INSURANCE

We would like to begin by noting that, as one of the key outcomes of the historical links between Portugal and Mozambique, which we discussed in Chapter 2, our legal framework is based on the Portuguese system. Although there have been a number of critical changes of most of the pieces of law in Mozambique during the different phases of development in the past, Portuguese law has maintained a strong influence on local legislation. In this Chapter, we shall discuss the current pieces of law covering insurance.

Besides the laws which cover insurance directly, we shall also outline other key pieces of legislation that have provisions relating to insurance. As we shall see in this chapter, legislation governing other economic sectors like aviation, marine, tourism, sports, security and transportation also have clauses that refer to some forms of compulsory insurance. Then, we shall look at the entity responsible for supervision of the insurance sector.

1. THE CURRENT INSURANCE LAW

The current insurance legislation is supposed to represent a refinement of previous legislation of 21 January 2003[1] and supporting regulations[2]. The principal Insurance Law which is currently in place consists of a legislative decree reference number 1/2010 of 31 December 2010[3]. This piece of legislation is supported by the following regulatory legislation:

- Decree number 30/2011 of 11 August 2011[4] containing the regulations in relation to access and operation of insurance business and respective intermediation

- Decree number 222/2010 of 17 December 2010 providing the approved chart of accounts

- Decree number 29/2012 of 26 July 2012 constituting the insurance regulatory body

- Ministerial Decree number 300/2012 of 14 November 2012 providing internal regulations of the insurance regulator

- Ministerial Decree number 101/2014 of 2 July 2014 approving models of insurance licenses

---

1. *Lei nº. 3/2003, de 21 de Janeiro*
2. *Decreto nº. 41/2003, de 10 de Dezembro*
3. Referred to in Portuguese as *Decreto-Lei nº. 1/2010, de 31 de Dezembro*
4. Known in Portuguese as *Decreto nº. 30/2011 de 11 de Agosto*

1.1. Key features of the Insurance Law of 31 December 2010

We would like to start by noting that we shall use the expression the **Insurance Law** to refer to the current principal legislation of insurance of 31 December 2010. It consists of the following four components:

- The Decree Law which provides the legal basis for the establishment of the law and formalises the process of approval of the law. Amongst the legal articles in this part of the law, there is definition of the scope of the law, specification that insurance business is governed by the Ministry of Finance, notification of formation of a new insurance regulatory body (ISSM) and of dissolution of the former regulatory authority (IGS). There is also a specification of the different rates of tax payable to the regulatory authority

- The First Book[5] of the Insurance Law which defines the legal conditions for registering and operating insurance business and respective intermediation. It has legal articles number 1 to 78 which are sub-divided into two parts[6]. The first part has the general legal provisions relating to registration and operation of insurance business. Then the second part has the

---

5. This is a literal translation for the expression *'Livro Primeiro'*, as noted in the law.

6. Referred to in Portuguese as *'Titulos'*

legal conditions for accessing and operating insurance, microinsurance, reinsurance and intermediation.

• The Second Book of the Insurance Law which is the legal regime of insurance contracts. It has the rest of the articles of the Insurance Law from number 79 to 260. This part of the law provides the legal conditions that must be satisfied by an insurance contract and also defines rules regarding treatment of premium and handling of claims. It also provides guidelines on how insurers can do coinsurance[7] and reinsurance[8]. Then, from article number 181, there are rules and regulations relating to legal conditions of different types of insurance contracts.

• The Glossary is the last part of the law where there are definitions of all key expressions covered in the Insurance Law.

Furthermore, it is vital to note some of the key requirements for legal reporting and notifications to the insurance regulator, as specified in the Insurance Law. This is intended to enable the regulator to monitor and review business practices of licensed operators in the market. You may

---

7   Coinsurance is a process where, on a large risk, insurers may agree to jointly underwrite it and share it (Silva, 2000: 118).

8   Reinsurance is a process in which insurers transfer a part of risk beyond their capacity to a separate entity (Portugal, 2007: 300).

find a list of all the key items in Appendix IV. Furthermore, the key statutory reports and notifications as required under the Insurance Law are as outlined in Table 7.

Table 7–Statutory Reports and Notifications as per the Insurance Law

What is required?	Where is this prescribed?	Who should do it?	How should it be done?
Application for a license to operate in Mozambique	Article 9	All prospective operators in insurance, reinsurance, microinsurance and intermediation	As per guideline from the ISSM and details outlined in Article 133 of the Regulations
Up-to-date policy and claim registers	Article 31	Insurers, Reinsurers & Microinsurers	No specific guidelines
Registration of microinsurance policies	Articles 43 & 53	Insurers and microinsurers	Presentation of all terms and conditions
Transfer of microinsurance portfolio	Article 55	Microinsurers	No specific guidelines
Notification of agents	Articles 57	All operators	As per guideline from the ISSM

The requirement for operators in the sector to submit reports and other notifications to the regulator is used for a supervisory function known as 'offsite inspection' (Hafeman & Randle, 2009: 14). This allows the regulator to monitor performance of the market in accordance with defined rules and to see if there are any trends requiring their intervention before further deterioration. We have also noted that, following expansion of our insurance market in the last 5 years, we are also seeing the authorities doing more regular 'onsite inspections'. This is a case where the supervisors go to the premises of the operator in order to attend to an area of focus. For instance, the regulator has been monitoring closely the levels of transfer of risks abroad, as we shall discuss later.

Besides considerations relating to traditional principles and practice of insurance, the new law also seeks to align the development policy of the insurance sector to emerging development initiatives of national policy-makers. This objective is reflected in the way the law has a clear focus on questions such as promotion of access to insurance services for the low-income population through a concept known as **microinsurance**. Articles 41 to 45 and 52 to 54 provide some of the key legal conditions for the setting up of a microinsurance company. Furthermore, Articles 364 to 365 provide legal provisions regarding intermediation of microinsurance. This specific treatment of microinsurance is a new feature which was not covered in previous legislation. We shall discuss further the concept of microinsurance in this book.

1.2. Regulations of Insurance legislation

The operation of the legislation of insurance is supported by regulatory legislation contained in Decree of 11 August

2011[9]. You could divide the Insurance Regulations into 5 key parts as follows:

- Part 1 is the Decree formalising the approval process of the Insurance Regulations.

- Part 2 has conditions for accessing insurance business

- Part 3 has conditions for handling of insurance business

- Part 4 has conditions for accessing and handling of intermediation

- Annex with a list of classes of insurance business

We shall not discuss all the key conditions specified in the regulations. We would like to highlight some of the key items below.

a. Statutory notifications

The Insurance Regulations contains a number of key requirements regarding items that should be communicated to the Insurance Regulator. Please find in Table 8, a summary of statutory notifications, as specified in the regulations.

---

9. Known in Portuguese as *Decreto nº. 30/2011 de 11 de Agosto*

**Table 8–Statutory Notifications as per the
Regulations of the Insurance Law**

What is required?	Where is it prescribed?	Who should do it?	How should it be done?
Notification of changes of articles of association or registered office or of mergers and acquisition	Article 3	All operators	As per conditions defined in the same article
Notification of all fronting transactions	Article 5	Insurers	By the 15th day of each month for previous month and as defined in the same article
Notification on shareholding structures	Articles 22-27	Insurers	As defined in the same articles
Notification of opening of a branch or change of address	Article 31	Insurers	As defined in the same article
Notification to ISSM of any irregularity detected	Article 137	Accounts, Auditing Committees, Internal & External Auditors of all operators	As defined in the same article

b. Statutory Actuary

We should also take special note of a crucial condition specified in Article 82 of the Insurance Regulations regarding the requirement for an **actuary**. According to the guideline for life business of Associação Portuguesa de Seguradores

(1997: 24), this is a fairly recent legal condition even in Portugal. Given the important role of an actuary, we should look at a definition of this profession and discuss some of its key functions. The Mathematics Department at Purdue University defines an **actuary** as follows:

> '*An actuary is a business professional who analy[z]es the financial consequences of risk. Actuaries use mathematics, statistics, and financial theory to study uncertain future events, especially those of concern to insurance and pension programs. Actuaries may work for insurance companies, consulting firms, government, employee benefits departments of large corporations, hospitals, banks and investment firms, or, more generally, in businesses that need to manage financial risk*'[10]

Furthermore, in doing their work, actuaries focus their attention on a range of 'interrelated factors that affect the ability of an insurer to generate and maintain sufficient capital to ensure that it can meet its obligations to policyholders' (Hafeman, 2009: 5). These activities are known as the **actuarial control cycle**. As illustrated in Figure 4, the principal preoccupation in this cycle is capital.

---

10. As per the following website consulted on 15 March 2014: http://www.math.purdue.edu/academic/actuary/what.php?p=what

Figure 4–Actuarial control cycle

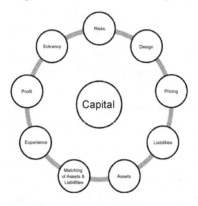

An actuary plays a central role in the handling of the broad range of risks to which an insurer is exposed. As we discussed in Chapter 4, in addition to risks assumed by clients, insurers, like all other entities are exposed to a broad range of risks. An insurer also has to plan how it will manage all the risks to which it is exposed. An actuary also provides critical mathematical input in designing of products as well as ensuring that appropriate prices are charged. Following the issuing of policies, an actuary assists in determining adequacy of financial provisions to cover future financial commitments (liabilities), as per the 'promise' in the insurance contract. These financial provisions are also known as **technical provisions** or **reserves**. Reserves are one of the key distinguishing features of financial accounts of an insurance company. The Insurance Law specifies minimum types of reserves that must be set up depending on type of insurance business

Furthermore, an actuary guides the financial management of an insurer by ensuring that it has sufficient and adequate resources (assets) to cover its future obligations and to satisfy rules specified in the Insurance Law. This process affects nature and types of investments that an insurer can make with premium received and its capital depending on nature and size of business. An actuary also ensures that the assets, as described above, match the liabilities, as provided for by the insurer.

Moreover, an actuary analyses claims experience of the insurer in order to see if there are any trends and if there is a need to review pricing or types of product or levels of reserves. An actuary also monitors profits or losses achieved by the insurer in the different lines of business in order to see if there are areas requiring review. At the same time, an actuary also tries to ensure that, in the course of its business and after settling claims due, the insurer retains financial capacity to meet future liabilities. This is known in insurance as **solvency** (Benjamin, 1977: 267). In order to prevent problems of insolvency or failure to meet their responsibilities, Insurance Laws in most countries including Mozambique define minimum levels of solvency that must be maintained by an insurer. Please have a look at Appendix V that has a presentation of a solvency margin report from the Insurance Market Report of Zimbabwe. We shall discuss later how we could consider new models to improve our market reports.

We shall not discuss in detail in this book the techniques involved in these key functions of an actuary. However, as you can see from the brief outline of the key functions of actuaries, they play an essential role. Unfortunately, as was observed by Hafeman (2009: 1), this profession is not well-known by most people and most countries like Mozambique do not have qualified professional actuaries and appropriate local associations to ensure quality of their work.

According to the Regulation of the Insurance Law, all **Life Insurance**[11] companies are required to have an actuary that has certain legal responsibilities and is expected to provide certain types of reports to the Insurance Regulator. Such a type of actuary is also referred to as a **statutory actuary**. The actuary does not have to be a full time employee of the insurer. It is possible to satisfy this condition by working with an actuary or an actuarial firm as an external contractor. This is a useful concession given scarcity of qualified actuarial professionals worldwide.

As specified in the same Article, **Non-Life** insurance companies are also supposed to comply with the same requirement within a time period of three years after the passing of the same piece of legislation. Since the regulations were passed on 11 August 2011, the requirement for an actuary should be also applicable for Non-Life insurance

---

11. Please see Chapter 7 for a description of difference between Life and Non-Life insurance companies

with effect from August 2014. Only microinsurance business is exempted from this requirement.

1.3. Statute on Approved Chart of Accounts

The approach and standards for handling and presentation of accounts of insurance business are as specified in the Statute of the Ministry of Finance reference number 222/2010 of 17 December, 2010. This measure was adopted as part of the reform exercise in the insurance sector. It is intended to align accounting practices in Mozambique to global standards as reflected in the International Financial Reporting Standards (IFRS). After completion of implementation of these new standards by all insurers, it will also be much easier for the regulator and the insurance association to compile market reports appropriately and timely. In the past, this has not been possible. The insurers in our market have been following common approaches and standards.

Before the implementation of IFRS, the market should also aim to have addressed some of the current issues which will limit effectiveness of this accounting model. One of the key areas that will need to be addressed is the problem of long-term payments of pensions in Workman's Compensation Act Insurance. As we shall discuss further in Chapter 9, this practice causes a miss-match with underlying classification of the same class of insurance. One of the key preoccupations of the emerging reporting standards is to ensure that insurers are appropriately classifying and accounting for liabilities assumed.

1.4. Statute on Models of Licenses

Licenses for approved financial service providers in the insurance sector are supposed to be according to the models presented in Statute number 101/2014 of 2 July 2014. This is one of the most recent pieces of legislation. The approved models are for the following categories of licenses:

- Insurance agent registered as a private individual

- Insurance agency registered as a company

- Insurance broker

- Reinsurance broker

- Insurance company

- Microinsurance company

- Reinsurance company

- Pension fund

The entities outlined above are in alignment with those defined in the Insurance Legislation. Besides the legislation described above, we should also note conditions relating to obligatory types of insurance, as we shall discuss below.

1.5. Legislation on Obligatory Classes of Insurance

From our research, we noted that there are a number of laws that refer to obligatory types of insurance as outlined in Table 9.

Table 9–Laws covering obligatory types of insurance

Legal Reference	Obligatory Types of Cover	Covering Entities
Law number 2/2003 of 21 January 2003[3] and the respective regulations[4]	Motor Liability	Insurance Market
Decree no. 41/2005 of 30 August 2005	Guarantees and Public Liability for Travel Agents	Insurance Market
Social Security Law no. 4/2007 of 7 February 2007	Pension Fund	Social Security Public Fund
Decree no. 9/2007 of 30 April 2007	Public liability and guarantees for security firms	Insurance Market
Regulations on Tourism Transport–Decree 41/2007 of 24 August 2007	Motor Liability for Tourism	Insurance Market
Civil Aviation Law no. 21/2009 of 28 September 2009	Aviation Liability	Insurance Market
Decree no. 49/2010 of 11 November 2010	Depositors Insurance	Central Bank
Insurance Law no. 1/2010 of 31 December 2010	Professional Indemnity for insurance intermediaries	Insurance Market
Decree no. 62/2013 of 4 December 2013[6]	Workman's Compensation Act Insurance	Insurance Market
Law no. 5/2014 of 5 February 2014	Professional Indemnity for law firms	Insurance Market

Besides the National Social Security Pension Fund and the Depositors Insurance Fund, there are no other government institutions or public funds to cover these obligatory types of insurance. As a result of this setup, we have a situation where the private sector insurance market tries to provide cover where there are no appropriate public funds. On this basis the private sector insurers try to take advantage of the force of law in order to underwrite these types of insurance, as public institutions would have done.

This situation where the market tries to provide a public service that should be covered by public funds creates a critical market distortion. It is not clear if the insurers trying to provide such types of social insurance should strictly follow the approach they would apply in normal commercial business or if they should treat such risks as public social insurance funds would cover them. It is not clear if rules applied to normal commercial business should be applied to such types of social insurance being provided by private sector operators.

When public funds in South Africa provide the compulsory Compensation for Occupational Accidents insurance, the pricing of such insurance is not based on any market related pricing mechanism. Would it not be a consistent approach for the local private sector insurers here to also fix the pricing for the same risk in our market, where there is no public fund? How would this fit with the emerging preference of regulators to prevent all forms of price fixing and related monopolistic practices?

It appears that we are still going to have many debates in our market on these questions. We are of the view that it is not sustainable for traditional commercial insurance companies to cover social insurance in the same way that they would underwrite traditional commercial insurance business. Some of the exposures involved in social insurance are of a nature that can cause failures right across the market. If the government is failing to provide such forms of social protection, the insurance market should handle the risks appropriately and avoid a situation where the smaller insured population is indirectly subsidizing other social services that should be covered by appropriate public funds. We shall discuss further the key characteristics of obligatory types of insurance.

1.6. Regulations on Complementary Pension Funds

In addition to the compulsory national pension scheme, there is now a legal framework for the setting up of complementary pension funds by pension fund administration companies from the private sector. This is provided for in the respective regulations covering complementary pension funds. These regulations are referred to as Decree no. 25/2009 of 17 August[12]. They define the rules for the setting up of pension funds and respective management. They also govern the rules for the setting up of pension fund administration companies.

---

12. Known in Portuguese as Decreto nº. 25/2009 de 17 de Agosto

As defined in Article 7 of the Insurance Law, such pension funds and administration companies are supposed to be supervised by the insurance regulator.

Furthermore, the regulations of the Insurance Law also specify that the pension funds can either be open to anyone interested or closed type of funds for a restricted group of people in a company or an association of some form. The types of pension plans can either be **defined benefit** or **defined contributions**. In the defined benefit model, the rules of the fund determine the benefits that are payable to each beneficiary and the fund has the responsibility of ensuring that adequate contributions and investments are achieved to cover the respective liability. In the defined contribution plans, the contributions from the members are determined upfront and then the benefits for each member depends on the sum of contributions for the respective member plus the return on investment of the fund, less respective administration costs.

2. TAXES AND FEES

We should now look at the treatment of Value Added Tax, Withholding Tax, Stamp Tax and the Insurance Supervisory Tax. We shall also look at the practice of charging of Administration Fees and Policy Fees. We shall complete this review with a presentation of a basic premium computation model.

2.1. Value Added Tax and Withholding Tax

In Mozambique, all supplies of import and domestic goods and services, in general, are subject to a Value Added Tax (VAT)[13] of 17%. Insurance premium is exempt from this tax. Although VAT is not applied on premium; when it comes to all other transactions on an insurance operation including calculation of sums insured and payment of services for local claims services, VAT is applicable. Furthermore, if an insurer were to generate any other form of revenue besides premium, it would also be subject to VAT.

In addition to the above, for any services provided by foreign firms, there is a requirement on the local company to apply a Withholding Tax. The current rate of Withholding Tax for non-resident service providers is 20%. It should be noted that reinsurance premium is exempt from this tax. Our insurance market relies significantly on foreign firms for key areas of service where there no appropriate local skills. Such areas of critical shortage of skills include claims assessment or adjustment, risk surveying, risk management, information technology services for insurance and actuarial services.

2.2. Stamp Tax

Insurance premium invoices and other specified documents that have a financial value are subject to an old form of tax developed from the Portuguese system known as Stamp

---

13. Referred in Portuguese as Imposto do Valor Acrescentado (IVA)

Tax. The word 'stamp' has been maintained from the ancient practice when people had to actually buy certain types of stamps that they needed to stick on the documents in question as physical proof of settlement of the required tax. Today, it is not required for insurance invoices to actually have a stamp. This tax is supposed to be applied on all documents, contracts, licenses, trade-marks, patents, financial guarantees, insurance premium and other items as defined in the law. In the insurance sector, the Stamp Tax is charged on both premium and on gross intermediary commissions, as outlined in Table 10.

Table 10–Stamp Tax Rates

Description of Covered Item	Rate
Life, Accidents and Health	1%
Obligatory Motor Third Party Liability and other Obligatory insurance policies	2%
Marine, Aviation, Good-in-Transit and Rolling Stock	2%
Guarantees and Credit Insurance	3%
All other classes	5%
Intermediary commission	2%

We have observed that insurers are not following a uniform approach in the application of some of the rates. There are different interpretations of this table of tax. There is a lack of clear categorization of some of the classes of insurance. For instance, the table refers to 'obligatory insurance policies'.

It is not clear if this refers only to classes of insurance that are specifically covered by pieces of law specifying the need for insurance as is the case of Workman's Compensation Act insurance. It is not clear if this applies if a construction company were to sign a construction agreement with the government which stipulates that there must be insurance of the construction works. Some insurers have been treating such a situation as obligatory insurance while others have been treating it as a normal class of engineering. It is unclear which interpretation of the law is correct.

Furthermore, there is also a need for this table to be reviewed in view of recent key developments in the financial sector with new emerging priorities such as Financial Inclusion of low-income people, as we shall discuss later in this book. We believe that the authorities could review tax for areas of interest such as microinsurance. At this stage, it appears that agriculture, which is not specified in any other category, by default, falls in other classes of insurance with a Stamp Tax of 5%. The development of agriculture insurance for the large population of small-scale rural farmers is as important as the other types of insurance which are more relevant for urban areas like obligatory motor liability, which enjoys a favourable tax rate of 2%.

Finally, some of the descriptions of classes of insurance tend to overlap. For instance, the insurance type described as 'Accidents' could be referring to a number of different types of insurance policies. In such cases, insurance operators end up making different interpretations of the same rules. Some insurance companies try to make conservative interpretations even if it means paying more tax than what others may charge for the same items.

2.3. Insurance Supervisory Tax

As stated in Article 7 of the Insurance Law, all insurance business and intermediary services are also subject to an Insurance Supervisor Tax or Surtax as presented in Table 11.

Table 11–Insurance Supervisory Tax

Business	Basis for application of Rate	Rate
Non-life insurance	Gross Premium Before Taxes (GPBT)	1.50%
Life insurance	Gross Premium Before Taxes (GPBT)	0.35%
Insurance brokers	Flat annual amount	Mt 10 000
Insurance agencies	Flat annual amount	Mt 3 000
Individual tied agents	Flat annual amount	Mt 1 000
Private pension fund administrators	Flat annual amount	Mt 30 000

It appears that it is fairly clear how this tax item should be applied. We shall discuss further in this chapter the breakdown of premium charged in our market and clarify the meaning of Gross Premium Before Tax. After reviewing the two tax items above, we should now look at the practice of charging of Administration and Policy Fees.

2.4. Administration and Policy Fees

Currently, all insurers in Mozambique also follow a generally accepted practice of charging of Administration Fees. The current standard **Administration Fee** in the market is 15% of the Gross Premium. In cases involving premium invoices for large amounts, insurers are willing to negotiate on the amount of fees to be charged and can agree to a level lower than the market standard. These fees are intended to cover the costs of doing business for the insurer. They are viewed as a critical item especially in transactions involving full or significant reinsurance through which most of the premium collected locally may be transferred to global reinsurance markets that support the local insurance market. Some of the insurers also charge a **Policy Fee** for any new policies.

2.5. Fire Brigade Levy

According to underwriting manuals from the period before independence, the insurance market used to also charge a Fire Brigade Levy on all insurance policies of property. It appears that the practice has been abandoned by the current insurance market. It also appears that in the early days of formation of insurance markets in Europe, there was a much closer association between Fire underwriters and the Fire Brigade. Nowadays, in most markets including Mozambique, the Fire Brigade is a public service that is financed from the national budget of the state. This is probably the most ideal way of handling this service given that it is part of what can be described in economics theory as a 'public good'. It is viewed as being ethically problematic if such services were privately owned and provided only to people that can afford to pay. Furthermore, these are also kinds of services where it is not feasible to selectively provide service to only those that have paid.

2.6. Proposed New Levy

There has been a recent proposal of a new tax on insurance. The Ministry of Health has proposed that someone needs to pay for the costs of handling victims of road accidents. They have been lobbying the National Government to pass a law instructing insurers to pay a new form of tax that is supposed to be charged on the motor insurance portfolio, as per the draft legislation. The insurance association was invited to discuss a white paper covering this theme. For administration of such a proposed fund, there was a proposal to setup a public entity called **Instituto Moçambicano de Emergência Médica (IMEM)**.

Following the presentation of this concept, the Insurance Association has not supported it. It has been suggested that nearly 80% of the vehicles on the roads in Mozambique do not have even the basic third party insurance. It would be unfair to create further burdens for the minority that are insured. It does not appear that this proposal has made any further progress. Given the lack of compliance by most motorists in respect of the obligatory road accidents motor insurance, it may be more useful for the government to find more suitable mechanisms to fund such types of social protection schemes. We shall discuss in Chapter 9 some of the options that could be considered.

2.7. Premium Computation

Following the review of the different tax items and fees that are charged in Mozambique, we should complete our review with a discussion on the **premium computation** model used in our market. A premium computation is a breakdown of the cost of insurance. Besides some of the different interpretations of classifications of taxes of certain classes of insurance, as discussed above, there are also different approaches in the process of summing up of insurance costs. The format of a standard premium computation used by most companies in Mozambique is as presented in Figure 5.

Figure 5–Sample of a Premium Computation

ITEM		DESCRIPTION	FACTORS	PREMIUM AMOUNT
A	C–B	Net Premium Income (NPI)		800.00
B	C x %	Local Gross Brokerage Commission	20.00%	200.00
C		Gross Premium Income (GPI)		1,000.00
D	C x %	Administration Fee	15.00%	150.00
E	C + D	Gross Premium Before Tax (GPBT)		1,150.00
F	E x %	Stamp Tax	5.00%	57.50
G	E x %	Surtax	1.50%	17.25
H	E + F + G	Gross Written Premium (GWP)		1,224.75

In the computation given above, the **Gross Written Premium (GWP)** is the total gross debit premium amount payable by the client. The Stamp Tax and Surtax rates depend on the class of business, as described above. The amount defined as **Gross Premium Income (GPI)** is the level at which reinsurance companies supporting the local insurers may quote, if there is reinsurance involved in the transaction. That is also the level where the total gross amount of premium payable by the client could have been defined if our market did not have the concepts of Administration Fees and the two premium tax items. The Gross Brokerage Commission also depends on the class of business and is also influenced by the rates of commissions applicable in each company. As noted above, Brokerage Commission is subject to a 2% Stamp Tax. Therefore, the broker or agent involved in the transaction retains 98% of the quoted gross brokerage commission. In the case of a **Direct Insurance** placement, the **Net Premium Income (NPI)** would be the same figure as the GPI, as there would be no commission payable.

As can be noted in the breakdown of premium presented above, the two obligatory taxes are applied on the sub-total of Gross Premium and Administration Fees. Not all companies apply taxes on this sub-total including Administration Fees. We believe that it is prudent to apply the taxes at this level because Administration Fees are part of income for the insurer. There are insurers in our market that do not apply the taxes on the Administration Fee component. These are some of the issues that the insurance regulator should try to resolve by issuing appropriate guidelines on this matter.

3 OTHER KEY REQUIREMENTS

After the discussion on the Insurance Law and the different forms of taxes and fees applicable in our market, we should now look at two other critical items that affect insurance business.

3.1.Foreign Exchange Control

As part of a process of financial markets liberalisation policy, a new foreign exchange law was passed in 2009. The new law[14] and respective regulations define the rules and regulations for inward and outward transfers of money. For the purposes of payment of reinsurance to foreign markets, the insurance only need to obtain clearance from tax authorities before requesting their commercial bank to do the respective transfer. There is no tax payable on reinsurance premium. However, all other payments for services provided by non-resident entities are subject to tax in Mozambique, as defined by the national tax laws.

1.2. Anti-Money Laundering Law

As noted above, the Regulations to the Insurance Law state that operators in the insurance market should comply with appropriate anti-money laundering legislation. In the last two

---

14. Referred to in Portuguese as Lei Cambial nº 11/2009 de 11 de Março

decades, there has been growing pressure from international development agencies to ensure that all countries adopt, implement and enforce legislation aimed at preventing organised crime and financing of terrorism. Such a group of laws are described as Anti Money Laundering/ Combating the Financing of Terrorism (AML/CFT) legal framework. For Mozambique, the AML aspect is covered in law number 7/2002[15]. There is not yet any legislation specifically criminalising financing of terrorism as per the CFT guideline of this framework. With regards to the current law covering AML, there are still many gaps which limit its effectiveness. The scope of covered entities does not include the full range of operators in the insurance sector that should be part of the process. There has been no adoption of any specific measures in the insurance sector to assist in making this law effective. Basic AML requirements such as Customer Due Diligence are not yet in place. The appropriate regulatory bodies have not yet been granted appropriate authority to enforce the law.

4 THE INSURANCE REGULATORY AUTHORITY

As we discussed in Chapter 2, in the early days of emergence of formal insurance business in Mozambique, insurance was regulated together with banking by an entity that was known as Inspecção de Crédito e Seguros. Then, after independence, the authority to regulate insurance business was transferred

---

15. Lei nº 7/2002 de 5 de Fevereiro

to the monopoly insurance operator–EMOSE. Following a critical shift of economic policy in the mid-1980s, the policy-makers decided to create a business environment for competition. Starting from December 1991, as part of this process of the opening up of the market and in order to ensure a level playing field for all operators in the market, the authority of supervision of insurance was shifted away from EMOSE to the Ministry of Finance[16]. Then, following the passing of a piece of law on 20 July 1999[17], the Government established a new insurance regulatory body—Inspecção Geral de Seguros (IGS) (Sigaúke, 2013: 5). It was expected to play a critical role in the process of modernisation of the insurance sector.

Then, following the passing of the insurance regulatory framework of 31 December 2010[18], the insurance general inspectorate, has been replaced by a new authority known as Instituto de Supervisão de Seguros de Moçambique (ISSM). The new regulatory body is intended to have more authority and responsibilities than the previous entity. In order to allow the new regulatory body to have more autonomy than the government departments in the past, the ISSM has a Board of Directors. This is in alignment with developments in other countries in the region where the regulatory authorities are

---

16. Lei nº. 24/91, de 31 de Dezembro
17. Decreto 42/99, de 20 de Julho
18. Decreto Lei nº. 1/2010, de 31 de Dezembro

located in more empowered entities such as the Financial Services Board (FSB) in South Africa. We should also note that insurance falls within the ambit of control of the Ministry of Finance. The respective principal Insurance Law and regulations are also governed by the same ministry.

Following the passing of the Insurance Law of 2010, the establishment of the new insurance supervisory authority has been formalised with the passing of regulations number 29/2012[19] of 26 July, 2012 (RSA Consultores, 2013: 143). These regulations define the rules and regulations of the supervisory authority and how it is supposed to function. The regulations have been followed by further supporting legislation reference number 300/2012[20] of 14 November 2012 which defines the organisational setup of the office of the insurance supervisor.

We would like to acknowledge that all the changes noted above from the new regulatory framework represent positive developments. We have experienced a more proactive involvement of the Insurance Regulator as an autonomous entity compared to the past. The organisation is playing a far more prominent role in promoting development of the insurance sector besides the supervisory function. There are also a few areas that can be improved. One of the key

---

19. Known in Portuguese as *Decreto nº. 29/2012 de 26 de Julho*

20. Known in Portuguese as *Diploma Ministerial nº. 300/2012, 14 de Novembro*

areas where a new approach could be considered is on the question of actuarial input. We support the recommendation by Hafeman (2009: 18) that an actuarial role is even more critical for supervisory authorities. Actuaries working for the regulator could assist in a number of critical functions (Mutenga, 2014: 75). They could provide critical technical input in the process of definition of regulatory requirements. They could assist in reviewing, explaining and assessing quality of material submitted by insurers. Finally, there will also be an even greater need for them in handling more complex processes in the near future due to an emerging key shift of the regulatory models, as we shall discuss in Chapter 14 under key trends.

CONCLUSION

We would like to note that a lot of progress has been achieved in the development of the legislative environment for insurance. This development has followed the liberalization of the insurance market in the 1990s and the subsequent changes in insurance legislation in 2003 and in 2010. We have also looked at all key pieces of law that refer to obligatory types of insurance. We shall discuss further the concept of obligatory types of insurance later in this book.

Furthermore, we have also looked at other key requirements such as taxes and the practice of charging of Administration Fees and Policy Fees. Then we also looked at other pieces of legislation affecting insurance including the Foreign Exchange Laws and the Anti-Money Laundering Law. As an overall observation, we have also noted that, in general, there is a need for preparation of guidelines in order to clarify a number of items that are not clear in the insurance legislation. Instead of waiting for appropriate changes of law, the market could also take the initiative of adopting some forms of self-regulation, wherever possible.

REFERENCES

- Benjamin, Bernard (1977). *General Insurance*. London: William Heinemann Ltd.

- Hafeman, Michael (2009). *The Role of the Actuary in Insurance*. Primer Series on Insurance, Issue 4, May 2009. Washington: The World Bank.

- Hafeman, Michael and Randle, Tony (2009). *On and Offsite Inspections*. Primer Series on Insurance, Issue 13, December 2009. Washington: The World Bank.

- Mutenga, S. (2014). *Enhancing Enterprise Risk Management in the African Insurance Industry*. In the African Insurance Bulletin. Issue no. 0005 of May 2014. Doala: The African Insurance Organisation. Pp. 75-77.

- RSA Consultores (2013). *Legislação do Sistema Financeiro de Moçambique*. Porto: Vida Económica, p. 143.

- Sigaúke, Abílio, Feliciano (2013). *Evolução histórica e papel da entidade de supervisão de seguros em Moçambique*. Paper presented at the Insurance Seminar of the ISSM.

CHAPTER 6

CONTRACT OF INSURANCE

Following the discussion on the foundational principles and the legal framework of insurance in Mozambique, we shall now discuss key characteristics of an insurance contract compared to that of other business activities. Then, we shall review the key legal requirements for a valid insurance contract. We shall also look at the difference between an insurance agreement and other types of commercial contracts. We shall also pay close attention to the section covering insurance contracts in the Insurance Law of Mozambique and highlight some of the key unique features in our system. Then, we shall discuss the key types of insurance agreements issued in our market. We shall conclude this chapter with a discussion on the concept of simplified plain language contracts.

1. CHARACTERISTICS OF AN INSURANCE CONTRACT

An insurance contract has a number of unique characteristics compared to other types of contracts, as we are now going to discuss.

1.1. Aleatory contract

According to Mehr and Cammack (1972), business contracts may be '**commutative**' or '**aleatory**'. Commutative contracts are those types of agreements where both parties in the agreement exchange things that are of equal value. For instance, when one buys a car, the selling price and the car are supposed to be of the same value for the parties involved. In fact, most contracts tend to be commutative. According to information on the website of the Financial Planning Body of Knowledge[1], in aleatory contracts, the parties to the agreement are not exchanging things of equal value. In a basic insurance agreement, an insured pays premium and could receive nothing if there are no claims. However, if the unexpected were to happen and the insured has a claim, then, he/she could receive a claim settlement which could be far much more than the premium that was paid. Due to this situation where the outcome is affected by chance and may not be equal, it is acknowledged that insurance contracts are aleatory (Thomas and Reed, 1977: 23)

1.2. Contract of adhesion

According to Mehr and Cammack (1972: 146), contracts can be agreed to on the basis of either '**bargaining contracts**' or '**contracts of adhesion**'. In bargaining contracts, the parties

---

1. As per the following website consulted on 1 march 2015: http://financialplanningbodyofknowledge.com/wiki/Contract_characteristics

to the agreement can discuss and agree on the conditions in the entire contract. In contracts of adhesion such as insurance, the agreement is drawn up by one party that presents it more or less on the condition of '**take-it-or-leave-it**'. An insured could request for alterations of some limits or specific parts of the terms of their proposed insurance contract. However, in general, the insurer has a standard insurance contract and forms that the insured clients should follow if they want cover. It is on this basis that courts will tend to rule against an insurer for any ambiguities that may exist in the contract since it is the insurer that would have drafted the agreement (Thomas and Reed, 1977: 24). This rule is known by the Latin name '*contra proferentem*'.

1.3. Unilateral contract

Contracts may also be either '**bilateral**' or '**unilateral**' (Mehr and Cammack, 1972: 147). In bilateral or reciprocal contracts, both parties to the agreement are bound to mutual performance without which either party could be viewed as having broken the agreement. In unilateral agreements, as is usually the case with insurance, only one of the parties is making a promise to perform in the future in accordance with the agreement. After the insured will have executed the act of paying premium, only the insurer is responsible for a promise that may be legally enforceable.

1.4. Conditional contract

An insurance contract is also defined as a conditional contract. A conditional contract is a type of contract where the performing party is only required to perform if the other party to the agreement would have satisfied certain conditions specified in the contract under consideration (Thomas and Reed, 1977: 23). For instance, an insured should notify the insurer of all claims within a defined period and provide proof of loss suffered in order to qualify for compensation. In other words, the performance in a conditional contract is limited by conditions defined in the contract. Even if a claim occurs, these conditions have to be met before the contract can be deemed to be legally enforceable.

1.5. Personal contracts

In general, insurance contracts of property are treated as 'personal contracts' (Mehr and Cammack, 1972: 148). This means that they are agreements between an insurer and a specific person or entity. This means that, usually, insurance contracts are non-transferable. If an insured person sells insured property, it cannot be assumed that the insurer automatically covers the new owner of the same property. The only exception to this rule is life insurance where an insured can transfer rights to benefits or proceeds under a life policy to another entity such as a bank as collateral or security to secure a loan.

As we shall discuss later in this Chapter, one of the legal principles in our Insurance Law refers to options of insurance policies that are not personal and can be transferred by the bearer. There may be a need for the local legal condition to be reviewed given that it appears to contradict this traditional rule that insurance agreements are personal contracts.

1.6. Executory contracts

Insurance contracts are also defined as executory contracts (Thomas and Reed, 1977: 23). An executory contract is a type of agreement where one of the parties only needs to perform if an agreed event occurs. In the case of an insurance contract, an insurer only has to indemnify an insured if the covered event occurs. This means that the performance of the insurer is suspended unless the covered event occurs.

1.7. Key issues arising from nature of insurance contract

As we have noted from our discussion above, insurance has very unique types of contracts. Given that insurance promises to provide indemnity in case of an event that may or may not occur, the respective contracts are aleatory, executory, conditional and unilateral. We believe that some of these key characteristics of an insurance contract are also part of the underlying reason why insurance, as an unintended consequence, can become one of the key targets of improper financial transactions, as we shall discuss later in this book. Based on these unique characteristics of insurance, it is a financial transaction where there is no need for the buyer to prove that they are receiving at the same time a specific service for their payment. Besides the promise given at the time of payment, the service could be provided in the future subject to certain unforeseen events. After discussing these key characteristics of insurance contracts, we should now discuss the legal requirements for valid insurance agreements.

2. LEGAL ELEMENTS OF INSURANCE CONTRACTS

An insurance contract plays a very significant role in an insurance transaction. It is essentially the principal item which is delivered after the conclusion of the agreement between an insurer and the insured client. The insurance contract is intended to define the legal conditions on the basis of which the insurer would 'make good' any of the losses that may be suffered by the client, as promised by the insurer. In order for this insurance contract to be a valid legal contract it has to satisfy the following five key legal elements:

2.1. Offer and acceptance

At the stage of entering into an insurance agreement, like in any other legal commercial contract, there should be an offer and acceptance at the beginning of that process. According to Cannar (1979: 10), presentation of a proposal form by the insurer does not constitute an 'offer' to insure. It is viewed as an *invitation to treat* in the same way as goods on display in the window of a shop. There is an appropriate offer process when the person or firm seeking insurance submits a completed proposal form. Then, the insurer can accept the offer or not. The insurer may quote terms and conditions of insurance following which the prospective buyer of insurance may accept or not, the proposed terms and conditions of insurance. In this process of offer and acceptance, it is vital to note the responsibilities of disclosure on the part of both the prospective buyer of insurance and the seller of insurance.

The Insurance Law provides disclosure conditions in Articles 91 to 97. The rules of disclosure are focused on the role of the proposing insured and the insurer, as we shall discuss below:

a.   Disclosure by the proposer

In alignment with the principle of Good Faith, our Insurance Law stipulates that the prospective buyer of insurance is required to make clear, complete and exact disclosure of all material information on the risk to be insured prior to placement of cover. Also in alignment with the emerging debates in international markets on issues of disclosure, the law qualifies the situations where the insurer can use the argument of non-disclosure so that this concept is not abused for the purposes of rejecting claims without due consideration of the nature of lack of disclosure. The law also provides guidelines on how an insurer could handle cases of negligent non-disclosure if discovered after placement of cover or after occurrence of a claim.

As part of the disclosure process, the law refers to the practice of completion of proposal forms by the insured. Although this practice is clearly provided for in the law, the majority of insurance intermediaries tend not to be too keen for their large corporate clients to complete proposal forms. Some observers in the market are concerned about the risk of excessive bureaucracy which reduces efficiencies and increases costs of doing business. For some types of operations such as engineering projects, some practitioners in the sector argue that the underlying engineering construction contract and technical specification documents of the project tend to contain far much more detail on the project than could be obtained from any standard proposal form. If the market becomes more organized in the future, there is scope for development of clearer guidelines on when proposal forms could be used or not and probably some element of standardisation in order to reduce paper-work and duplication of efforts from the different operators in the market.

b. Disclosure by Insurer

As stipulated in the Insurance Law, prior to inception of cover, the insurer should disclose the following:

- Designation and legal status of the company.

- Nature and scope of risk to be insured.

- Restrictions of insurance cover.

- Premium amount or premium rate applicable for the risk in question for the period of proposed cover.

- Methods of payment of premium and consequences for lack of payment.

- Basis for any loading or discounting of premium that may be applied in the contract.

- Minimum sums insured for obligatory insurance covers.

- Duration of insurance contract, renewal conditions and methods how the contract could be terminated.

- Conditions regarding transfer of rights under the contract to another party.

- Complaints procedure including the option for referral to the insurance regulator for review, without prejudice of rights to go to courts.

- The option for insurers and their insured clients to agree on a choice of law on any insurance contract except for obligatory types of insurance for which the law of Mozambique should always be applied.

According to Article 94 of the Insurance Law, failure by the insurer to disclose all this information prior to commencement of an insurance contract gives the policyholder the right to cancel the insurance contract within 30 days after receipt of the insurance policy. However, such a right is only applicable if the lack of disclosure is of a nature that would influence the decision of the policyholder to accept or not the proposed insurance terms and conditions.

2.2. Consideration

Consideration is an essential element for any business agreement to be legally enforceable (Vaughan, 2009: 161). It is 'what each side to a contract does, or promises to do, for the benefit of the other' (Cannar, 1979: 141). According to Sadler (2012: 10/2), consideration usually takes the following two common forms:

- 'a promise to pay for goods in return for a promise to supply them; or'

- 'a promise to pay for a service in return for a promise to provide it.'

As such, in an insurance contract, consideration from the insured is payment of premium in exchange for which the insurer promises to settle any valid claims during the period of the policy, in accordance with the terms and conditions of the insurance policy. The rules regarding treatment of premium in insurance are defined in Articles 120-135 of the Insurance Law. In this section of the law, there is definition of how such a price should be stipulated as well as when and how it could be paid. It appears that, in terms of the law, insurance premium is payable with effect from the date of commencement of insurance cover or within thirty days after submission of the respective insurance premium invoice by the insurer. There are different interpretations of the meaning of the specified time limits and obligations especially in cases where an insurance intermediary is involved. It appears to us that this is another area where the insurance association could play a critical role of facilitating the development of appropriate guidelines.

2.3. Legal capacity

The next key legal element for a valid insurance contract is **legal capacity**. Article 84 of the Insurance Law reinforces the general legal principle that an insurance contract is only valid if the parties entering into the insurance agreement have legal capacity. For clarification of what sort of persons do not have legal capacity in Mozambique, you may consult the Mozambican Civil Law[2]. In accordance with conditions applied in Portugal and all other territories, minors do not have legal capacity. In the Civil Law, a minor is defined as, in general, a person with less than 21 years of age (Plural Editores et al. 2009: 50). The law also outlines exceptions such as the case of a minor that might have gone through a process of emancipation.

It is also vital not to look at legal capacity of only the insured or prospective buyer of insurance. The legal capacity of the entity assuming risk should also be scrutinised. As

---

2.   Referred to in Portuguese as *Código Civil*

noted by Waty (2007: 72), the Insurance Law defines the legal capacity of authorised operators of insurance and intermediary services. Firstly, insurance business can only be conducted by companies that have been appropriately registered and licensed in Mozambique. Secondly, within the insurance sector, there is a clear separation of the different capacities and functions of different forms of insurers, intermediaries and reinsurers. This means that, for instance, a company that is registered as only a life insurer has only legal capacity for life insurance.

2.4. Legality of object

The next essential legal element that we should review is **legality of object** of insurance. According to Cannar (1979: 12), '*[a]s a matter of public policy, the common law does not uphold contracts whose objects it regards as illegal.*' By law, insurers are not supposed to '*indemnify a policyholder against the criminal as opposed to the civil consequences of a wrongful act which led to a claim against him. Wrongful actions may have both a criminal and civil facet to them.*' Insurance will only cover costs of legal defence and indemnities to third parties. It will not protect the insured from prosecution, conviction or a fine that may be applied by the court for what may be defined as criminal offence in terms of the law. This also means that insurance does not pay for bail. These are all critical items to note. We have witnessed cases where clients expected the insurer to cover such items.

2.5. Legal form

We should now look at **legal form** as another essential legal requirement. In general, contracts can be made 'in any form, i.e. orally, in writing, or even implied by conduct' (Sadler, 2012: 10/2). However, for certain specified activities such as hire purchase agreements, sales of property and insurance, only written contracts are legally enforceable. The form and content of insurance contracts is defined in Articles 102 to 107 of the Insurance Law. As defined in Article 102, an insurance contact must be reduced to a separate written document which must be clearly labelled as an insurance policy.

a.   Key parts of an insurance policy

Furthermore, there is also a breakdown of key parts of an insurance policy in Article 103 of the Insurance Law as follows:

- *General terms and conditions* of insurance cover with all the appropriate conditions of the type of insurance contract in question.

- Exceptions, exclusions and all other special conditions restricting cover for the type of insurance contract in question.

- *Schedule* of specific terms for the specific client and subject matter of insurance.

From the elements discussed above, we should note that exceptions and exclusions are very important aspects of an insurance agreement. They are often the source of misunderstanding at the time of claims. It has been noted that in relation to insurance cover, it tends to be more 'the exclusions rather than the inclusions that really count...' Kirkham (2008: 21). We shall discuss claims and related issues in Chapter 13.

b.   Rules on delivery of policies

Furthermore, there are also rules in the Insurance Law on the delivery of insurance policies. Policies must be delivered to the policyholder in a period of up to a maximum of 30 days following agreement for the issuing of the policy (Article 6). If the policy is not delivered within this time period, the policy can be rendered void. This means that, the policyholder can declare the insurance contract of no legal force or validity. In such a case, the policyholder is entitled to a full refund of any premium that may have been paid. However, it is not clear what is the positioning of an insurance intermediary in this rule. What happens if the insurer delivers just within the defined period but the broker or agent takes a few more days reviewing the policy document, as part of their service? Is delivery to an appointed insurance broker or agent defined as delivery to the policyholder? We do not believe that there is clarity on these questions in the law. The insurance association could take the initiative of developing guidelines covering this and other critical items.

c. Issuing of certificates and proof of insurance

We have also noted that the Insurance Law does not make reference to a common market practice of issuing of certificates. For Workman's Compensation Act insurance and Motor Third Party Liability, the market has a practice of issuing an insurance policy as well as a one-page type of *certificates*. This document is used as proof that the item or business unit in question has valid insurance. This is vital especially for compulsory insurance like motor third party liability for which road traffic authorities try to enforce the law (Chiejina, 2004: 108). It would not make sense to give every driver a copy of the insurance policy of a large company with a large fleet of vehicles that are insured under one policy. Therefore, the innovative solution of the market has been to develop simple types of certificates with basic details of the insured item and period of cover as a basic form of proof of insurance in a format which is not cumbersome to handle.

Furthermore, in some markets in our region such as Malawi and Zimbabwe, they have developed something which is probably even better. The proof of insurance for motor liability cover is in the form of a disc which has to be displayed in an appropriate place on the windscreen like other items such as car inspection, car radio tax and the annual motor municipal tax. Portugal has a similar system of a disc for proof of insurance (Associação Portugesa de Seguradores, 2001: 12). Some insurers in our market have started following a similar system of insurance discs although this is not specifically covered by our insurance legislation.

d.   Cover Notes and Hold Cover

We have also noted that our Insurance Law does not make reference to the practice of issuing of **Cover Notes**. This is a provisional insurance document which is usually issued for a defined short period in order to confirm a **hold cover** situation whilst waiting for the issuing of the proper policy (Cannar, 1979: 57 and Chiejina, 2004: 108). To hold covered means that the insurer has assumed risk and will treat any claims occurring as though an insurance policy had been issued. Cover Notes may be issued by an authorised intermediary. The practice of issuing of cover notes is not very common in our market. When insurers agree to hold covered any risk, they may simply send a written message stating that cover is in place at terms quoted or on the basis of terms and conditions of expiring period whilst waiting for a final agreement and issuing of the final policy. Given the lack of specific provisions in our law on cover notes and holding covered, the Insurance Association could take the initiative of drafting guidelines for the market.

e. Problematic rule on transfer of policies

We should discuss one more critical issue regarding legal forms of insurance policies, as defined in our Insurance Law. In Article 105, the law makes reference to the following forms of insurance policies:

- *Nominative policies*–are supposed to specify the insured party but can be transferred by the insured.

- *Elective policy*–where the insured party is supposed not to be specified and the policyholder can transfer it by endorsing the policy in favour of a new insured

- *"For the bearer"*- is supposed to be a type of policy which does not need to be endorsed but can just be delivered to the next new insured.

We believe that the rules regarding capacity of one party (the Insured) to transfer legal rights of a policy to a third party without the knowledge and consent of the Insurer is very problematic. It is not aligned with the general principles and practice of insurance. As we discussed above, in general, insurance policies are 'personal contracts' which cannot be transferred. Part of the reason insurers would not want the insured to transfer covers to other parties as they wish include the following:

- The pricing of insurance for most types of risk is connected to a certain technical risk categorisation process. Things such as values at risk, age of covered items/ persons and nature of use of a subject of insurance are very critical underwriting conditions.

- Some clients may have a bad record of negligence or bad debts. An insurer may not want to continue giving them cover indirectly through other persons that could accept a policy on their behalf and then transfer to them.

- These options of transferring of a policy from one party to another also contradict, to some extent, the spirit of disclosure, as defined in Articles 91 and 92 of the same Insurance Law.

- Most importantly, what mechanism is in place to protect the insurance policy from fraud or abuse if the insured can transfer ownership and there is no obligation to notify or secure consent of the insurer? There is also a risk that, in some instances, some people could try to transfer a policy to another party by deliberately noting a date prior to an uncovered accident?

For the reasons noted above and in order to avoid ambiguities in the regulatory environment, this clause needs to be reviewed. Fortunately, at this stage, we are not aware of any insurers that offer policies in the form as described above where one insured party can transfer a policy to another party. We shall now look at types of agreement between insurers in relation to the issue of pricing of compulsory types of insurance.

3. MARKET AGREEMENTS

Following the termination of the monopoly insurance market, the companies which have been established in the emerging market are supposed to compete for business like in any other economic activity. However, there are cases where insurers have setup **market agreements**. In Mozambique, we have a market agreement covering the Motor Third Party Liability Insurance for foreign registered vehicles. The agreement defines the minimum amount of premium which should be charged for this type of insurance.

In addition, the Insurance Association has been in the process of setting up a new market agreement covering another compulsory insurance intended to cover work-related accidents and illnesses. The Insurance Association is of the view that this approach is required for compulsory types of insurance which are sold as stipulated by the law. The association sees this as not being a worse practice than approaches of other more sophisticated markets such as South Africa that have public monopolies such as the political risks fund and the fuel levy. Other market observers see this local market agreement as a form of **cartel** where insurers are colluding in order to maximize profits. As such they see this as an **anti-competitive** practice which is contrary to emerging public policy in Mozambique. The Insurance Law, in its current form does not provide any specific guidelines on this debate.

4. EXECUTION OF INSURANCE CONTRACTS

Given the importance of contracts in business, the mercantile law provides rules regarding execution of all legal contracts. Insurance contracts play an even more significant role in insurance such that, in addition to general rules in the mercantile law, there are specific additional provisions in the Insurance Law. The rules regarding how an insurance contract should be structured are provided in Articles 108 to 119 of the Insurance Law. There is specific treatment of various critical questions including the following:

- Nature of insurable risks.

- Risks which can be excluded such as war, insurrection and terrorism.

- What should be done if there is evidence that the risk does not exist.

- How to handle a situation of worsening or reduction of the nature of covered risk.

- Duration and renewal of contract

- Transfer of insurance rights.

We should also note the rule regarding renewals as defined in Article 116. It is stated in the law that all insurance contracts should have an automatic renewal. It appears that the condition is intended to protect the insured from being unintentionally exposed when a policy expires and they do not realise that they have to renew. However, the concept of automatic renewals has tended to have other un-intended consequences. There have been cases of clients that have disposed of insured items or have transferred their insurance covers from one company to another. In such cases, if the insured clients do not inform their previous insurer that they no longer require insurance in subsequent years, that insurer could continue renewing and invoicing in each subsequent year, without express consent of the customer. It is not part of global best practices for any type of business to continue raising new invoices without express consent to renew and without settlement of debts from the previous year(s).

We believe that this rule of automatic renewals needs to be reviewed. Besides the issues of bad debts, there is also a problem of distortions of revenue in the market. Insurers following this practice end up over-stating their revenue. When a client places insurance with another insurer whilst a previous insurer continues to renew the same contract, in principle, we could also end up with the fundamental problem of contribution, as described in Chapter 3. We should now look at one more key feature of the Insurance Law of Mozambique.

5. PLAIN LANGUAGE

One of the key reasons insurance is not trusted by many people is the use of complex technical language which only insurance people can interpret. The lack of a clear understanding of the language applied by insurance companies also contributes to conflicts after occurrence of claims. While insurers tend to assume that they are providing valid reasons for the way that they handle claims in accordance with traditional principles of insurance and legal rules; the insured persons may tend to see such actions as manipulation of the policy to avoid claims or to reduce their financial loss. In order to avoid these problems, there is now a growing global consensus that agreements for services such as insurance should be written in a language which is simple, clear and concise.

According to Burt and Gordon (2008: 33), use of plain language was also identified by Dullar Omar, a former Minister of Justice in South Africa, as part of a broader process of 'democratising language'. Tied to wider political transformation processes in that country from 1995, it became a policy requirement for insurers to use plain language as a means to enable access, promote participation and empower the consumer (ibid. 34).

The current Insurance Law of Mozambique already contains a number of rules related to the concept of plain language. In Article 103 of the Insurance Law, it is specified that an insurance policy should be written and issued in the following manner:

- clear and comprehensible language;
- legible text;
- in Portuguese;
- signed and stamped by the insurer.

From the rules stated above, it is clear to us that the policy-makers are concerned about the traditional problems of technical jargon in insurance. Furthermore, in Article 104, it is a requirement of the law that all conditions that exclude, reduce or restrict any aspect of insurance cover must be in bold letters. This is supposed to ensure that such conditions can be easily identified by the insured persons. This is part of local efforts to combat the general concern about bad practices of insurers that are accused of hiding in *fine print* conditions that remove most of the cover that many clients believe is in place. It is alleged that, for instance, on "All Risks" types of policies, most clients believe that all risk situations are covered at the time of buying insurance. Then, if they are unfortunate to suffer a loss or damage, at the time of presenting a claim, they suddenly discover certain "hidden" conditions that were not highlighted at the time of purchase of cover. Therefore, this rule is aimed at improving transparency of what is not covered in an insurance policy.

Finally, we would like to also note that, in our opinion, the standard Portuguese insurance policy contracts from Portugal and Brazil, which are used by some of the insurers in our market, tend to satisfy many of the key features of plain language. They have a clear structure and layout. They follow a consistent approach and have a glossary which explains key expressions and all clauses are number-referenced in a coherent and logical way. Typical English policy wordings such as Multi-mark and Assets All Risks, which are used by some of the local insurers, do not comply with most of the rules of plain language. We shall further discuss these forms of wordings later in this book.

CONCLUSION

In this chapter, we have covered key aspects regarding insurance contracts. At first we discussed the key legal requirements for a legal insurance contract. The legal requirements are offer and acceptance, consideration, legal capacity, legality of object and legal form. Whilst looking at these elements, we have also discussed how these are treated in the Insurance Law of Mozambique and other appropriate legislation. Then, we also noted how the Insurance Association has set up market agreements relating to obligatory types of insurance, which we shall review later in this book.

Furthermore, we discussed the legal conditions regarding execution of an insurance agreement. We have observed some of the key legal conditions that may need to be reviewed such as the question of transfer of policies from one party to another. We also noted that there is a need for a clear guideline in relation to the involvement of intermediaries in the legal rule regarding delivery of policies.

Finally, we discussed the concept of plain language. We noted how the Insurance Law in Mozambique is fairly progressive as far as this theme is concerned. We have noted that some of the policies issued in our market satisfy conditions of plain language whilst others do not. After this discussion regarding insurance contracts, in the next Chapter, we shall look at the key conditions for setting up and running an insurance or microinsurance company in Mozambique.

REFERENCES

* Associação Portuguesa de Seguradores (2001). Seguro Automóvel. Lisboa: Associação Portuguesa de Seguradores

* Cannar, Kenneth (1979). *Motor Insurance Theory and Practice*. London: Witherby & Co. Ltd.

* Chiejina, Ezekiel, O. (2004). *Foundations of Insurance: Law, Agency and Salesmanship*. Lagos: Mbeyi & Associates Ltd.

* Kirkham, Sharon. (2008). Going for Broke(r). in RiskSA, February 2008, Vol. 05 Issue 04. Pages 20-24.

* Madge, Peter (1990). *Indemnity and insurance: a guide to the aspects of building contracts*. London: RIBA Publications

- Mehr, Robet, I. and Cammack, Emerson (1972). Principles of Insurance. 5th Edition. Illinois: Richard D. Irwin, Inc.

- Plural Editores and KPMG (2009). Código Civil. 3rd Edition.Maputo: Plural Editores

- Sadler, John (ed.) (2012). The Insurance Manual. West Midlands: Insurance Publishing & Printing Co.

- Silva, Carlos, Pereira (2000). *Da economia e da gestão nas empresas de seguros*. Porto: Vida Económica (Grupo Editorial Peixoto de Sousa

- Thomas, Paul, I. and Reed, Prentice, Sr. (1977). Adjustment of Property Losses. 4th Edition. New York: McGraw-Hill, Inc.

- Vaughan, Emmet, J. (1992) *Fundamentals of risk and insurance*. 6th Edition. New York: John Wiley & Sons Inc 2009: 161

- Waty, Teodoro, A. (2007). *Direito de Seguros*. Maputo: W&W Editora Lda

CHAPTER 7

COMMERCIAL INSURANCE OPERATIONS

Following the presentation of the historical background, of the key concepts and respective regulatory framework of insurance, we should now look at key conditions for accessing and operating commercial insurance business in Mozambique. We shall review key legal characteristics of the different types of entities that can be established in the commercial insurance area. We shall also discuss issues relating to training and development in our market as well as the role of other service providers besides financial intermediary services which we shall discuss in more detail in the following chapter.

1. SELLERS OF INSURANCE

We shall look at the basic requirements for the setting up of different forms of insurance companies depending on the intended type of business entity, on location of head office and on type or class of insurance business to be covered. We shall look at key features of the different options and we shall also identify the types of operators that may already be doing business in each of the segments of the sector.

1.1. Type of business entity—Capital Stock Company vs. Mutual

According to Article 13 of the Insurance Law, an insurer can be in the form of a capital stock insurance company or a mutual society (RSA Consultores, 2013: 352). The key difference between the two types of business entities is that while a capital stock company belongs to a group of 'stakeholders', a mutual is owned by 'policyholders' (Vaughan, 2009: 67). On the one hand, the owners of a capital stock company provide the capital for formation and running of the business with the aim of making a profit after settlement of claims and costs of doing business. On the other hand, a mutual is formed for the purposes of providing insurance to members. The surplus remaining after settlement of claims and expenses are supposed to be returned to the policyholders as 'dividends' (Silva, 2000: 56). The minimum capital requirements for the different types of licenses are as outlined in Table 12:

**Table 12–Minimum Capital Requirements
for Insurance Company Licenses**

TYPE OF LICENSE	AREA	TYPE OF BUSINESS	MINIMUM CAPITAL
Mutual	Non-Life	Non-Life only (excluding Health & Assistance)	Mt 7,500,000
		Health only	Mt 7,500,000
		Assistance only	Mt 7,500,000
		Any 2 of Non-Life Types of Business	Mt 12,500,000
	Life	Life	Mt 25,000,000

Capital Stock Insurance Company	Non-Life	Non-Life only (excluding Health & Assistance)	Mt 15,000,000
		Health only	Mt 15,000,000
		Assistance only	Mt 15,000,000
		Non-life including Health and Assistance	Mt 33,000,000
	Life	Life	Mt 67,000,000
	Life & Non-Life	Life, Non-Life, Health & Assistance	Mt 100,000,000

We should note that at the time of writing of this book, there were not yet any registered mutual companies operating in Mozambique. It is also very crucial to note that all the insurers in Mozambique were registered as limited liability companies, in accordance with our Mercantile Law[1]. The meaning of this legal status is that liability of the investors in these companies is limited to the maximum amount of capitalisation of the company, if there were problems of bankruptcy. In my opinion, this is also an important legal basis to explain why insurance companies should never offer insurance policies with unlimited liability as was the case regarding certain types of social insurance which were covered by the private sector insurance market in the absence of appropriate public funds. We shall discuss further the key issues involved in these classes of business.

---

1. Known in Portuguese as Código Comercial (*Decreto-Lei nº. 2/2005 de 27 de Dezembro*)

1.2. Status of License—Authorised vs. Unauthorised

According to Article 7 of the Insurance Law, only companies that have appropriate authorization by the regulatory authorities in Mozambique are permitted to do insurance business in Mozambique. This rule is further reinforced by other laws relating to areas such as foreign exchange and company tax laws. Under the foreign exchange laws, all entities in Mozambique requiring insurance are not permitted to make payments of premium to foreign insurers for property located in Mozambique. With regards to company tax laws, unauthorised payments to foreign insurers are not admitted as approved expenses for the purposes of determining financial performance of a company.

However, appropriately established insurers, are permitted to transfer abroad payments of premium for risks where they may not have adequate financial capacity to retain them on their own. Such a transaction is part of what is known as reinsurance, as we shall briefly discuss later in this chapter. This same legal facility for the local insurance market is also used by some insurers to carry out a quasi-reinsurance transaction known as fronting, as we shall discuss in the next segment.

1.3. Fronting

The word **fronting** is used to refer to a situation where an appropriately authorised insurer in Mozambique underwrites a local risk on behalf of another insurer abroad.

DEVELOPMENT OF INSURANCE IN MOZAMBIQUE

It is a mechanism that global underwriters in international markets try to use in order to bypass the restriction that only locally registered insurers can underwrite local business. The local insurer is used to legitimise the local issuing of the policy documents and collection of premium for an agreed administration fee. In most cases, such arrangements are usually made on the understanding that, after legitimately issuing the policy locally, then, the local insurer could transfer the entire risk to the foreign insurer as reinsurance using the authorised process of reinsurance transfers.

Furthermore, in most cases, the foreign underwriter accepting the risk has full control in the assessment and underwriting of the risk as well as the handling of any claims that may occur. The local insurer may be required to use a form of policy wording from abroad. The policy wording may contain conditions designed to allow the foreign underwriter to have control in the underlying insurance transaction. There may be a **Claims Control Clause** which allows the external underwriter to play a direct role in the handling of any claims that may occur. There could be a **Cut-Through Clause** which allows the foreign insurer to negotiate and settle claims directly with the local client (Sharp, 2009: 34). The local insurer could also apply a **Nominated Reinsurer Clause** or **Pay as Paid clause** which are intended to only put obligation on the local insurer to settle claims to the client only after settlement by the appointed reinsurer on the same account.

Although fronting is not illegal, the regulators do not view it as a core business activity of insurers. In such a transaction, the local insurer becomes a conduit or an intermediary for transferring risks as opposed to being an insurer or underwriter of risks, as per the normal function of insurers. In cases where a local insurer may want to do it, the insurance regulator requires appropriate justifications for such operations. Regulators are preoccupied about this practice because it can be used to extract financial resources. This can contribute to the economic problem of **capital flight** (Adepoyigi, 2005: 113). Unwarranted exit of capital can affect the balance between income earned by a country and payments abroad. In economics this is known as **Balance of Payments**. Insurance is one of the elements under the category of services in these national accounts. As part of effective management of the welfare of a country, economists try to maintain a positive balance between net inflows and outflows.

Notwithstanding the argument of supporting balance of payments, it should be noted that policy-makers should not restrict transfers for legitimate reinsurance. This is vital because it ensures that local markets do not expose themselves to ruin through retention or accumulation of retained risk beyond their financial capacity. If you will remember, one of the key conditions for a risk to be insurable is the 'law of large numbers.' Some of the assets in our country are very unique and have very high values such that it is not feasible for any insurer only covering local risks to generate adequate premium to cover any of the claims that may occur in that portfolio. This is the situation for specialist types of business such as insurance of large commercial aircraft, major mineral-extraction projects, ocean-going vessels, energy, oil and gas sectors. Furthermore, in the event of a claim on a major reinsured risk, the inward claim settlement from reinsurers becomes a vital inflow of foreign exchange which is usually what is required to absorb the shock of large losses or catastrophic loses affecting various key risks at the same time.

We believe that, as part of the process of monitoring of fronting, the focus should always be directed at unwarranted reinsurance for risks which can be retained locally or other questionable practices such as schemes of **money laundering**, **tax evasion** and **transfer pricing**. As we discussed in the previous Chapter, some of the unique features of insurance contracts create a situation where insurance and connected processes of reinsurance can be manipulated. This is a subject which requires a detailed research. We are aware that the African Insurance Organisation (AIO) has commissioned an international auditing firm to carry out a study of this phenomenon and how to prevent abuse of insurance markets for illegal financial activities.

Some of the global risk consultants and large companies may tend to force the local insurance market to transfer certain types of risks. This may be due to the fact that multi-national companies tend to want to fully control the area of financial risk transfer through mechanisms such as captive insurance companies as described below in the section on alternative risk transfer. These types of placements are usually done on mega-projects that are unique and require types of cover beyond risk appetite, know-how, experience and financial capacity of locally licensed operators.

1.4. Location of Head Office—Local vs. Foreign

As provided for in articles 21 to 23 of the Insurance Law, it is possible for an insurer or reinsurer that is domiciled or has a head office based outside of Mozambique to apply for authorization to setup and run a local operation as a branch office of an offshore operator. Up to the beginning of 2014, there were no insurers operating as branch offices controlled by parent companies outside Mozambique. However, it appears that, at the end of 2014, an insurer from Portugal had been granted authority to setup a branch office in Mozambique.

It is not very clear how such arrangements are supposed to work because there are no clear guidelines on a number of issues concerning such types of operations. This is also likely to create new distortions in a market that already does not have a level playing field in other areas, as we shall discuss further in this chapter. There are certain critical advantages to be gained by any company that will be able to only setup minimal local structures and compete with other companies that have had to fully incorporate a local subsidiary. Some of the critical challenges in the local market include high costs of doing business and lack of skills and supporting services.

Notwithstanding this recent development, all the other local insurance subsidiaries of international insurance groups have onshore head offices. This means that these insurance companies have setup fully registered principal offices for their local operations in Mozambique. Being subsidiaries, it means that they have been fully established in Mozambique with all required structures, governance bodies, systems, policies, processes and personnel. It also means that all their business activities should satisfy first and foremost the local laws, rules and conditions of doing business in Mozambique before considerations from anywhere else.

1.5. Type of business—Life vs. Non-Life

Insurers are required to manage and account separately for Life and Non-Life insurance business (Article 6 of the Insurance Law). It should be noted that, in the transition phase from 1991 to 2003, it was possible to operate as a composite insurance company handling both life and non-life business under one license. The first three insurers that were established before and during the transition period were set up as composite insurers. For such companies, it was expected that they would separate the two portfolios within a certain time period and that the two types of business would be managed separately. This has not yet happened. However, all new investors that may want to operate both types of business are now required to apply for separate licenses and capitalise two distinct entities. This lack of consistency on the question of separation of licenses does not contribute to the maintaining of a level playing field between the already established and the recently licensed companies.

Furthermore, for each type of insurance business, the law provides a list of classes of insurance that belong to each category, as per Article number 84 in the regulations of the Insurance Law. This list could be improved in alignment with global classifications as well as key growth areas in the market. Pension funds are also listed as one of the classes of Life insurance. Pensions are a separate type of business which should be accounted for separately, in accordance with international accounting standards of insurance business.

In addition to the above, the classification in the law also separates certain things that are classified together in conventional insurance accounts. For instance, in the law Business Interruption is being classified as a separate class from Property Damage. That is not in alignment with how insurance companies in Mozambique and all other markets treat the two items. Usually, material damage and consequential financial loss are classified as sub-categories of the same class of business. Furthermore, financial reports from the insurance companies and the market reports issued by the regulatory authorities themselves follow different forms of classification. We would like to propose a basic classification of non-life insurance business for our market based on a traditional model used in other countries in our region as presented in Appendix VI. We shall look at the classes of life insurance business in Chapter 11.

1.6. Microinsurance

The Insurance Law of 2010 also introduces a new concept of **microinsurance**. The key emerging concern in the microinsurance initiative is how to cover effectively the majority low-income population which is neglected by traditional financial markets. We would like to acknowledge that, with this reference to microinsurance in our insurance legislation, we are one of the first few markets in Africa to take such an initiative. Microinsurance business can be provided by either conventional insurance companies or by companies that can register as microinsurers (Article 42). The minimum capital requirements for companies that may want to exclusively underwrite only microinsurance are as outlined in Table 13.

Table 13–Minimum Capital Requirements for Microinsurance

TYPE OF LICENSE	AREA	TYPE OF BUSINESS	MINIMUM CAPITAL
Mutual Microinsurance Company	Composite	Life & Non-Life for only Members of the Mutual	Mt 3 million
Mutual Microinsurance Company	Composite	Life & Non-Life not restricted to only Members of the Mutual	Mt 10 million
Public Limited Microinsurance Company	Composite	Life & Non-Life	Mt 10 million

Currently, some of the existing insurance companies are doing some forms of microinsurance business. According to the market report of the Insurance Regulator of 2014, only one entity had been registered as a dedicated microinsurance company. However, there were no records of business performance indicators in this area in the annual reports of the authorities. If the regulators believe that microinsurance is an important aspect of the development policy of the sector, it will be essential for them to also provide reports on this type of business from both the traditional insurance companies doing microinsurance and dedicated microinsurance operators. We shall discuss further in Chapter 14 the development trend connected to microinsurance.

1.7. Risk pools

After the discussion on insurance and microinsurance companies, we should now discuss risk pools, as another form of insurance. A risk pool can be used in order to create underwriting capacity for areas of critical need not covered by traditional insurance and reinsurance markets (Portugal, 2007: 313). A pool is supposed to underwrite and accept risks using joint capacity from a group or pool of different entities as well as reinsurance that may be arranged on behalf of the pool. Usually, such an arrangement is formalised in an agreement that outlines the basis on which the members of the pool can introduce risks into the pool and take a share of liability and respective premium after deduction of agreed fees and expenses of the pool. An underwriter or a financial consultant may be appointed as a pool manager with the responsibilities of handling of the accounts of the pool on behalf of the members.

We do not yet have any local risk pools in Mozambique. One of the best examples of an effective risk pool in our region is the South African Nuclear Risks Pool (SANP). It was formed by the South African government in order to place insurance of the Koeberg Nuclear Power Station into a global nuclear risks pool. There are also risk pools at regional level in Africa. The African Insurance Organisation (AIO) has established two key risk pools as follows:

- The African Aviation Pool
- The African Oil and Energy Insurance Pool

We also believe that risk pools could be one of the most appropriate mechanisms for achieving three critical goals. Firstly, in a country such as Mozambique where we have a limited number of skilled and experienced personnel, it creates a platform to pool technical resources and skills. Secondly, it creates space for building of collective financial underwriting capacity from participating insurers. Thirdly, there is improved bargaining power of the local market when negotiating for reinsurance as a group.

2. INSURANCE ASSOCIATION

The local insurance association, referred to in Portuguese as Associação Moçambicana de Seguradores (AMS), was officially registered on 11 July 2002 (Oliveira, 2013: 2). In the early years of its formation, it was not very active. There have been attempts to make the association more active starting from 2007. The principal goals of the association, as outlined in its articles of association[2], can be described in brief as collaboration of insurance companies in order to support development of skills, knowledge and capacity of the local market.

Besides the national insurance association, there are also regional organisations that could support the local market in its development initiatives. In the past, local companies have not played an active role in regional activities on the continent. The focus was on learning from mainly Portugal, given the historical links. However, some of the members of the local association have now begun to participate in regional initiatives such as the Organisation of Eastern and Southern African Insurers (OESAI) and the African Insurance Organisation (AIO). Through these organisations, our association could have an opportunity to share insights with counterparts in other territories that face similar challenges as we do.

---

2. Published under official gazette with reference: BR nº. 45 III Series, 9 de Novembro de 2007

3. REINSURANCE

The next key feature of our insurance market that we should review is reinsurance. Reinsurance is an essential tool for the management of risk by an insurer and for purposes of stabilising its results (Garand and Wipf, 2008: 263). As such, through reinsurance, an insurer can expand its underwriting capacity for a specific risk or for an entire portfolio. This capacity is usually in the form of financial capacity which enables the insurer to assume more risks with higher values at risk than it would do if it relied only on its own financial resources. Reinsurers may also provide technical support to insurers by providing guidance on how to handle covered risks.

Besides providing capacity, reinsurance contracts can also be used to protect risks retained by the insurer. We should also note that only appropriately licensed insurance companies can place reinsurance abroad, if there is no capacity in the local market. The principal reinsurance markets on which our insurance market relies are located in the key international financial centres of London, Zurich, Munich and Paris. There are also key regional reinsurance markets in Johannesburg, Harare, Kenya, Lagos and Mauritius. We should also note that, at the time of writing this book, there was one local reinsurance company registered in our market known as Moçambique Companhia de Seguros (MozRe). It appears that other regional reinsurers might also set up offices in Mozambique in the near future.

4. SUPPORTING SERVICES

Besides the entities that are directly involved in insurance business, as we have discussed up to now, there are also a number of other key supporting services that make it possible for insurance to function properly. In addition to service providers that any other business in any other sector may require, the following are particularly essential to the functions of insurance:

- Loss assessors or adjustors—These are professional service providers required for assessment of claims on insurance contracts, as we shall discuss in more detail in Chapter 13

- Risk surveyors and risk managers—These are professionals that are required for purposes of identifying, assessing, analysing and proposing means of controlling risks, as we discussed in Chapter 3.

- Salvage dealers who buy from insurers remaining material after an insured event. By buying what is left and trying to re-use it, they reduce financial costs of claims and assist in disposal of items salvaged from the insured entity, as part of the claims settlement process.

- Panel beaters, property evaluators, plumbers, builders, well control experts for the oil and gas sector and other contractors that may be required to assist in the event of a claim

Furthermore, we should also note that there is still limited or no service in other key areas of the insurance sector of Mozambique. There is a lack of skills for essential activities such as actuarial services, risk management and loss assessment. In order to cover this gap, most of the companies rely heavily on foreign contractors. The bulk of foreign firms contracted locally are based mainly in South Africa and in Portugal.

5. TRAINING AND DEVELOPMENT

We do not yet have in Mozambique professional courses for training and development of skills in insurance such as the Chartered Insurance Institute of London, as we discussed in Chapter 1. It appears that key stakeholders in the insurance sector are aware of this problem and have indicated their commitment to support initiatives aimed at development of local solutions. In the interim, the insurance sector could consider collaborating with the training institute of bankers known as the *Instituto de Formação Bancária de Moçambique* (IFBM). They already have infrastructure as well as training programmes that were designed for the banking sector. They are willing to collaborate with the insurance sector given that some of the banks handle insurance products, as we shall discuss in the next chapter.

6. MARKET REPORTS

One of the key features of reliable and solid financial markets is the compilation of up-to-date market reports with appropriate indicators of financial soundness. Market reports are vital tools to ensure transparency and to assure the public of the financial soundness of the operators involved in the market. According to a presentation by the President of Board of the office of the insurance regulator, it is also one of the legal duties of the regulatory authorities to produce market reports (Santos, 2013: 3). This is defined in item number 3k) in Article 11 of the Decree number 29/2012 of 26 June 2012, which provides legal basis for the formation of the new regulatory authority.

Following the first formal seminar of the national insurance market of 5 December 2013, the ISSM started producing an annual insurance market report. This has been a significant achievement. We would like to contribute to this critical process by making a few recommendations for the improvement of the report. We have compared our market report to those from Botswana, Swaziland and Zimbabwe. We believe that our authorities could improve the quality of our report by adopting some form of model that would allow them to appropriately benchmark performance locally and in comparison to global standards. We would like to propose a model called CARAMELS.

6.1. CARAMELS Model

The CARAMELS model is presented in a paper of the International Monetary Fund written by Das and others (2003). In this paper, they propose for the insurance sector a model derived from a bench-marking concept that was first developed for the banking sector. This benchmark from banking is widely known by the acronym—CAMELS. This is derived from the following indicators: Capital Adequacy, Asset Quality, Management Soundness, Earnings and Profitability, Liquidity, and Sensitivity to Market Risk. There are a number of ways of measuring all these financial aspects in a bank in order to assess financial soundness. CARAMELS is an adaptation for insurance business of the concept of CAMELS. The insurance version of the model is also aimed at measuring equivalent indicators in insurance as well as two additional items that are unique to our business: Reinsurance and Adequacy of Reserves. We shall not discuss details of these indicators in this book. This theme requires a complete book of its own. The key point to note is that this model allows us to focus on risk and appropriate financial management, which are key conditions for 'long-term success' in our business (Garand and Wipf, 2008: 254).

6.2. Financial Reporting Standards

The insurance association has a critical role to play in supporting the regulator in the process of improving financial reporting in our market. One of the major challenges that we need to overcome is to ensure that financial reports are finalized within a reasonable time period after the year-end and that there is a consistent approach in the presentation of financial information. Part of this problem should be addressed in the near future since the local insurance sector is now supposed to adopt the International Financial Reporting Standard (IFRS).

CONCLUSION

We have had an opportunity to discuss the business operations of the commercial insurance market. We discussed the types of business entities that can be established. We observed that besides setting up of an insurance company, it is also possible to set up an insurer in the form of a mutual. At this stage, our market only has public limited companies. We also noted that the law of Mozambique permits the setting up of insurance branches that may be controlled by principal offices domiciled abroad. There is a need for guidelines on how the local rules and conditions of doing business should be applied for such branches. We have also noted that there is no level playing field between the older companies that were able to setup as composite insurers and the newer investments that are now required to setup as two separate licenses for life and non-life insurance business.

Furthermore, we also discussed the contentious question of fronting and connected problems of illicit financial transactions. This subject also requires clear guidelines in order to clearly distinguish between unwarranted transfers and proper external placements which the market itself may require in order to access certain forms of financial and technical support. We also noted key developments concerning microinsurance business. The business activity of reinsurance is also part of our Insurance Law. These areas require guidelines in order to ensure clarity.

Finally, we also looked at the critical role played by the insurance association. There is a lot of work to be done by the association in its efforts to contribute to the development of insurance in Mozambique and to support the regulatory authorities. One of the key areas requiring attention as soon as possible is training and development of skills at all levels. There is also scope for improvement of our insurance market report. After this review of the situation of the suppliers of insurance service, we should now look at distribution channels of insurance in the next Chapter.

REFERENCES

- Adepoyigi, Tola (2005). *Oil & gas construction insurance in Nigeria.* Lagos: Peniel Ventures.

- Das, U.S., Davies, N., and Podpiera, R. (2003). *Insurance and Issues in Financial Soundness.* IMF Working Paper, WP/03/138. Washington: IMF.

- FinMark Trust (2009). FinScope Mozambique 2009. Cape Town: FinMark Trust

- Garand, Denis and Wipf, John. (2008). 'Risk and financial management' in Churchill, Craig (ed.) Protecting the poor: a microinsurance compendium. Geneva: Internationational Labour Office and the Munich Re Foundation: Munich. Pp. 254-269.

- Muchena, Israel (2012). *The Mozambican insurance market*. In The African Reinsurer. Lagos: The African Reinsurance Corporation. Volume 26. Pages 32-35

- Oliveira, Rui (2013). *Papel da Associação Moçambicana de Seguradores* in a paper presented at the Insurance Seminar of the ISSM.

- Portugal, Luís (2007). Gestão de Seguros Não-vida. Lisbon: Instituto de Formação Actuarial

- RSA Consultores (2013). *Legislação do Sistema Financeiro de Moçambique*. Porto: Vida Económica.

- Santos, Monjane, Maria, Otília, (2013). *Mensagems da Presidente do Conselho de Administração* in Insurance Market Report of 2012. ISSM.

- Sharp, David (2009). *Upstream and Offshore Energy Insurance*. Livingston: Witherbys Insurance

- Silva, Carlos, Pereira (2000). *Da economia e da gestão nas empresas de seguros*. Porto: Vida Económica (Grupo Editorial Peixoto de Sousa

- Vaughan, Emmet, J. (1992) *Fundamentals of risk and insurance*. 6th Edition. New York: John Wiley & Sons Inc.

CHAPTER 8

INSURANCE INTERMEDIARIES

Intermediaries play an important role in supporting the development of insurance and other types of economic activities. There are two pieces of legislation that can help us to understand what are intermediaries and how they work. Firstly, there is a general definition of the business of intermediaries in the Mercantile Law[3] of Mozambique, as covered by Law no. 2/2005 of 27 December[4] and subsequent alterations[5]. However, given the special nature of insurance business and the unique roles of the different types of intermediaries or agents, the Insurance Law provides further rules and guidelines on this activity.

1. THE ROLE OF INSURANCE INTERMEDIARIES

Insurance intermediation is one of the most critical elements contributing to the expansion of insurance business worldwide. According to McCord (2008: 357), insurance agents (one of

---

3. The current Mercantile Law is known in Portuguese as *Código Comercial*.
4. Referred to in Portuguese as *Decreto-Lei nº. 2/2005 de 27 de Dezembro*.
5. Lei nº. 10/2005; Decreto-Lei nº. 2/2009; and Lei nº. 3/2009

the forms of intermediaries), have been in existence for as long as there has been insurance'. An insurance intermediary can be defined as a firm or individual that serves as a 'go-between' that offers to provide some service between two parties that are trying to exchange something. The intermediary offers this service for a fee that may be provided by the supplier or buyer of the service or good under consideration. Intermediaries can be found in businesses such as the stock exchange, sales of property, insurance and other areas. However, the concept of an intermediary is more widely practiced in insurance business than other activities given the complexities of insurance contracts (Mathonsi, 2013: 5).

The buyers of insurance require assistance and advice in order to make sure that they are arranging appropriate types of cover depending on their needs. Insurers, as suppliers of insurance, want access to consumers through the distribution channels of the insurance intermediaries. According to a manual on insurance intermediation from the IISA (2011E, 49-55), the five main functions of intermediaries can be summarised as follows:

i. Assessment of risks and execution of a 'needs analysis' of the client. The exercise of risk assessment could also be complimented by risk survey exercises , as we discussed in Chapter 4.

ii. Selection of an insurance company that will provide the most adequate form of cover depending on the needs of the client. It is essential for the intermediary to consider questions such as financial strength, quality of service and sustainability of proposed solutions.

iii. Issuing of instructions for the binding of a valid insurance agreement that satisfies all essential legal elements, verifying that the insurer issues covers as required and arranging for collection of agreed premium on time.

iv. Provide administrative services.

v. Assist the client in handling of any claims that may occur.

2. TYPES OF INSURANCE INTERMEDIARIES

There are three basic types of intermediaries in the insurance market of Mozambique. The simplest form of an insurance agent is an **Individual Tied Agent**.[1] This is that is contracted as an intermediary by a specific insurance company. This type of intermediary usually works on an **exclusive agency agreement**. This means that they can only work with one insurance company.

Then, at the next level we have an **Insurance Agent**. This type of insurance agent may be an individual or a company. Such an agent may also have an exclusive agency agreement with a specific insurer or could be operating as an independent intermediary. The company could be set up

---

1. Known in Portuguese as *Angariador* or *Promotor*

as a sole proprietorship[2] or a private limited company[3]. An insurance agent may also have other business activities besides insurance. It is through this approach that entities such as banks, micro-finance institutions, travel agencies and other types of business may arrange insurance agency agreements, as we shall discuss later.

Finally, at the highest level in the area of insurance intermediaries, we have an **Insurance Broker**. This is a type of intermediary that has insurance intermediation as an exclusive business activity. Insurance brokers are supposed to be dedicated insurance professionals. They tend to be independent firms that may have access to more than one insurance company for purposes of placement of insurance.

As at the end of December 2014, there were 45 authorised insurance brokers and numerous individual tied agents and insurance agencies. Most of the registered intermediaries are based in Maputo. The only intermediaries that have some form of country-wide distribution network are banks and micro-finance institutions that use their existing branch network to

---

2. A 'sole proprietorship' or 'sole trader' is the most basic form of a business entity. It is owned and run by an individual that is fully responsible for the business and there is no separation between his/her interests and that of the business.

3. A 'private limited liability company' is a business entity that is legally recognised as a distinct legal entity and should not be seen as the same thing as the owners.

provide insurance products in some form of partnership with insurance companies.

3. REMUNERATION OF INSURANCE INTERMEDIARIES

Insurance intermediaries are supposed to earn their remuneration through what is known as **commission** or **brokerage**. This commission is calculated as an agreed percentage of the premium charged and collected (Chiejina, 2004: 155). In most cases in our market, the clients are not aware of how intermediaries are remunerated for their service. In countries such as South Africa, it is now obligatory for intermediaries to disclose to the clients how much they are earning. This is covered in a piece of legislation known as the Financial Advisory and Intermediary Services (FAIS) which was passed in 2002. It is believed that it is vital for the person that is actually paying the cost to be aware how much they are paying in order for them to be able to understand what value for service they are obtaining. Mozambique and most countries in our region do not yet have such forms of legislation. Given the concerns of the policy-makers to protect the interest of the consumers as alluded to in the Insurance Law, it is vital for our market to have a debate on this question.

Furthermore, there are no consistent practices in our market in the handling of commissions. In Mozambique and other Portuguese-speaking markets, some of the insurers follow a practice of breaking down intermediary commissions into the following three categories:

- Intermediation commission for introducing business to an insurance company

- Collection commission earned for services of collection of premium on business placed by an agent

- Brokerage commission for the complete service of placing business and collection of premium

In such a system, a tied agent could be paid only intermediation commission for providing only the service of placing insurance. Such agents are not supposed to receive premium on behalf of the insurer. The client is supposed to pay the insurer directly. This arrangement where an agent is not authorised to receive premium is also known as **cash agency** in insurance markets such as Malawi and Zimbabwe. Brokers are expected to receive the full brokerage commission for providing a full range of service of advising the client, placing business and collection of premium. The arrangement where an insurance agent or broker is permitted to collect premium is also known as **credit agency** in some of insurance markets in neighbouring countries.

Besides the system of splitting commissions described above, the majority of insurers in our market now work with a simplified commission model. In most instances, insurance intermediaries are paid commission on the basis of an agreed commission rate defined by the insurers (sellers of insurance) for the different types of insurance business. However, on insurance agreements involving large companies, some of the buyers of insurance (instead of sellers) try to bargain with the insurance intermediary in order to fix an amount of annual **brokerage fees** payable to the broker. With the approach of a commission rate, brokerage commission is proportionate to amount of premium. As a result, brokerage commission is also proportionately large on large accounts. As a result of this observation, some of the very large corporate buyers of insurance try to achieve a saving of costs by defining a fee proportionate to actual service provided by the broker. In such instances, after accepting the **fee-based remuneration**, the intermediary would pay back to the client any commissions paid by the insurer or would discount commissions in premium charged by the insurer. This process is what is known as **rebate** of commission.

Furthermore, we would like to also note that insurance companies in our market have different levels of commissions. In some cases, some of the insurance companies do not offer a consistent set of commission rates for the same insurance business to different brokers! Other insurers appear to offer some forms of administrative fees. We believe that there is a loophole in the treatment of respective taxes. It also appears that some insurers offer intermediaries what is known as **Profit Commission**. This is an additional form of commission which is paid at the end of an agreed insurance period for any positive balances remaining in the account of the insurer after settlement of agreed expenses and claims.

Finally, we would like to note that it is not necessarily an entirely bad thing that different operators are handling remuneration of intermediaries as they see fit. That is part of an appropriate situation in a free market where authorities are not supposed to apply any forms of controls. However, we believe that policy-makers need to be aware that, if there are no guidelines, some of these market practices can degenerate to a level where they start posing major threats to consumer protection and stability of the affected markets. It is on this basis that we believe that our market could benefit from disclosure conditions and many other critical elements of financial advisory intermediary services legislation, which we do not yet have.

4. KEY LEGAL CONDITIONS

According to Article 7 of the Insurance Law, it is prohibited to operate as an insurance agent or insurance broker or insurance intermediary without authorisation by appropriate authorities in Mozambique. Violation of this law can be punished by application of a prison sentence of at least one year for involved persons as well as financial penalties as stipulated in the law. Only locally admitted or licensed insurance intermediaries can handle placement of insurance on local risks.

a. Conflict of interest

Furthermore, in order to avoid issues of **conflict of interest**, it is not permitted for any person involved at any level in an insurance company or claims assessment firm or the insurance regulatory office to work, to own or to have any direct or indirect interest in an insurance intermediary. In the same way, people involved in an insurance intermediary are prohibited from working, owning or having any financial interest directly or indirectly in an insurance company. This rule is stipulated in Article 62 of the current Insurance Law.

b. Commission Stamp Tax

Insurance intermediaries are required to pay a Stamp Tax of 2% of all commission processed. Like in the case of accounting for tax on premium, refunds and cancellations are also credited appropriately in the respective Stamp Tax submissions. Intermediaries are also required to pay an annual insurance regulator fee as follows:

- Insurance brokers: Mt 10 000

- Insurance agents: Mt 3 000

- Individual tied agents: Mt 1 000

5. INSURANCE BROKERS

In accordance with the Insurance Law, the highest level of insurance intermediation is occupied by professional insurance brokerage companies. According to the licenses that some of the operators in this area have, they can deal with all classes of business in general and life insurance including pensions. As reflected in Article 60 of the Insurance Law, the company name of an insurance brokerage firm should clearly identify the company as an 'insurance broker' so that there is no ambiguity about the function of the company.

Some of the brokerage licenses also refer to brokerage of reinsurance. However, there is very little reinsurance trading besides a few individual placements that some of the local brokers try to control on behalf of the national insurance market. Local insurance companies tend to rely on either international reinsurance brokers or direct placements in either the local reinsurance company or in foreign reinsurance markets. Article 60 of the Insurance Law, states the minimum capital requirements for insurance and reinsurance brokers as follows:

- Mt 450 000 for an insurance broker
- Mt 600 000 for a reinsurance broker

Given the rapidly growing number of registered insurance intermediaries in Mozambique, insurance intermediation has some of the fiercest competition. Not all the registered brokers are fully functional due to, amongst other issues, the fact that some of the firms have proved not to be viable businesses. Some of the insurance brokers are former agents of some of the insurance companies that have upgraded their licenses. We have provided in Appendix VII a list in alphabetical order of the licensed insurance brokers as at the end of 2014, as per the website of the Insurance Regulator.

At the moment, none of the major brokers appear to have setup any branch network besides offices in Maputo. Some of the large provincial cities like Beira and Tete are covered by new emerging local brokerage firms. It appears to us that the more established brokers do not yet find it economically viable to setup operations outside of Maputo. Part of the reason for this situation is because we are still in a highly centralized economy. Decision-making for most economic activities and the national government is mainly located in Maputo. Given that the decision-makers are in Maputo, most businesses tend to prefer to focus on Maputo.

However, we believe that this is going to change with the new key projects outside of Maputo such as the coal mines in Tete, the oil and gas exploration projects in Pemba and increasing trade at ports in central and northern parts of the country. These projects will also put pressure on the policy-makers to speed up the development of infrastructure and facilities such as roads, bridges, airports, railways and other key services that will make these zones more accessible and reduce costs of doing business there. With all of these developments, there will be more brokers and agents willing to expand outside of Maputo. In some respects, the insurance regulator can also consider certain measures to promote expansion of insurance service outside of Maputo. The insurance regulator could offer incentives such as lower taxes for intermediaries that may setup outside of Maputo. It is vital to support the development of insurance services in other parts of the country as part of the wider policy of supporting economic growth in other parts of the country besides the capital city. This would help to create employment opportunities in different locations as well as create conditions for improved supply of service such as insurance that could contribute to making other parts of the country as hospitable as Maputo.

6. INSURANCE AGENTS

From the period of opening up of the insurance market in the early 1990s, there has been a rapid growth of insurance agencies. There is also a new trend of development of new agency models. The key agency agreements in our insurance market today are as outlined in Table 14.

Table 14–Insurance Agency Models

	TYPE OF AGENCY	MAIN OPERATORS	TYPICAL PRODUCTS
1	Tied Agents	Mainly individuals working on an exclusive basis with insurer that has appointed them	**Mono-line agencies** for policies like Motor, Travel, Life, etc
			Multi-line agencies that can handle different types of insurance
2	Independent Insurance Agencies	Sole Proprietor or Private Limited Companies	All types of insurance business
3	Bancassurance	Commercial Banks	Credit Life, Funeral, Hospital Cash, Mortgage Life, Travel
4	Microinsurance	Micro Finance Institutions and other forms of Partner-Agents	Micro-Credit, Weather Index Insurance

a. Tied Agents

We have two basic types of tied agents in our market. We have the **mono-line type agencies** that are permitted to only handle one type of product. Then, we have the general agents or **multi-line agents** that are permitted to handle more than one type of product.

Furthermore, the route of tied agencies is also the model that has been applied for firms that are not dedicated to insurance intermediation. They may want to distribute insurance besides the other services that they usually provide to their clients. This has been the approach applied for travel agents that are interested in distributing travel insurance. Finally, we should also note that, the option of registering as a tied individual agent is seen by the policy-makers as a means of facilitating entry of national citizens into insurance intermediation business. The expectation of the authorities is that, with the growth of their insurance portfolio, tied agents should develop their business and take it to the next level of an independent insurance agency firm.

b. Independent Insurance Agents

An independent insurance agent is supposed to be a formally established business entity dedicated to insurance intermediation. As an independent intermediary, it is not required to be limited to only handling insurance products of only one insurer, as is the case of a tied agent. The conditions for setting up such an agency and obtaining a license are less onerous than those applicable for insurance brokers. The minimum capital requirement is Metical 150,000.00, as noted in Article 121 of the Regulations to the Insurance Law. According to the website of the Insurance Regulator, the licensed independent insurance agents in our market are as follows:

- Tayob Hassan Agente de Seguros Sociedade Unipessoal, Lda
- Mais Vida Agente de Seguros, Lda

- Maputo Seguros Agente de Seguros Sociedade Unipessoal
- Integrity Agente de Seguro

c. Bancassurance

Bancassurance can be defined as 'the joint effort of banks and insurers to provide insurance services to the bank's customer base' (Swiss Re, 2007: 5). In Mozambique, from the different types of agency models outlined above, bancassurance has grown to be the largest and most diverse source of insurance business. Banks tend to have a far more extensive infrastructure in all key urban areas across the country than insurance companies and intermediaries. In addition, there is also the convenience to the customer of having a one-stop shop for accessing banking and insurance service. There are a number of models that can be followed in bancassurance arrangements. We have a presentation of some of the key global models in Figure 6.

Figure 6–Global Bancassurance Models (Source: Unknown)

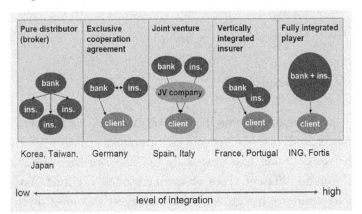

Not all the models presented above are applied in Mozambique. On the basis of the regulatory framework in Mozambique, banks are not expected to follow the concept of a 'Pure Distributor' where they would have agency agreements with different insurers at the same time. It appears to us that part of the consideration for this restriction is that then the bank would need to satisfy a far more complex role of providing advice on insurance. Such an approach would require a high level of skills and insurance would need to be the core focus, as is the case of traditional insurance brokers.

The most prevalent model amongst banks in Mozambique is the 'Exclusive Cooperation Model'. However, there are some commercial banks that have opted for the model of 'Vertical Integration' and seem to be evolving towards some form of full integration in some areas. There is not yet any 'Joint Venture' type of arrangement where a bank and an insurer would co-invest into a separate entity that would serve as a vehicle for distribution of bancassurance type of products. According to the Swiss Re Sigma Report on Bancassurance (2007: 5), there are also further developments in other markets of variations to bancassurance. There are business cases of financial institutions offering fully integrated financial services. This is also known as *allfinanz*. There are also cases where, contrary to bancassurance, it is the insurer providing or distributing financial or banking services from an insurance business. This is what is known as **assurbanking**. We do not have in our market any companies applying the last two models described above.

d.   Microinsurance Intermediaries

Besides insurance brokers and insurance agents that are specifically set up as insurance intermediaries, it is possible for micro-finance institutions and non-governmental organizations to operate as microinsurance agents. According to McCord (2008: 358), this form of intermediary, which he describes as the 'partner-agent model', is now being extended to other services that are not traditional distribution channels of insurance such as retail shops, post offices and mobile telephone services. According to Article 57 of the Insurance

Law, this can be done on the basis of a microinsurance agency agreement.

7. UNDERWRITING MANAGEMENT AGENTS

We should now look at a new development of the model of underwriting management agents (UMAs). A UMA is a business unit operating under an insurance license and doing insurance business on behalf of an insurer that grants it authority and capacity to accept risks. The Insurance Law in Mozambique does not contain any specific conditions on such forms of agencies. There are business entities in our market that are already using agency models similar to basic forms of underwriting management agency. With increasingly fierce competition, there are also signs that some insurers are granting limited authority to some brokers to quote and accept business automatically on their behalf. This approach to placement of business is part of what is described as insurance **binder agreements**.

As one of the key outcomes of the emergence of underwriting management agencies, the boundaries between intermediation and insurance underwriting can become blurred. In South Africa, the regulators have taken measures in order to ensure that there is clarity on the roles and responsibilities of the different parties involved in the processes of advice, guidance, placing and underwriting of risks. Part of the motivation for seeking this clarification is to reduce risks of what could appear as 'ambivalent' roles of an intermediary. Kenneth Cannar (1979: 41) argues that the ambivalence arises from *'the practical difficulties that face agents when trying to balance their duty to a client with their sense of obligation to the insurer.'*

8. DIRECT BUSINESS

To complete our discussion on intermediation, we should now look at cases where insurance is not purchased through intermediaries. Direct business is the word used to refer to a portfolio of insurance business placed directly with an insurer without involvement of an intermediary (Chiejina, 2004: 170). The Insurance Law of Mozambique does not prohibit direct placements of insurance by buyers of insurance at all levels. However, there are not yet any pure Direct Insurers in Mozambique. All the registered insurers tend to rely on both direct as well as placements by brokers and agents.

Furthermore, we should note that the significance of direct portfolios in our market is as a result of two key factors. Firstly, insurance intermediation is still at an early stage of development following the unbanning of the activity with the reforms of 1991. Secondly, most of the traditional insurance intermediaries are located only in Maputo and do not have appropriate representation across the country. In most of the cities and towns in Central and Northern parts of the country, consumers have access only to branch offices of insurers which have a more extensive network than most of the intermediaries besides banks involved in bancassurance.

Finally, we should note that in some markets there are restrictions on type of insurance business that can be placed directly. For instance, in Lloyd's of London which is the largest global insurance market, it is not permitted to place directly with the underwriters. Placement of insurance business should be done though Lloyd's Brokers (Cannar, 1979: 41). We believe that there is a need for our policy-makers to review the rules regarding direct placements. We are of the view that permitting direct placements for large projects and business enterprises creates a loophole for foreign intermediaries to bypass the locally established intermediaries by instructing the client to place insurance locally on a 'direct' basis. In such arrangements, the non-admitted intermediary would then try to extract commissions by instructing the local market to front the risk through them, as a 'reinsurance broker' for that specific account.

CONCLUSION

In this chapter we have discussed the key role played by intermediaries in the distribution of insurance. We noted that Mozambique already has a fairly broad range of types of intermediaries. We observed that most major intermediaries are based mainly in Maputo. We believe that we shall see some of them setting up branches in other key areas of development in the country. Then, we looked next at the different types of insurance agency arrangements that exist in our market.

Furthermore, we believe that there is a need for improved legislation covering intermediary services. However, instead of waiting for the required legislative changes, the registered intermediaries could take the initiative of drafting guidelines for intermediation, codes of conduct and professional training manuals. Through such an initiative, the market could voluntarily start applying some form of self-regulation.

Finally, we should also note that there is an issue in the Insurance Law regarding types of insurance covers that are supposed to be arranged by brokers as part of the conditions for doing business. On one hand, insurance intermediaries are supposed to provide some form of protection to their client in case they misuse premium from their clients. On the other hand, intermediaries are also supposed to protect their clients from financial prejudice that may arise from inappropriate insurance advice. In the next Chapter, we shall discuss the two different types of financial protection that are required by intermediaries as well as other forms of obligatory insurance in Mozambique.

REFERENCES

- Cannar, Kenneth (1979). *Motor Insurance Theory and Practice*. London: Witherby & Co. Ltd

- Chiejina, Ezekiel, O. (2004). *Foundations of Insurance: Law, Agency and Salesmanship*. Lagos: Mbeyi & Associates Ltd.

- IISA (2011 E). *Insurance Broking*. Insurance Institute of South Africa

- Mathonsi, George (2013). Cobrança e Canalização de Prémios às Seguradoras—Paper presented at the Insurance Seminar of the ISSM.

- McCord, Michael, J. (2008). 'The partner-agent model: Challenges and opportunities' in Churchill, Craig (ed.) Protecting the poor: a microinsurance compendium. Geneva: International Labour Office and the Munich Re Foundation: Munich. Pp. 357-377.

- Swiss Re (2007). *Bancassurance: emerging Trends, Opportunities and Challenges*, Sigma No. 5/2007. Zurich: Swiss Reinsurance Company Ltd.

CHAPTER 9

SOCIAL INSURANCE AND OTHER OBLIGATORY TYPES

We shall now begin our review of the principal types of insurance products by looking at different forms of obligatory insurance. We shall look at the compulsory insurances that are provided by both the public and private sector. We shall also compare approaches of handling of this type of insurance in Mozambique and other markets. We shall also identify some of the critical gaps in the local legislation for such classes of insurance. In order to address some of the challenges that we are seeing, we have also recommended self-regulation initiatives that the insurance market could consider besides waiting for improvements of the regulatory framework.

1. SOCIAL INSURANCE

1.1. Defining social insurance

As we have already discussed in Chapters 4 and 7, **Social Insurance** is a type of insurance which is obligatory by law. It is intended to provide financial protection to society against mainly fundamental types of risks that traditional insurance markets might not be able to cover adequately (Vaughan, 2009: 51). It is usually treated differently compared to **Private Insurance** or **Commercial Insurance** which may be arranged in conventional insurance markets and for which there is no legal requirement for them to be obligatory by law. According to Mehr and Cammack (1972: 379), social insurance can be defined as:

'A device for the pooling of risks by their transfer to an organisation usually governmental, that is required by law to provide pecuniary or service benefits to or on behalf of covered persons upon the occurrence of certain predesignated losses...'

Such types of funds exist in insurance markets such as Botswana, Brazil, Namibia, Portugal and South Africa. However, as was noted by Lester (2009: 20), the setting up of such funds also requires strong governance and supervision.

1.2. Key characteristics of social insurance

As defined by Mehr and Cammack (1972: 379-380), the key characteristics of social insurance are as follows:

- 'Coverage is compulsory by law'

- 'Eligibility for benefits is derived, in fact or in effect, from contributions having been made to the program by or in respect of the claimant or the person as to whom the claimant is dependent'

- 'The method for determining the benefits is pre-scribed by law'

- 'The benefits for any individual are not usually directly related to contributions.' There may be an element of redistribution of income.

- The cost is borne primarily by contributions which are usually made by covered persons, their employers or both'

- 'The plan is administered or at least supervised by the government'

We should add to the characteristics of social insurance one emerging item which has been raised mainly by researchers in the area of microinsurance. They believe that subsidization is another key distinguishing feature of social protection. It does not appear to us that there is clarity of how many and which of these characteristics have to be satisfied before a product can be seen as more of social insurance as opposed to normal commercial insurance business.

Furthermore, we should also note that the idea of social protection is not only a preoccupation for developed rich countries. As part of emerging global development trends, we have noted that there is an acknowledgment that it is also crucial to have some form of protection of the majority low-income population in the Developing World. According to a publication from the World Bank on Poverty Dynamics in Africa, it was noted that, besides economic conditions, the low-income population is unable to benefit from economic growth due to neglected factors of 'location, social exclusion and exposure to uninsured risk' (Christiaensen et al, 2002: 3). Therefore, appropriate social protection could assist in resolving a key national development preoccupation regarding how economic growth could be enabled to also address problems of poverty.

2. PUBLIC SOCIAL INSURANCE

We shall start our review of compulsory insurance in Mozambique with types of social insurance that are covered by public funds. As a result of the situation described above, most countries in Africa provide only bare minimum forms of social protection. At the moment, we are aware of the existence of only the following two public funds:

2.1. Social Security

Mozambique has a national scheme for social security as provided for by Law number 2/2007 of 7 February 2007. According to this law, the national scheme is supposed to provide the following forms of social protection:

- **Basic non-contributory social security** for vulnerable segments of the population without capacity to cover their basic needs. The funding for this level of cover is supposed to be by contributions, donations, subsidies and other forms of finance from the public or private sector. This basic level of support for the needy does not yet appear to be functional.

- **Obligatory contributory national social security system** which is intended to cover all people that have any form of employment. The principal contributions for this scheme are supposed to come from both the employers and employees.

- **Complementary social security schemes** that may be arranged by employers and employees as additional voluntary schemes besides the obligatory national social security system. Such complementary schemes are supposed to be registered with the Ministry of Finance and to operate in accordance with basic rules provided in this same law.

The total contributions to the obligatory contributory scheme are supposed to be 7% of gross salary. The allocation between employee and employers of these contributions are 3% by the employee and 4% by the employer. It also appears that only a few large enterprises have managed to secure exemptions from contributing to the national scheme. Although the government has created legal provisions for the formation of private pension funds, such options are supposed to be only supplementary to contributions to INSS.

2.2. Depositors Insurance

As part of social protection mechanisms, we also have a local equivalent of what is known as **Depositors Insurance Fund** (DIF) or **Deposit Guarantee Fund** (DGF). Such types of funds are intended to reimburse people who may lose money deposited in banks and related institutions following their failure. In Mozambique, such protection exists only for deposits in registered financial credit institutions. Through a Decree reference number 49/2010[1] of 11 November 2010, all deposits in local currency and of private individuals are covered up to a limit which is regulated and controlled by the Central Bank of Mozambique. The fund is financed through:

- Contributions from the State and covered institutions that are part of the scheme,
- Fines and penalties charged to covered institutions,
- Donations and any other sources permitted by law.

We have noted that this local deposit guarantee fund does not cover deposits or contributions in insurance companies and pension funds. We believe that policy-makers could consider extending deposit guarantees to the following two cases that we believe also deserve some form of protection like any other deposit by private individuals:

- Pension funds
- Savings and investment-linked life insurance

---

1. Referred to in Portuguese as *Decreto nº. 49/2010 de 11 de Novembro*

Pensions and contributions to savings and investment-related life insurance products should be seen more like deposits by the insured for the long term and not pure risk premium for the account of the insurer. Such types of insurance fit perfectly the definition of deposits as defined in Article 5 of the law covering Guarantee Fund for Deposits of Credit Institutions, as discussed above. We believe that the same solution is required for pension claims from one of the types of social insurance that is covered by the private insurance market, as we shall discuss later in this Chapter.

Besides the issue of protection of money belonging to insurance policyholders and beneficiaries of social insurance, we shall also discuss later in this book the key development trend in international markets of policyholder protection. We should now discuss some of the areas of social risks for which we do not have public funds.

3. UNFUNDED AREAS OF SOCIAL RISK

We should start by acknowledging that, given the universal problems of very poor distribution of scarce economic resources, society is not able to provide adequate protection to all people against all fundamental risks that pose a constant threat to our welfare and wellbeing. However, most nations have attempted to provide basic minimum cover for key risks such as the two outlined above. We would like to discuss a number of other critical areas that do not have any form of systematic protection in Mozambique. We shall focus on the major group of fundamental perils for which there are good examples of effective solutions in the SADC region and in international markets.

3.1. Political Risks and War Damages

War and related problems of political risks along with the two perils of fire and water constitute the three most feared risks since the early days of emergence of insurance in ancient time, as we discussed Chapter 1. While the commercial insurance markets here and abroad have developed solutions in relation to perils of fire and water; most have tended to avoid the risks of war and politics. Given this **market failure**, in most industrialised countries, war and political risks are covered by public funds. In Mozambique, we do not have a public fund to cover these risks. In SADC, the only countries that provide some form of social protection against these fundamental risks are South Africa and Namibia. You may read more about the South African fund on their website: www.sasria.co.za

In Mozambique and most other African countries without such funds, commercial insurance markets tend to offer a very limited form of protection on the basis of a condition known as the 'riot and strike extension'. This extension only covers what is defined as non-political riot and strike cover. As you can imagine, the definition of what is political and non-political is very contentious. Following major claims events such as the **Food Riots of September 2010** in Maputo and other cities, there were disagreements about whether this was covered or not. There have also been other major disputes concerning this exclusion in other territories. According to Gamal Sakr (2012: 5), there were major legal disputes between the insurance market in North Africa and their reinsurers following the Arab Spring revolution starting in 2010. The main dispute was due to the fact that insurers assumed that they could cover a broader range of risks than that for which they had capacity. As a result of the event, the estimated losses for insurers in North Africa were as follows:

- Tunisia: $700 million
- Egypt: $150 million
- Libya: $400 million

Besides the insurance losses noted above which are in dispute, it is also estimated that there was an economic loss of more than $42.5 billion in the 3 countries. Then there was the impact of human suffering, injuries and deaths of many people. Given this critical impact of political risks, it is vital for us in Mozambique and other countries to consider this major risk and look at some of the mechanisms that have been setup in other territories such as SASRIA in South Africa and NASRIA in Namibia.

3.2. Redundancy

In many of the developed countries in Europe as well as in South Africa, there also exist public funds to provide insurance for redundancy or unemployment. We do not yet have such a type of cover in Mozambique and the rest of Africa. In some respects, the basic non-contributory social security component of the national social security of Mozambique is supposed to provide some form of cover in this area. However, this part of the fund will only function with appropriate funding.

3.3. Natural Disasters

We have already noted that Mozambique is highly exposed to natural perils of cyclones, flooding and droughts. The country has been affected by a number of disasters caused by such natural phenomena. For purposes of coordinating responses to such types of events, there exists a National Disasters Management Institute[2]. Its work is focused on coordinating activities such as early warning systems and channelling of relief assistance. There is not yet a fund for compensation of victims of such events.

---

2. Known in Portuguese as *Instituto Nacional de Gestão de Calamidades (INGC)*

3.4. Road Accidents

In Mozambique and other countries in the region, there has been a rapid growth of vehicles on the roads. There has also been a sharp increase in the number of road accidents causing injury to people and massive damage to property. In order to combat this fundamental problem, it is vital to have some form of national fund to cover victims of accidents. We do not have a public fund for compensation of third party victims as is the case in countries like Portugal, Namibia, South Africa and Swaziland. The fund in Portugal is known as the **Fundo de Garantia Automóvel** (FGA), as noted in the manual of Motor Insurance from the Associação Portuguesa de Seguradores (2001: 22).

The fund is intended to cover claims of third parties caused by uninsured vehicles or cases where the culprits are unidentified. If the party responsible for the accident has third party motor liability insurance, then that policy would cover the accident. In Mozambique, there is no public motor liability scheme. All motorists are expected to buy the obligatory motor third party liability from the commercial insurance market. Notwithstanding this legal requirement and the availability of insurers to cover this risk, many vehicles do not have even the basic compulsory third party liability insurance.

3.5. Public Health

We also do not have a public health insurance scheme in Mozambique. Following rapidly increasing cases of extreme injuries affecting numerous people without health insurance and without financial means to cover their own costs, the Ministry of Health recently proposed the formation of a fund to cover medical emergencies[3]. They have proposed that such a fund could be financed by the government or by introducing a new tax that could be collected through the insurance market. The insurance association has advised the authorities that, although it supports the idea, it is important for the authorities to find appropriate sources of funding instead of relying on the small minority of the population that has already taken the initiative of buying insurance. The insurance association sees this challenge as one more motivation for the government to find ways of arranging systems that ensure cover for as many people as possible so that the costs of the scheme are shared across a broader population base.

4. SOCIAL INSURANCE IN THE PRIVATE INSURANCE MARKET

As we have already discussed in Chapter 7, the commercial insurance markets tries to offer certain types of insurance for some of the obligatory types of insurance that are not covered by any form of public funds. In this 'grey area' of overlap, as presented in Figure 7 below, insurers offer Workman's

---

3.   Known in Portuguese as *Instituto Moçambicano de Emergência Médica*

Compensation (WCA) Insurance, Road Traffic Act (RTA) Insurance and other types of obligatory insurance that are not covered by public funds. As we shall discuss below, the nature of exposure in this area of overlap creates a number of critical ambiguities.

Figure 7–Grey Area of Social Insurance

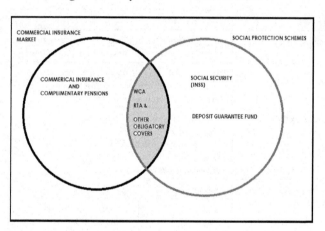

4.1. Workmen's Compensation Act Insurance

The Workmen's Compensation Act (WCA) Insurance is one of the key social insurance covered by private insurers in our market. Before discussing the key challenges of this class of business, we should look at key definitions of this type of insurance.

a. Scope of Cover

The nature and scope of Workmen's Compensation Act (WCA) insurance is as presented in Table 15.

Table 15—Basic policy Specification for Workmen's Compensation Act Insurance

ITEM	DESCRIPTION	
Subject of insurance	All employees in all businesses and organisations except for the government and local authorities	
Scope of cover	All work-related accidents including occupational illness that may occur whilst the employee is working or in transit to or from work	
Main exclusions	• Intentionally self-inflicted injuries • Negligence • Not following established safety procedures • Insanity • *Force majeure*	
Principal benefits	Basis of Claim	Benefit
	Death	• Pension to defined beneficiaries • Death subsidy & funeral expenses
	Total Permanent Disability (TPD)	• Life pension • Supply of adequate artificial limbs
	Temporary Total Disability (TTD)	Indemnity of costs of remuneration for period of disability
	Medical Expenses	Unlimited liability for medical expenses

The model described above also represents the most common approach to this insurance policy in most markets in Africa with a few variations of structure and benefits.

b.   Regulatory framework in Mozambique

Up to 2014, the insurance market had been using an archaic piece of legislation from the colonial period to regulate Workmen's Compensation Insurance. This original law had been in place since 1957[4]. The old law has now been replaced by a new piece of law of December 2013[5]. The Ministry of Labour, as a principal sponsor of the new law, had the view that it was necessary to update legislation of this type of insurance for the following reasons:

- To update limits and benefits
- To review the scale used to determine compensation in the event of a covered claim scenario
- To provide a solution to the historical problem of compensation claims from the past which had lost value as a result of problems such as the rising cost of living as well as currency re-evaluation exercises in the past. The

---

4.   Designated in Portuguese as Diploma Legislativo nº. 1706, de 19 de Outubro de 1957

5.   Referred to in Portuguese as Decreto nº 62/2013 de 04 de Dezembro de 2013

previous system did not include any mechanism to protect value of compensation with time. This process of linking payments of pensions to some form of indicator such as the inflation rate is called **indexation**.

As a result of this review, insurers are facing a situation where they have to cover higher levels of liability as a result of the revised levels of compensations. The authorities have also pegged the minimum amount of pension payable in the future to minimum levels of salaries in the respective sector of the worker. This means that insurers have to increase levels of financial provisions to cover these changes. We believe that all these new changes and complex financial implications require a review of methods of supervision of financial reserves for this class of insurance. We believe that the authorities should have appropriate tools to identify situations where an insurer might not be setting aside appropriate levels of provisions. The current insurance regulatory framework does not yet provide any guidelines on this issue.

Furthermore, the changes are supposed to apply on pension benefits of the past on a **retroactive basis**. It does not appear to us that there is clarity on how and who pays for the difference between the provisions from the past and significantly increased obligations as a result of the revision of historical liabilities. In our opinion, it should not be premium for current policyholders paying for this because that could be the beginning of a huge **pyramid scheme**. We should avoid a situation where contributions made today would be used to cover commitments of the past without due regard to the future liability that comes with the risks accepted today.

c.   Occupational illness

We have noted that, besides injury resulting from accidents, WCA insurance is also intended to cover occupational illness. According to the website of the World Health Organisation (WHO), occupational illness is 'any disease contracted primarily as a result of an exposure to risk factors arising from work activity'[6]. This type of exposure can result in major catastrophic losses with liability payable over a long period. This exposure over a very long period is also referred to as **'long tail liability'**.

Furthermore, we have observed that the local market runs the risk of being exposed to pre-existing occupational illnesses from previous employment. Given higher standards of monitoring in South Africa, it is possible that some workers that may already have symptoms of occupational illness from operations there such as mines could relocate to Mozambique after being retrenched. Given that labour from South African industries is perceived to have better skills than locally-based labour, such workers might be able

---

6.   As noted on the website of the WHO on 05/05/2015: http://www. who.int/occupational_health/activities/occupational_work_diseases/ en/

to find another job in Mozambique. Although Mozambique can gain required skills in such processes of labour mobility, it is imperative for the protection of local risk carriers that we are able to distinguish pre-existing illnesses arising from prior employment elsewhere and make sure that it is treated separately from cases of local exposure.

Following rapid expansion of insurers in our market, we are also seeing increasingly fierce competition aimed mainly at capturing market-share by reducing premium. In insurance business, this practice of reducing prices in order to gain market share is referred to as '**undercutting**'. We believe that this issue is made worse by the fact that there are no guidelines that could be used as a basis for determining appropriate pricing. The Insurance Association is trying to address this problem by developing a guideline for this class of business.

d.   Solutions for the future

We have also noted that, amongst numerous other recommendations for this class of business, Waty (2007: 58) also observes that the lack of a public fund is a critical gap. This situation where the private sector insurance market tries operate as a substitute for a public fund poses many challenges. This model is based on the not so realistic assumption that all the insurers will continue to be operational and financially viable in the future. What happens to compensation beneficiaries if an insurer becomes insolvent? What mechanisms are in place to ensure continuity of the settlement of compensation in the future? Given the current situation where such exposure is covered by private sector insurance operators, there are limited guarantees of protection in the future.

Furthermore, we believe that while waiting for the government to setup this recommended fund, the private insurance market should define limits of liability. It does not make sense for companies registered as limited liability entities to issue policies offering unlimited liability. There is also very limited reinsurance to support such types of exposure. It used to be possible to cover policies with unlimited liability with appropriate reinsurance financial support from some of the underwriting syndicates in Lloyd's of London. However, capacity for unlimited liability was withdrawn from that market following failures of some of the underwriting syndicates in the 1980's that were affected by major claims that accumulated in a rapid and highly unexpected manner. This large accumulation of losses was known as the **London Market Excess of Loss spiral** or **LMX spiral**.

In addition to the measures outlined above, we also believe that it is essential for the authorities to define occupational health and safety standards and to establish respective institutions for regular monitoring and effective enforcement of rules and regulations for safe work-places. We believe that more emphasis should be placed on preventing and minimising injuries as opposed to just relying on a transfer of risks or the problems to insurance. Transfer of risk to insurance is only a very small fraction of management of risks, as we discussed in Chapter 4. We believe that the Ministry of Labour could play a critical rule in driving this process. Please have a look at websites[7] of the following organisations that present initiatives aimed at developing a holistic approach to treatment of risk at work:

- The Occupational Health and Safety Programme of the Ministry of Labour in Brazil: http://portal.mte. gov.br/seg_sau/

- The National Occupational Safety Association (NOSA) of South Africa: http://www.nosa.co.za/

Finally, we believe that there is a need for a case study on the handling of this class of business in the Developing World. We believe that the International Labour Organisation (ILO) is best positioned to support such an initiative. We have also observed that there are good case studies from countries also without public funds like Botswana and Macau that appear to have developed more effective approaches. In the models applied in these two countries, they have avoided exposing limited liability companies to unlimited liability. In the case of Macau, the regulatory authority has also developed comprehensive guidelines on the handling of this class of

---

7. Website references as consulted on 9 May 2014

business. Macua also represents one of the best models to consider for Mozambique given that they also use Portuguese as one of their official languages. However, Macau has been able to appropriately refine local laws for areas such as WCA Insurance starting from the same source as us, the Portuguese legal system.

4.2. Road Traffic Act Insurance

The **Road Traffic Act (RTA) insurance** is an obligatory form of insurance to cover third parties that may be affected by motor vehicle accidents on public roads. This type of obligatory insurance is part of the **Highway Code**, which is a group of laws relating to use of public roads by vehicles and pedestrians. From the early stages of introduction of motor vehicles, there was a realisation that they were far much more dangerous to the public than other means of transportation. In the early days of the motor industry, it was required by law that a man had to march in front of a car in order to prevent accidents (Cannar, 1979: 5). Although there is evidence of existence of motor insurance from as early as the 1890s; motor third party liability was only made obligatory in the United Kingdom in 1930.

There is a broad range of models used for obligatory motor insurance in the SADC region. Compulsory motor liability insurance can be divided into two types of insurance cover. Firstly, there is the cover for injury or death of persons as a result of an accident, also known as **Third Party Bodily**

Injury (TPBI). Secondly there is cover for damage to vehicles and property belonging to other people, also known as **Third Party Property Damage (TPPD)**. The compulsory motor third party liability in Mozambique is supposed to cover both types of exposure.

a. Pre-independence Highway Code

The first forms of legislation on motor liability insurance in Mozambique were laws number 40/079 of 8 March 1955[8] and number 28/81 of 20 May 1969[9] (Firmino, Luísa et al. 2011: 134-140). The first piece of law introduced alterations to the Highway Code at that time in order to include Motor Third Party Liability Insurance. The second piece of law related to the requirement for foreign registered vehicles entering Mozambique to have local motor third party liability insurance. The temporary motor third party liability insurance cover for foreign registered vehicles connected to this law has continued up to today. It is sold at the border posts and is usually for a maximum period of 30 days. This time period is also the maximum amount of time that one is permitted to temporarily import a vehicle into Mozambique without having to arrange import guarantees or pay import duty taxes.

---

8. Referred to in Portuguese as *Decreto-lei nº. 40/079 of 8 March 1955*
9. Referred to in Portuguese as *Diploma Legislativo nº. 28/81, de 20 de Maio de 1969*

b.   Highway Code of 2003

Given the rapidly increasing number of vehicles on public roads, a sharp rise in numbers of road accidents causing massive amount of injury to people and damage to property and the lack of mechanisms for compensation, the government decided to make motor third party liability insurance obligatory for all locally registered vehicles. The new requirement for all vehicles to have at least third party liability is covered in Law number 2/2003 of 21 January 2003[10] and the respective regulations[11]. After the passing of this legislation, motor third party liability became clearly obligatory for all vehicles on the roads in Mozambique besides the focus on foreign registered vehicles as had been the case in the law of 1969.

The same law specifies loss or damage situations that should not be covered by the compulsory insurance including the following:

-   Injury to the driver and to non-fare paying passengers in the insured vehicle

-   Damage to property of the driver of the insured vehicle and any owner of the vehicle or policyholder of the insured vehicle or of their legal representatives as well as spouses, ascending and descending relatives including adopted children of all the persons stated above

---

10. Referred to in Portuguese as Lei nº. 2/2003 de 21 de Janeiro
11. Designated in Portuguese as Decreto 47/2005 de 22 de Novembro

- Loss or damage as a result of accidents involving malicious damage and theft of vehicles

Furthermore, we should note that if a vehicle is insured for third party only, the same policy does not cover loss or damage of the insured vehicle itself and any property that might be transported on it. If the insured wants to cover damage to his own vehicle, he/she has to arrange additional insurance cover which is known as Own Damage insurance. For property transported in his/her vehicle, the insured should purchase appropriate insurance known as Goods in Transit insurance.

In addition to the exclusions noted above, the law also specifies that the insurer has the right to recover losses from responsible parties in the following situations:

- Any person that may have wilfully caused an accident

- Any driver that might not be appropriately licensed to drive or might have been driving under the influence of alcohol or drugs or who might have fled the scene of an accident

- Any person that might not have taken their vehicle for periodic vehicle inspections, as stipulated in the Highway Code and complementary legislation[12]

---

12. Regulations covering periodic inspection as covered in Diploma Ministerial Nº. 56/2003 de 28 de Maio

Following our discussion above regarding the scope of cover for motor third party liability, we should also note that there are a number of critical gaps in the laws covering this class of business. We have observed that the current legislation on compulsory motor liability does not specify a minimum limit of obligatory cover. As a result of this situation, we are not able to make the same distinction as insurers can do in Portugal between the basic minimum compulsory insurance for purposes of **Road Traffic Act (RTA)** and the **Optional Motor Third Party Liability** which has higher limits (Associação Portuguesa de Seguradores, 2001: 17). This Optional Motor Third Party Liability is also what is referred to as **Full Motor Third Party Liability** in countries like Malawi, Zambia and Zimbabwe

Furthermore, there are no guidelines regarding the nature and type of insurance contract that should be applied. As part of the outcome of this situation, there are no consistent approaches in the underwriting of this risk. However, we are also aware that the insurance association has taken the initiative of drafting a standard policy document and guidelines for this type of insurance. It is hoped that, even before appropriate improvements of the law, the insurance market could take the approach of voluntarily adopting a standard insurance policy contract and guidelines, as some form of self-regulation.

Furthermore, it also appears that most vehicles on the roads remain without at least the basic motor third party liability insurance. Although motor third party liability is now supposed to be obligatory, there is not yet any effective mechanism to ensure enforcement. Some people continue to avoid buying insurance. There is also a huge danger that traffic police officers could be shown fake insurance documentation. There is no way for them to verify which document is valid or not. There can also be cases where the insurance documentation could be genuine but, unbeknown to the authorities, the insured might not have paid premium for the cover to be effective. As specified in the Insurance Law, if the insured does not pay premium within specified periods, there is no cover.

c.   Motor Liability Public Fund

Besides the issues discussed above, we do not have a **motor liability public fund** to cover situations where victims of an accident might not be able to obtain compensation from the private insurance market. This might happen as a result of a failure by the insurer to meet its financial obligations (insolvency). This could also happen because the claim is excluded as a result of the specified exclusions or that the driver simply avoided placing insurance. In such situations there is a need for some form of public guarantee fund (Oliveria, 2013: 10). We should now look at systems used in southern Africa.

i. Fuel levy system

The fuel levy system is used in the Southern African Customs Union (SACU), which consists of Botswana, Lesotho, Namibia, South Africa and Swaziland. They have public funds which collect a form of tax on fuel and gas in order to cover costs of motor road accidents. In South Africa, this type of a fund is known as the **Motor Vehicle Act (MVA)** Fund. The MVA fund is not intended to cover TPPD for which separate cover should be arranged from the private sector insurance market. Given that all vehicles require fuel, it tends to be one of the best systems for ensuring that all motorists are making equitable contributions to the fund. It helps to reduce the problem of avoidance of insurance, which is one of our key current problems. However, the key challenge for countries using such a system is that there is a high risk of financial losses through fraudulent claims.

ii. Vehicle Disk system

In countries like Zimbabwe, the public vehicle tax system has been combined with the placement of compulsory third party liability. The price of insurance of each type of vehicle depends on category of vehicle. The pricing mechanism does not take into account the differences of amount of road usage per type of vehicle. The main advantages with this system is that it helps to reduce problems of avoidance of insurance for all registered vehicles and it improves efficiency of collection.

iii. Border Insurance System

Mozambique and other countries in SADC that do not have the fuel levy system have a system of temporary third party liability insurance which is sold to all foreign registered vehicles at the point of entry into the country. The pricing mechanism tends to be fairly simplified and does not also take into account the different levels of intensity of use of the covered vehicles. For countries such as Malawi, Mozambique and Zambia, locally registered insurers can compete for this business through agencies or some form of representation at the border. Zimbabwe has adopted a system whereby the selling of the motor liability insurance policies for foreign registered vehicles has been integrated in the processes of customs and immigration. Furthermore, they only have one entity at each border post issuing the compulsory policy on behalf of a consortium of insurers.

iv. The Yellow Card Scheme

The Yellow Card Scheme is intended to cover countries of the regional organisation known as the Common Market for Eastern and Southern Africa (COMESA). It is a concept similar to the 'Blue Card' in the European Union and the

'Brown Card' in West Africa. According to the COMESA website[13], the scheme is operating in the following countries: Burundi, Democratic Republic of Congo, Eritrea, Ethiopia, Kenya, Malawi, Rwanda, Uganda, Tanzania, Zambia and Zimbabwe. Although Mozambique is a member of this regional grouping, it is one of the few key countries in this region that has not yet adopted the scheme. This is a major issue given that Mozambique is a key trade route for a number of land-locked economies in this region.

The scheme is intended to cover both motor third party liability and medical expenses for occupants of the insured vehicles. Since a motorist can arrange insurance cover for the whole region at point of destination, it reduces paper-work and costs at border posts. If a foreign registered vehicle covered on this scheme were to have an accident in the covered territory, a 'claims bureau' in that area is supposed to handle the claim locally. Then, the claims bureaux are supposed to have a mechanism for settling of claims in the region. The calculation of premium for this system tends to be highly simplified and is linked mainly to category of vehicles.

We believe that concepts such as the Yellow Card system present an opportunity to support regional development initiatives. There is a need for more dialogue between key stakeholders in the region in order to see how the effectiveness

---

13. http://programmes.comesa.int/index.php?option=com_content&view
=article&id=79&Itemid=107

of this system could be improved in order for all territories to support it. For a country like Mozambique, which serves as a key transport corridor for a handful of land-locked economies in the region, adoption of such a system would represent a loss of significant revenue compared to the current system applied at the points of entry.

4.3. Aviation Liability Insurance

Aviation liability insurance is another type of mandatory insurance as defined in Article number 43 of the Civil Aviation Law number 21/2009 of 28 September 2009[14]. The law does not provide any definition of scope of cover and minimum limits of liability for such insurance. We also believe that it is vital for operators in the aviation sector to look at guidelines and standards in the international treaty for aviation known as the **Montreal Convention** of 1999.

Furthermore, we are aware that aviation insurance is a highly specialised type of insurance. Our market has very limited local underwriting capacity. We shall not discuss any details on this business in this book. We should now look at some of the obligatory types of insurance for certain types of professions.

---

14. Known in Portuguese as Lei de Aviação Civil, Lei nº. 21/2009 de 28 de September

5. STATUTORY COVERS FOR SPECIFIC PROFESSIONS

Like other insurance markets in our region, we also have a requirement for compulsory insurance for certain professions. The specific professions that require placement of obligatory insurance by law are insurance intermediaries, security firms, travel agents, sportsmen and law firms. We shall discuss these obligatory covers and also identify some of the challenges experienced by the insurance market in this area.

5.1. Professional Indemnity

In Mozambique, we have found two cases of pieces of law that make it obligatory for insurance intermediaries and law firms to have professional indemnity insurance. The requirement for Professional Indemnity for intermediaries is defined in the Insurance Law. Professional Indemnity insurance is intended to provide financial protection for individuals and firms that provide advice and professional service (Vaughan, 2009: 481). The standard professional indemnity policy covers all or part of the following situations:

- Negligence, errors, omissions, misrepresentation and misstatement

- Unintentional breach of confidentiality, trust, authority or privacy

- Defamation

- Accidental loss or damage of third party documents and property intrusted to the professional
- Violation of good faith and fair dealing
- Other extensions of cover as may be defined in the policy

Furthermore, we should note that the risk of professional service is not covered under other normal liability insurances such as Public Liability and Products Liability. Clients of professional service providers could sue these entities for things such as negligence, misrepresentation, miss-selling, bad faith and inaccurate advice. Such types of claim events are not covered in typical liability policies. It has also been observed that due to increasing risks of legal liability and growing awareness by consumers of their rights, there is a growing demand for this type of insurance, in general (Associação Portuguesa de Seguradores, 1999: 27). We should now look at the handling of compulsory Professional Indemnity insurance in Mozambique and some of the issues that need to be addressed.

a. Professional Indemnity for Lawyers

According to Article 32 of law number 5/2014 of 5 February 2014 relating to operations of legal firms, it is obligatory for such firms to have Professional Indemnity insurance to cover them for liability arising from their professional services. The law in question does not specify a required minimum amount of cover. It states that the association of lawyers will define the minimum amount of cover that is required.

b.   Professional Indemnity for Insurance Intermediaries

The need for professional indemnity insurance for intermediaries in Mozambique is specified in Article 64 of the Insurance Law. This cover is required for all insurance brokers and agents that are authorised to handle premium collections on behalf of insurers. Although it is an obligatory insurance, there is no uniform specified policy and there are no guidelines on how this risk should be handled. This leaves too much room for different insurers to provide covers with varying nature and scope of cover. Such a situation could undermine the purposes of making it obligatory. The minimum amounts of cover, as stated in the regulations to the Insurance Law, are as presented in Table 16.

Table 16–Minimum cover for Professional Indemnity for Intermediaries

TYPE OF INTER-MEDIARY	BASIS OF DEFINING COVER	MINIMUM COVER
Insurance Broker	10% of average annual premium projected to be received in the next 3 financial years net of commissions to be retained	Mt 300 000
	10% of annual premium received in the last financial year net of commissions	

Insurance & Microinsurance Agents authorised to collect premium	10% of average annual premium projected to be received in the next 3 financial years net of commissions to be retained	Mt 90 000
	10% of annual premium received in the last financial year net of commissions	

From the way this cover is defined in the Insurance Law including the references to collection of premium, it appears that the policy-makers had in mind a different type of cover. It appears that when the law refers to professional indemnity, the regulators are actually referring to what are known as **Premium Guarantees**. These are not part of insurable risk, as we shall discuss below.

Furthermore, we believe that it is problematic to request the same insurance market that needs this protection to then also cover the same risk, as is stipulated in Article 101 of our insurance regulations. The same piece of law also gives the insurance regulator the authority to forcibly place such cover with insurers that it may select and at terms that it may define. The law does not seem to take into account any form of risk assessment of the intermediary that seem to have a right to have this cover through even enforcement by law.

c. Premium Guarantees

We should discuss the concept of Premium Guarantees referred to above. In order to provide an appropriate protection from abuse of premium held by intermediaries, the insurance market of South Africa has an **Intermediaries Guarantee Facility (IGF)**[15]. Cover on the facility is not required for intermediaries that do not receive premium on behalf of insurers. To 'receive premium' means that premium is paid through an account belonging to an intermediary. In the case where the intermediary is simply collecting cheques that are drawn in favour of the insurers, premium guarantees may not be required.

It is in alignment with the approach described above that some of the brokers in Mozambique avoid receiving payments from clients through their accounts. They argue that, as part of their business practice, they can only present to the client the original invoice from the insurer and they always instruct the client to issue the cheque in the name of the insurer or make direct bank transfers to the account of the insurer. They see this approach as a definite solution around the problem of lack of appropriate premium guarantees in our market. Furthermore, some brokers believe that by not issuing their own additional invoices they avoid some of the ambiguities regarding taxes such as IVA, the local value added tax.

Finally, we would like to say that, besides insurance intermediaries and lawyers, there are many other professions where professional indemnity is a critical requirement. We believe that with appropriate advice from professional

---

15. For more information you may check the website of the IGF http://igfsec45.co.za/#!/igf

intermediaries, other professionals that require such insurance would be given appropriate advice.

5.2. Sportsmen

Sports are the next area that we should look at that has some form of obligatory insurance. According to regulations reference number 65/2007[16] of 24 December 2007, which are part of the regulatory framework for sports under Law number 11/2002 of 12 March 2002, all people involved in sports should have an obligatory sportsmen insurance. This is another example of a type of insurance which is supposed to be obligatory but there is no reference to it in the insurance regulatory framework. There is also no agreed market policy wording and there are no guidelines on how such business should be handled.

Furthermore, we have noted that the Personal Accident guideline of the Associação Portuguesa (2000: 23) refers to a Personal Accident Insurance for Sports, Culture and Recreation. However, it is clear from the definition that this is not intended for professional sportsmen. It appears that there is some form of contradiction between our local law on sports and the approaches in Portugal on this question. In fact, traditional insurance policies for classes such as Personal Accident specifically exclude injuries arising from participating in professional sports. With support of specialist

---

16. Referred to in Portuguese as *Decreto nº. 65/2007 de 24 de Dezembro*

underwriters in international markets such as Lloyds, it is possible to find appropriate insurance cover for sportsmen.

5.3. Security firms

There is also reference to obligatory guarantees and insurance in the law regulating private security companies. According to Articles 8 and 9 of the regulations number 9/2007 of 30 April 2007, security firms are required to have the following minimum covers:

- A guarantee of not less than Mt 500,000.
- A Public Liability insurance policy of at least Mt 750,000. The law also states that this policy should cover 'illicit' events.

As we shall discuss later in this book, in respect of specialist types of insurance, guarantees can be arranged through either banks or insurance companies. With regards to the Public Liability which is intended to cover illegal activities, this requirement creates a major dilemma. It is not the intention of insurance to cover illegal activities, as we discussed in Chapter 6 when we looked at the essential elements of legal contracts. It appears that this requirement was not clearly structured and could be improved.

5.4. Travel Agents

As specified in regulations number 41/2005[17] of 30 August 2005, travel agents are required to have the following obligatory covers:

- Guarantee of Mt 500,00
- Insurance of Mt 100,000

There are no guidelines on what type of policy is supposed to be insured and how it should be handled. The types of perils described in the law quoted above are not insurable in the traditional insurance market. Even for the few insurance companies that have some form of underwriting capacity for guarantees, travel agency bonds are specifically excluded.

5.5. Tourism Transportation

According to regulations number 41/2007[18] of 24 August 2007, licensed transporters of tourists are required to have motor third party liability. There are no minimum limits of cover specified. The regulations state that the operators should insure up to the limits specified for normal motor third party liability. Unfortunately, in the law for motor third party liability, minimum limits of cover have not yet been defined.

---

17. Decreto 41/2005 de 30 de Agosto
18. Decreto 41/2007 de 24 de Agosto

5.6. Other Areas

In addition to the pieces of laws quoted above, there are a number of other laws that specify some forms of compulsory insurance policies for areas such as educational institutions, driving schools and marine activities. Most of the obligatory policies referred to in these laws need to be referred to in the Insurance Law. This is part of a process in the development of law known as **codification**. In doing such an exercise, it would also be vital to ensure that the prescribed policies are appropriately defined and that there are clear guidelines on how the policies should be handled.

Besides the obligatory types of insurance that we discussed above, we would like to also recommend other types that could be considered in the future. Our recommendations are focussed on areas of risk where insurance tends to already be obligatory in other more structured markets. We have also focussed on types of risks that are becoming increasingly critical in our economy with the continued rapid economic growth. We believe that our authorities need to consider the following areas:

    a.   Directors and Officers of Companies

Directors and Officers (D&O) Liability insurance is one of the highly recommended types of cover for large businesses. It is intended to provide indemnity for financial losses caused by error and omissions by key decision-makers in the business. This type of insurance is not yet obligatory in our

Company Law as is the case in other countries in our region. With an increasing number of large investments with Boards of Directors making decisions that affect multi-million dollar projects and operations, it will become increasingly vital to have this insurance to protect the interests of investors and other key stakeholders.

b.   Trustees of Pension Funds

Following the reform of pension funds legislation, it is now possible to setup complementary private sector pension funds, as we discussed in Chapter 5. Given this development, it is also crucial for workers and employers contributing to these funds to be protected from risks of lack of due care by the trustees of pension funds. In other markets in our region, it is a key requirement for pension fund trustees to have a Trustees Liability Insurance.

c.   Other professions

For other professions such as engineers, architects and medical practitioners, it should also not be possible to have a license without appropriate Professional Indemnity insurance. The market tends to only see opportunistic requests for cover when professionals from some of these sectors are tendering for work on large projects where the principal party may demand such covers as part of their risk management processes. That is part of a problem described in insurance as **selection**. This is when an individual or a company only wants to arrange insurance only when they feel a claim might happen or only for a temporary period when they need to demonstrate that they have insurance. Insurers have a difficulty assessing such risks given the lack of experience with such a customer. Insurers tend to load their rates for more premium and apply tougher conditions for such inquiries, if at all they agree to even look at them.

6. PUBLIC CONTRACTS

We should now discuss situations where the government may take the approach of making certain types of insurance obligatory by contract as opposed to relying on the force of law. This is the approach used mainly for public contracts controlled by the government, municipal authorities and other public enterprises. This is usually applied in engineering projects, and concession agreements.

In the case of engineering projects, we can see evidence of contractual obligations in our market in standard public construction contracts such as the **FIDIC**[19] type of agreement. In such agreements, professional service providers in

---

19. FIDIC is the abbreviation of the French name *Fédération Internationale Des Ingénieurs-Conseils* which stands for the International Federation of Consulting Engineers. This is an international standards organization for the construction industry which has developed, amongst other things, templates for construction agreements.

this agreement are normally required to arrange Professional Indemnity Insurance amongst other types of insurance including in particular Contractors All Risks (CAR) and Guarantees. We shall review these specialist types of insurance later in this book.

CONCLUSION

In this Chapter we have discussed the area of social insurance and other forms of obligatory insurance. Mozambique has only bare minimum public social insurance through the social security and the depositors insurance. We have also identified a grey area consisting of obligatory insurance provided by the commercial insurance market, due to the lack of public funds. As we discussed, this creates a moral dilemma where it is unclear how obligatory products are supposed to be provided by private limited liability companies. The laws which transfer this liability to the private insurance market need to be supplemented with appropriate guidelines.

Furthermore, some of the obligatory types of insurance transferred to the private sector have a high potential to cause financial ruin. As result of the various major issues identified in this Chapter, we believe that there is a need for a critical review of the legal framework of obligatory insurance classes underwritten by the private-sector insurance market.

We have also noted that the depositors insurance fund which currently only covers bank deposits could be extended to also cover savings type of contributions and pensions from the insurance sector. In our view, these funds from insurance are not different from bank deposits. They are another form of deposit or fund belonging to covered individuals and not the financial institutions through which they are held.

Finally, we also identified numerous gaps of fundamental risks that are covered by neither the government nor the commercial insurance market. There is a need for policy-makers to review these risks and explore prospects of setting up of basic mechanisms of simple forms of social protection. The principal motivation for considering these mechanisms of social protection is because fundamental perils are one of the key factors contributing to lack of development for the majority of the population. Besides the impact on vulnerable unprotected people and infrastructure, these fundamental perils are also responsible for causing major shocks at the macro-economic level.

REFERENCES

- Associação Portuguesa de Seguradores (2000). *Seguros de Acidentes Pessoais*. Lisboa: Associação Portuguesa de Seguradores

- Associação Portuguesa de Seguradores (1999). *Seguros de Responsabilidade Civil*. Lisboa: Associação Portuguesa de Seguradores

- Cannar, Kenneth (1979). *Motor Insurance Theory and Practice*. London: Witherby & Co. Ltd

- Christiaensen, Luc; Demery, Lionel and Paternostro, Stefano (2002). *Growth, Distribution and Poverty in Africa: messages from the 1990s*. Washington: The World Bank.

- Firmino, Luisa; Saturnino, Eduardo; Neves, Alexandre and Chongo, Angelina (2011). *Colectânea de Legislação Sobre Seguros*. Maputo: Centro de Formação Jurídica e Judiciária—Ministério da Justiça

- Mehr, Robert, I. and Cammack, Emerson (1972). *Principles of Insurance*. Illinois: Richard D. Irwin, Inc.

- Oliveira, Rui (2013). *Papel da Associação Moçambicana de Seguradoras* in a paper presented at the Insurance Seminar of the ISSM.

- Lester, Rodney (2009). *Consumer Protection Insurance*. Primer Series on Insurance, Issue 7, August 2009. Washington: The World Bank.

- Sakr, Gamal (2012). Political risks, riots and civil commotion Insurance: the African Dimension in The African Reinsurer, Vol. 026. Lagos: African Reinsurance Corporation (pp. 5-13)

- Tadaro, M. P., & Smith, S.C. 2003. *Economic Development*. Pearson Addison Wesley—Essex.

- Vaughan, Emmet, J. (1992) *Fundamentals of risk and insurance*. 6th Edition. New York: John Wiley & Sons Inc.

- Waty, Teodoro, A. (2007). *Direito de Seguros*. M Maputo: W&W Editora Lda

CHAPTER 10

STANDARD COMMERCIAL NON-LIFE BUSINESS

As already defined in this book, insurance business in our market is divided into two portfolios: **non-life insurance** and **life insurance**. In other insurance markets in our region-the non-life is referred to as **short-term insurance** while the life is referred to as **long-term insurance** business. In this book, we are further sub-dividing the non-life portfolio into general and specialist non-life insurance. In this Chapter, we shall focus on the basic types of insurance in the general non-life category of business. This consists of the majority of types of products underwritten in our market. This general category of non-life insurance is also mainly composed of types of insurance that fit normal underwriting capacity of the local insurance market. This is in contrast to the specialist types of insurance for which there is limited local market capacity.

1. MULTI-MARK III POLICY WORDING

We would like to begin by noting that there are a number of types of policy wordings used in our insurance market for the different types of insurance. The principal models of insurance policy wordings that we use in our market were developed mainly in the United Kingdom, Portugal and South Africa. For the purposes of this book we shall use the South African model of insurance policy wordings known as Multi-mark. The policy wording had gone through revisions up to the third version in South Africa before that market abandoned the approach of standard market wordings. The regulators there are concerned that such an approach could be seen as **market collusion**. As part of preoccupations of global business policy-makers, such conduct is perceived as being contrary to the interest of consumers. It is believed that business entities are not supposed to cooperate in such a way that they prevent competition and are concerned about serving only their interests.

However, the last edition of the wording (Multi-mark III) has remained a key reference for insurers in mainly the southern and eastern Africa region. At this stage, some of the insurers in Mozambique have adopted this version and customised it for use in the local market. Notwithstanding some of the local adaptations, the structure, approach and content of the policy has remained significantly the same as per the original wording.

2. GENERAL EXCEPTIONS CONDITIONS AND PROVISIONS

The first and most critical part of the Multi-mark policy wording contains the General Exceptions, General Conditions and General Provisions applicable to this contract. These terms and conditions are applicable to the different types of insurance types that are contained in the full set of the wording. These underlying types of insurance, referred to as sections, are optional and the client may choose to have only one type of cover or a number of different combinations depending on their nature of business and their insurance requirements. In other policy systems such as the standard wordings from Portugal, each insurance type may be insured as a complete insurance policy on its own.

2.1. General Exceptions

The general exceptions consist of events and situations that are not covered by all the types of insurance covered under the Multi-mark III wording. These exclusions are all part of standard exclusions that are not covered in conventional insurance policies. In general, the principal risk situations which are not covered are as follows:

- War, riot, civil commotion, terrorism, sabotage and related events as defined in the exclusion condition

- Losses as a result of nuclear exposure or contamination as defined in the respective condition

- Losses arising from legal liability following exposure to asbestos

- Losses or damages caused by failure of computers. This exclusion is as a result of the concern that existed at the turn of the Century in 1999 when it was feared that some computers would fail to process the change after the digits 999. It was not known if some of the old technology in the computers would be able to process this change and understand the logic of the sequence of time

- Insurers are not supposed to settle claims to any entity or country on which sanctions may be applied by appropriate international organisations.

2.2. General Conditions

The general conditions of the policy wording define all the key conditions and rules governing the insurance policy in general. Some of the terms and conditions are connected to the traditional principles of insurance, as we discussed in Chapter 3. In alignment with the principle of good faith, it is noted that the policy will not cover any claims in cases where there is lack of disclosure of material facts on the insured item by the insured. There are also terms and conditions relating to the average condition, the duty of the insured to act 'as if uninsured'.

The other general terms and conditions are intended to ensure that the insurance policy only covers policies that satisfy criteria of legal contract as we discussed in Chapter 6. The general conditions also define the procedures to be followed by the client in the event of claims. They also specify the territory of the legal system on which the contract is based and steps that could be followed in the event of a legal dispute.

2.3. General Provisions

The general provisions contain the other terms and conditions that enable the insurance contact to operate as intended. It explains how to handle questions such as costs of preparation of claims, the concept of excess or first amount payable by the client, approaches to settling of premium and ways of handling certain types of claim situations.

Following the discussion on the general terms and conditions of an insurance policy, we should now look at each of the specific types of insurance. Whilst looking at each of the following types of insurance, we should remember that general exceptions, conditions and provisions apply on all the policies, in general.

3. THE FIRE GROUP OF POLICIES

Fire insurance is a basic cover for insuring property at specified premises against loss or damage caused by fire and other specified perils. The additional specified perils are often described as '**allied perils**'. In the early stages of development of this policy, it covered only the peril of fire damage (Vaughan, 2009: 56). With time, cover on this policy has been extended to include a number of other perils.

Furthermore, Fire insurance can be used to insure property used for residence, business, public companies, government and any other organisation or association. Besides the obligatory classes of insurance, this is one of the most highly recommended types of insurance for any person or entity that owns or has a financial interest in any property that can be insured on this policy. We should now review the different types of Fire policies that make up the Fire group of insurance policies.

3.1. Standard Fire policy

The Standard Fire policy is the simplest form of policy in the Fire group of policies. The basic summary of scope of this simple Fire policy is as outlined in Table 17

Table 17–Policy Specification of a standard Fire policy

Item		Description
a.	Subject of insurance	Standard policy usually covers the following items: • Buildings, fixtures and fittings, walls, gates, posts and fences • Loss of rent • Plant, machinery and equipment • Stock and materials in trade • Any other specified items
b.	Covered perils	The standard policy covers the following perils: - Fire - Lightning or thunderbolt - Explosion
		It may also be extended to cover the following perils: - Earthquake - Storm, wind, water, hail or snow - Aircraft and other aerial devices or articles dropped therefrom - Impact by animals, trees, aerials, satellite dishes or vehicles

In addition to the perils outlined above, a standard Fire policy may also be further extended to cover the following:

- Discharge or leakage from any sprinkler or drencher system
- Subsidence and landslip
- Malicious damage
- Riot, strike, civil commotion, labour disturbances and lockout
- Other perils as per the policy wording

Besides the extensions noted above, we have also observed that the standard Portuguese Fire policy used in our market also has an extension for 'electrical risks'. According to that form of policy wording, this extension is intended to cover damage to electrical machines as a result of electrical faults including short-circuits, damage by electrical currents and electrical breakdown. This extension is not part of the scope of cover on the standard Multi-mark policy wording and most other traditional wordings in English-speaking markets. This is something that should be reviewed by an appropriate technical committee in the future.

3.2. Other Forms of Fire Policies

In addition to the basic Fire policy as described above, there are other optional forms of Fire policies covering the same perils as noted above and additional specified perils that may be required for specific situations. It is on this basis, that the Multi-mark III policy wording offers the following optional customised versions of Fire policies:

- **Office contents**—this covers Fire and Allied Perils as well as burglary, loss of rent, accidental damage of glass and legal liability relating to office documents. It is intended to provide some form of comprehensive cover for an office setup.

- **Buildings combined**—this policy covers the same perils as a Fire policy plus other specified perils including legal liability, burglary and accidental damage of sanitaryware. It is a combined type of policy which is intended to insure only low risk situations such as residential property, offices, schools, hospitals and churches. Properties involving any form of industrial activity should not be insured on this policy. They should be covered under the Fire Section.

- **Houseowners** insurance which covers residential buildings for risks of Fire and Allied Perils as well as other specified perils including accidental damage of glass and public liability.

- **Householders** for insurance of contents of residential buildings. Besides standard Fire and Allied Perils, it also covers additional incidental risks that are of critical interest for a household. The key additional perils which are covered are burglary and public liability. On other types of policies personalised for private individuals, this policy could have many other extensions including even contingent liabilities such as loss of credit cards, emergency assistance and **hole-in-one cover**[1].

3.3. Business Interruption

In addition to the optional policies described above which have been developed from the basic Fire policy, there is also a related type of insurance cover known as **Business Interruption** or **Consequential Loss** or **Loss of Profits**. This policy is intended to provide compensation to the insured for loss of profits as well as increased costs of operating which may arise following material damage of insured assets (Valsamakis, 2010: 206). This interruption cover may be issued as an extension of a Fire policy or as a separate policy which is triggered following a claim on a connected Fire policy covering material damage.

---

1. This is a type of cover where the insurer reimburses expenses of the insured as a result of one of the traditional rules of golf. According to this rule, the player that accomplishes the unusual achievement of sinking the ball in one stroke is supposed to buy a round of drinks for fellow players.

3.4. Fire Technical Committee

We should also note that in other markets in our region, Fire is one of the key classes of insurance that tends to have a standing committee to handle a number of critical issues connected to this class of business. For instance, the underwriting of Fire risk is done on the assumption that there is an appropriately equipped fire-fighting public entity in key areas such as city centres. Through the technical committee, the insurance sector could monitor performance of such entities. It can also play a more proactive role in the development of property insurance and supporting standards of housekeeping and fire prevention.

4. MOTOR

Insurance of motor vehicles has a broad range of types of policies and variations of cover. The different types of motor insurance covers can be divided into the following three broad categories: **Road Traffic Act (RTA) Insurance, Full Motor Third Party Liability** and **Own Damage Insurance**. As we discussed in the previous Chapter, the RTA basically covers motor third party liability only up to the minimum required by law. In some of the territories like South Africa, this basic legal insurance only covers **Third Party Bodily Injury** and does not cover damage to vehicles and property of other parties.

4.1. Full Motor Third Party Liability

The **Full Motor Third Party Liability** has a broader form of third party cover and higher limits than what is required by law. Given that the Road Traffic Act in Mozambique does not have a defined limit of basic minimum RTA cover, there tends to be no clear distinction in our market between the basic minimum compulsory cover and the optional third party liability with a broader cover and higher limits of liability.

4.2. Motor Own Damage

There are fairly different approaches between underwriters in our market in the underwriting of Motor Own Damage. On the one hand, there is the concept of 'comprehensive' cover which is the predominant approach in companies influenced by models from English-speaking international markets. On the other hand, there is the approach of specified perils cover which tends to be the preferred approach in, amongst others, mainly Portuguese-speaking markets. The key features of the two types of Motor Own Damage policies are as outlined in Table 18.

Table 18—Models of Own Damage Cover

	ITEM	DESCRIPTION OF TYPES OF COVER	
a.	Type of policy	**Specified Perils Policy**	**Comprehensive Policy**
b.	Covered perils	The standard policy covers: • Crash, collision and overturning • Fire, lightning and explosion • Theft or robbery • Natural phenomena • Isolated damage of glass	The policy is covers 'All Risks' that may occur except for the specific exclusions.
c.	Principal exclusions	The principal exclusions are: • Consequential Loss • Depreciation in value • Wear and tear, mechanical break-downs, failures or breakages • Damage to tyres by application of brakes or by road punctures, cuts or bursts	

For both models of policy wordings, cover is usually up to the maximum value of the vehicle. The basis for defining sum insured of the vehicle is usually market value. In a few cases, the insurer can agree to issue on the basis of **agreed value**. However, it is also important to ensure that an appropriate policy wording with the right types of conditions is used.

Furthermore, standard Motor insurance policies in our market have amounts payable by the client in the event of any claim. As part of standard market practice in Mozambique, there is no excess applied on Third Party liability claims. For the areas of cover where excesses are applied, they may be in the form of one simple excess for all claims or there could be different types of excess depending on type of claim.

4.3. Extensions of Motor Insurance

In addition to the broad types of Motor cover described above, we should also note that most policies offer additional cover for other risks or unexpected situations that may affect an insured vehicle. There are a number of such extensions of insurance cover including the following, as outlined in the manual of the Associação Portuguesa de Seguradores (2001: 18-19):

- **Loss of use** cover for consequential financial impact as a result of not having access to a car affected by a covered insurance claim

- **Motor Occupants** cover for death or permanent disability as a result of a motor accident

- **Emergency assistance** cover as a result of a breakdown or accident following which there may be a need for emergency evacuation of the people and/or breakdown service for the vehicle

Please have a look at Appendix VIII where we have presented a comparative review of types of insurance covers on the basic Motor Insurance from the compulsory Third Party Liability to Comprehensive Cover. We would like to also note that motor insurance is one of the classes of insurance for which there tends to be a lot of aggressive competition. It is vital for the authorities to monitor the risk of insurers applying reckless pricing aimed at securing market share. As can be noted from some of the failures of insurers in our region, such practices can lead to financial ruin. If there were to be failure of any insurance company in Mozambique, the concerned policyholders would be completely exposed since there are no formal financial protection mechanisms. Such a situation can cause a loss of credibility in the entire insurance system, including companies that are financially sound.

5. GENERAL LIABILITY

General liability is a word used to refer to a group of third party liability policies that may be arranged as separate policies or may be packaged as one global policy. Liability insurance is one of the highly recommended types of cover for any individual, company or organisation. A standard liability policy is intended to protect the insured against legal liability arising from bodily injury and property damage suffered by third parties. A third party is defined in the Merriam—Webster Encyclopaedia as 'someone who is not one of the two main people involved in a legal agreement but who is still affected by it in some way'. In other words, a third party is a 'stranger to both the agreement and the consideration', although he/she may be affected by it. The main parties involved in an insurance agreement are the insurer and the insured. In alignment with this definition, standard liability policies exclude from cover people or entities that are viewed as having a legal connection to the two main parties. We should now discuss the different types of general liability covers.

5.1. Public Liability

A standard Public Liability policy is intended to settle compensation to third parties arising from the legal liability of the insured for personal injury or property damage suffered at the premises of the insured party (Sadler, 2012: 2/23). In the Multi-mark policy wording, the insured event is defined as:

> *'Damages which the INSURED shall become legally liable to pay consequent upon **accidental death of or bodily injury to or illness of any person** (hereinafter termed injury), or accidental loss of or **physical damage to tangible property** (hereinafter termed damage) which occurred in the course of or in connection with the business within the territorial limits and on or after the retroactive date shown in the schedule, and which results in a claim or claims first being made against the INSURED in writing during the period of insurance.'*

We have highlighted in bold letters the following words that need some clarification:

- **'Accidental'**: From this it can be interpreted that the policy is intended to cover unintended actions.

- **'Death of or bodily injury to or illness of any person'**: This is intended to limit covered events in relation to **physical** harm to people. As such, the policy is not intended to cover events such as discrimination, defamation, intimidation, stress, shock, fear, mental distress and other similar occurrences unless there has actually been physical harm.

- **'Physical damage to tangible property'**: There must be physical damage before a claim is covered. This policy is not intended to cover pure financial losses. The damaged property must also be 'tangible'. It is intended to cover physical assets.

In alignment with the definition of a third party defined above, this policy does not cover the following:

i. Persons employed or contracted by the insured. They are supposed to be covered under WCA Insurance or Employers Liability.

ii. Damage to property belonging to the insured or in the custody or control of the insured

iii. Professional service (because this is intended to be covered under Professional Indemnity)

iv. Claims arising from ownership, possession or use of:

- Motor vehicles (because this is supposed to be covered specifically under the Motor Third Party Liability)

- Aircraft, airports, airstrips or helicopter pads (because they should be insured appropriately under Aviation insurance)

- Boats, ships and ports (because they should be insured correctly under Marine insurance)

vi. Damage or injury caused by goods or products of the insured and happening elsewhere other than premises of the insured.

vii. Claims arising from seepage, pollution or gradual contamination unless as a result of a sudden and accidental event.

viii. Fines, penalties, punitive, exemplary or vindictive damages are not covered. This is partly because they do not represent damages suffered by the third party. It is not the intention of insurance to protect the insured persons or entities from punishment as may be determined by the courts.

ix. Standard policies in our market usually restrict cover to claims awarded in courts of Mozambique. Our Insurance Law permits the insurer and insured to choose any other law and location of arbitration, as they may see fit. This is defined in Article 163 of the Insurance Law.

Furthermore, standard liability policies in our market offer a number of extensions of cover that can be granted subject to negotiation with the insurer.

5.2. Products Liability

As described above, the Public Liability policy specifically excludes damages occurring elsewhere as a result of selling or supplying of goods or products. Products liability is intended to cover this legal liability that may occur outside the premises of the insured as long as they do not occur in countries that are specifically excluded in the policy (Associação Portuguesa de Seguradores, 1999: 29). Our standard market policies exclude products liability claims from the USA and Canada. Most insurers in our region tend not to have underwriting capacity for these areas given the issues of, amongst other things, high costs of litigation and what are seen as exaggerated awards by courts there.

Besides the territorial restrictions and the standard exceptions in the public liability policy, as we discussed above, the Products Liability policy also has additional specific exceptions. The policy does not also cover the following:

- *'[T]he cost of repair, alteration, recall or replacement of the goods or products.'* This risk can be insured under a separate specialist insurance cover known as **Product Recall** or **Product Guarantee**. Such types of insurance policies are not available in our market

- *'[T]he cost of demolition, breaking out, dismantling, delivery, rebuilding, supply and installation of goods or products (including containers and labels) and any other property essential to such repair alteration or replacement unless physically damaged by the goods or products'*

- *'[D]effective or faulty design, formula, plan, specification…'*

- *'[I]nefficacy or failure to conform to specification…'*

- Claims arising from use of goods or products in aircraft.

5.3. Employers Liability

As noted at the beginning of the section on General Liability policies, employees are not viewed as third parties and as such they are usually excluded from coverage under general liability policies. In some territories such as the United Kingdom, there is a legal requirement[2] to have Employers Liability insurance. It is not obligatory to have this insurance in Mozambique, besides the WCA Insurance that we discussed in the previous Chapter. The standard Employers Liability policy is intended to cover the following type of events:

---

2. As per the Employers' Liability (Compulsory) Insurance Act 1969 (UK)

'Damages which the insured shall become legally liable to pay consequent upon death of or bodily injury to or illness of any person employed under a contract of service or apprenticeship with the insured, which occurred in the course of and in connection with such person's employment by the insured within the territorial limits…'

The standard policy does not cover the following specific situations:

- 'Liability assumed by the insured under any contract, undertaking or agreement…'

- 'Liability for disease or impairment attributable to a gradually operating cause which does not arise from a sudden and identifiable accident or event'

Furthermore, in some territories such as South Africa where there exists a public fund for settlement of claims of occupational injuries and illnesses, there are some restrictions on employees taking their employers to normal civil courts for work-related accidents and illnesses. Employees are required to present their claims to the fund. In terms of the rules of that fund, employees do not have to prove negligence by the employer for their injury. They only need to prove that the 'injury or illness arose during the course of employment and that it resulted in personal injury to the employee.' Thereafter, if this requirement is satisfied, the fund automatically starts the compensation process. As a result of this situation, in

South Africa, the Employers Liability policy is not viewed as a completely critical policy to consider for all businesses and organisations.

In our market, although WCA cover is obligatory as was discussed in Chapter 9, there is no public fund to cover this fundamental social risk. There are also no clear guidelines on the treatment of such cases if presented to courts other than the labour courts overseeing calculation of compensation claims. Given this scenario, there are very different opinions in our market on whether it is necessary to recommend the insurance of Employers Liability. Some people believe that it is of little or no value when there is obligatory WCA Insurance. Others believe that it is better to play it safe by also arranging this cover. It is feared that there is always a risk that injured employees could go for civil litigation if they are not happy with the treatment of their claims by the Labour Tribune, under WCA insurance.

6. MISCELLANEOUS

The miscellaneous class of insurance consists of an assortment of policies besides the principal four types described above. Insurance coverage in these policies relates to items that usually already have basic cover under property damage insurance. In the market reports from the ISSM, engineering is also treated as part of miscellaneous risks. We believe that it is not the most suitable classification of Engineering Insurance. In this book, we shall maintain the traditional classification of miscellaneous which consists mainly of the types of policies, as discussed below.

6.1. Theft

Theft Insurance is one of the types of policies that has a slightly misleading traditional name. It should be more appropriately called Burglary insurance. The definition of 'theft' in the standard policy is restricted to an event *'accompanied by forcible and violent entry or exit.'* The principal exclusions of this policy are as follows:

- 'Loss or damage which can be insured under a Fire policy except in the case of explosion caused in an attempt to effect entry'

- 'Loss or damage insurable under a Glass insurance policy'

- Loss or damage of items that should be specifically insured under the Money policy. Things such as money, cheques, mobile telephone vouchers and other documents or certificates with a financial value should be insured under a Money policy.

- Theft involving any employees, principal, partner, director or any member of the insured's household is not covered. This should be more specifically insured under the Fidelity insurance policy.

6.2. Fidelity Insurance

Fidelity Insurance is another type that also has a misleading name. For types of insurance policies such as Fire and Theft, their names refer to what the insurer is insuring against. For Fidelity Insurance, it is not the intention of insurance to insure against fidelity or honesty. This policy is intended to insure against infidelity or dishonesty. It provides cover against theft, fraud and dishonesty by any employee of the insured. Such insurance cover can be arranged on the basis of a 'blanket' cover of all employees or on the basis of specified names of people or specified positions.

The Fidelity policy does not cover the following risk situations:

- The owner of the business
- Non-executive Members of the Board of Directors of the Insured company. Such members are not viewed as employees
- Any acts of fraud or dishonesty from employees that have already been caught but still remain as employees of the Insured
- Any consequential losses arising from a case of fraud or dishonesty.
- Any company or legal entity acquired by the insured

- Any interests of partners, principals or directors that are involved in fraud or dishonesty

- Computer fraud

We should note that this is one of the types of insurance for which completion of an insurance proposal form is an essential requirement. Appropriately structured proposal forms are very useful for purposes of highlighting critical controls that should exist in a company in order to mitigate the risk of fraud or dishonesty. Unfortunately, in the mad rush to capture business, most intermediaries and insurance underwriters do not have time to carry out such fundamental exercises.

Furthermore, this is one of the types of insurance where the underwriting approach has become over-simplified regardless of nature of risk under consideration. The insurance market tends to charge more or less the same premium rate regardless of nature of risk under consideration. The cost of insurance and conditions applied should take into account type of activity, risk control, values at risk, number of people covered, basis of cover and claims experience.

In addition, there is also a habit in our market of underwriting Fidelity Insurance for all types of business. In more developed markets, institutions such as banks are not covered under FG policies. Given the complex nature of fidelity risks in a bank and the kinds of specialised risk control measures that are required; such exposures are best handled by specialised markets. The most appropriate type of policy for banks and related financial services is a specialist type of policy known as Bankers Blanket Bond (BBB). It is not part of the scope of this book to try to provide details on this and other types of specialist policies.

Finally, we also believe that fidelity insurance is one of the classes of insurance where the market could agree on underwriting guidelines and create a mechanism for sharing of information on problems of financial crime. This is vital in order to protect the sector from fraud and abuse. The one product of insurance which is intended to protect the insured clients from fraud and dishonesty can easily be turned around into a tool for extracting claim payments from a naïve insurance market. Part of the solution to this problem is for the market to return to basics of insurance underwriting. This includes the practice of appropriate completion and review of proposal forms as well as informed review of risk.

6.3. Accidental Damage

The Accidental Damage policy is an 'all risks' type of policy. It is intended to provide insurance cover for 'accidental physical loss or damage' to insured property which is not specifically insured or insurable on any other insurance policy. In this policy there is also a clear specification that this policy cannot be expected to contribute in indemnifying for a claim covered by any other policy, as is usually supposed to be the case in the event of dual insurance, as per the principles of contribution that we discussed in Chapter 3.

This policy does not cover the following situations:

- Any shortfall of cover or first amount payable from another policy. If there is an alternative cover from the same insurer, any claim that should be covered under that policy is not supposed to be covered on the Accidental Damage policy

- The policy does not pay the full value of a pair set or collection of things if only a part of such a set or collection is damaged. This means that the policy only pays for the damaged part and does not have to replace the full set. This is also known as the '**pairs and sets clause**'.

- Losses caused by legal acts of any legal authority.

- 'Unexplained disappearance or shortage'. It is not the intention of insurance to cover what are known as '**trade risks**'. This means that this policy does not cover problems arising from mistakes, errors and omissions in the doing of business by the covered entity.

- The risk of fraud, dishonesty or being tricked

- Damage to vessels, pipes, tubes or similar apparatus as a result of 'overheating, implosion, cracking, fracturing, weld failure, nipple leakage or other failure'. Some of these perils are more specifically covered under the Engineering classes of insurance.

- Breakdown or derangement of electrical, electronic and/or mechanical machines

- 'Altering, bleaching, cleaning, dyeing, manufacture, repair, restoring, servicing, renovating, testing or any other work thereon'

- 'Fault or defect in design, formula, specification, drawing, plan, materials, workmanship or professional advice, normal maintenance, gradual deterioration, depreciation, corrosion, rust, oxidation or other chemical action or reaction, frost, change in temperature, expansion or humidity, fermentation or germination, dampness, dryness, wet or dry rot, shrinkage, evaporation, loss of weight, contamination, pollution, change in colour, flavour, texture or finish or wear and tear

- Any cosmetic damage which does not cause the insured item to stop functioning. As such there is no cover for only superficial damages of 'denting, chipping, scratching or cracking not affecting the operation of the item'

- 'Termites, moths, insects, vermin, inherent vice, fumes, flaws, latent defect, fluctuations in atmospheric or climatic conditions, the action of light'

- 'Settlement or bedding down, ground heave or cracking of structures or the removal or weakening of support to any insured property'

- 'Loss of or damage to chemicals, oils, liquids, fluids, gases or fumes due to leakage or discharge from containers'

- 'Loss or damage resulting from leakage or discharge of chemicals, oils, fluids, gases or fumes'

- 'Failure of and/or the deliberate withholding and/or lack of supplies of water, steam, gas, electricity, fuel or refrigerant'.

- 'Collapse of plant and machinery, buildings and structures'. This should be more specifically insured under the Engineering classes of insurance

Furthermore, the standard Accidental Damage policy also specifies that it only covers 'tangible' property. This means that it only covers physical things that one can touch. The policy also identifies items which cannot be covered under Accidental Damage because they should be insured more specifically on appropriate policies. The list of items that cannot be covered on this policy is as follows:

- Coins, bank and currency notes, cheques and other money related items including all documents with a financial value. These items are supposed to be covered on the Money policy.

- 'Furs, jewellery, bullion, precious and semi-precious metals and stones, curiosities, rare books and works of art.' There are different types of more appropriate policies that could be considered.

- Property being transported by any means. These should be covered under Goods in Transit or Marine Cargo insurance policies

- 'Railway locomotives, rolling stock and other railway property, aircraft, watercraft, mechanically or electrically propelled vehicles, motor cycles, mobile plant, caravans and trailers'. These items should be covered specifically in appropriate policies.

- 'Standing or felled trees, crops, animals, land (including topsoil, backfill, drainage and culverts), driveways, pavements, roads, runways, dams, reservoirs, canals, pipelines (external to the premises), tunnels, cables (external to the premises), cableways, bridges, docks, jetties, wharves, piers, excavations, property below the ground or explosives'.

- Items that should be specifically insured under Electronic or Computer Insurance policies.

- 'Property in the course of construction, erection or dismantling including materials or supplies related thereto'. This should be covered under the Engineering classes of insurance.

- 'Property in the possession of customers under lease, rental, credit or suspensive sale agreements'.

- 'Glass, china, earthenware, marble and other fragile or brittle objects'

6.4. Glass

Glass insurance is intended to cover loss or damage of glass at insured premises. This is a critical type of cover for types of business with large shop display windows, signwriting, mirrors, glass shelving, etc. This would be a useful type of insurance for businesses located in city centres where there is a high danger of accidental breakage of glass. Please also note that the Accidental Damage policy does not cover damage of 'glass.' The Glass policy defines glass as all plain glass or float glass not exceeding 6 millimetres in thickness or 6.5 millimetres thick of laminated safety glass. Armoured and bullet-proof glass is not covered in this definition. However, it is possible for the insurer to endorse or alter the policy to cover glass which does not fit this definition, if all parties are in agreement.

The Glass policy does not cover the following situations:

- Loss or damage as a result of claims related to a Fire policy. This exception does not apply in the case of tenants that are responsible for loss or damage to glass, as part of their lease agreement

- 'Glass forming part of stock in trade'. This is due to the fact that for companies such as glass manufacturers and retailers, such an exposure would be part of their normal 'risk of trade.'

- Glass which is already broken or cracked prior to placement of insurance

- Any superficial damage. Only fractures or breakage through the entire thickness of the glass is covered.

6.5. Accounts Receivable

We should start by noting that Accounts Receivable insurance has become increasingly less relevant with modern technological advances in the area of capturing, storage and accessing of business information. This type of policy is intended to indemnify the insured for money due to the insured business and which the insured is unable to collect as a result of damage of their books of accounts. It tends to be very useful for companies that supply goods or services to other companies on credit whilst awaiting payment at a later stage.

The Accounts Receivable policy does not cover the following situations:

- Damage to books of accounts caused by 'wear and tear or gradual deterioration or moths or vermin'

- Loss or damage as a result of legal actions of a legal authority

- Loss or damage resulting from lack of duplicate backup to electrical or electronic or magnetic data storage.

Furthermore, the definition of the calculation of indemnity also discounts bad debts. It is not the intention of the policy to cover the problem of debtors that are unwilling or unable to pay.

6.6. Business All Risks

The Business All Risks is also known simply as the "All Risks" in some underwriting policy systems. When included in Personal Lines policy packages, it may be referred to as '**Personal All Risks**.' The policy covers any loss or damage occurring anywhere in the world as a result of any accident or misfortune besides the specific situations defined in the policy. The specific situations which are not covered are as follows:

- Theft of things left in a car without making an effort to lock in a boot where they are not visible and to leave the car locked and in a secure place. Insurance is not intended to cover recklessness. The insured is expected to take measures to protect their property 'as if un-insured', as per the principle of loss mitigation covered in Chapter 3

- Specified activities that may lead to inevitable loss or damage. These include processes of 'cleaning, repairing, dyeing, bleaching, altering or restoring.'

- Losses arising as a result of 'inherent vice or defect, vermin, insects, damp, mildew or rust.' These events are caused by the very nature of the insured item or are within the control of the insured that could take measures to avoid the loss. A peril such as dampness is part of what is known as a 'gradually operating cause.' This means that it is not a sudden loss event.

- Loss as a result of fraud or dishonesty by the employees or other people directly involved in the business. This should be covered appropriately under the Fidelity policy, as described above.

7. Personal Accident & Related Covers

We should now review key types of general non-life insurance policies that are intended to cover people. It is vital to note that such policies have a few critical differences to insurance for property and liability. As we discussed in Chapter 3, in general, insurance of people is done on the basis of contracts of compensation as opposed to indemnity. This is due to the fact that there are no practical means of defining insurance value of life or limbs of a person. As a result of this, insurance policies of persons are not subject to conditions of average, contribution and subrogation. We shall now look at four key types of insurance of persons provided in our market.

7.1. Personal Accident

This policy is intended to cover death or bodily injury to covered persons as a result of a sudden and unexpected accident caused by 'accidental, violent, external and visible means.' The policy is referred to as Personal Accident (PA) when covering one person or Group Personal Accident (GPA) in the case of more than one person. Benefits under such a policy can be expressed either as a specified amount or as a multiple of annual salaries of the covered persons as illustrated in Table 19.

Table 19—Basic Policy Specification for Personal Accident

AREA	DESCRIPTION OF SCOPE OF COVER	
Type of Cover	Fixed Sum Insured	Stated Benefits
Death	Compensation is a **fixed sum insured** amount	Compensation is a **multiple of annual earnings**
Total Permanent Disability	**Fixed sum insured** amount. Compensation calculated as defined in the Table in the policy	**Multiple of annual earnings**. Compensation calculated as defined in the Table in the policy
Temporary Total Disability	**Fixed payable amount per week** up to a specified maximum of weeks	**Percent of average weekly earnings per week** for a period not longer than specified maximum number of weeks & **subject to deductions of amounts received from WCA.**
Medical expenses	As per specified maximum amount of cover.	As per specified maximum amount of cover and **subject to deductions of amounts received from other policies.**

The standard Personal Accident policies do not cover the following:

- Aircraft crew who are supposed to arrange a specialised Aviation Personal Accident

- Suicide or intentional self-injury

- 'Pre-existing physical defect or other infirmity'

- Claims caused by 'influence of alcohol, drugs or narcotics.'

- Claims as a result of active involvement in any 'riot or civil commotion'.

- Problems peculiar to women such as pregnancy, childbirth, abortion or miscarriage

- Extreme sports and other high risk activities. High risk activities specified on standard policies are 'motor cycling', 'racing of any power-driven vehicle, vessel or craft', 'mountain climbing', 'winter sports', 'polo on horseback, steeplechasing, professional football or hang-gliding'.

Finally, we should also note one critical legal condition pertaining to this type of insurance in Portugal and other international markets. As noted in the Personal Accident manual of the Associação Portuguesa de Seguradores (2000: 17), on the basis of conditions specified in law, there are restrictions on types of covers that can be arranged for minors. In our legal framework, it does not appear that there are any restrictions. Some insurers avoid covering minors on Personal Accident insurance due to a lack of underwriting capacity since international reinsurers would not encourage such products.

However, given that a number of schools demand some form of cover, some insurers offer a certain type of Personal Accident for schools. In our view, this creates fundamental problems of conflict with the principle of insurable interest. We are of the view that schools should only focus on legal liability, which is one of the covers of Schools Insurance[3] defined in the same manual from Portugal.

7.2. Hospital Cash

Hospital Cash insurance is a fairly new type of insurance policy in our market. It is intended to provide covered persons with a fixed amount of compensation per day in the event of being hospitalised as a result of an accident or illness. The maximum period of cover in the standard policy in our market is 30 days of hospitalisation. The defined daily benefit is usually payable if hospitalisation is in excess of a specified minimum amount of time or days. This minimum period of time before activation is known as a **franchise**. A franchise is a 'point below which claims are not payable but above which

---

3. Referred to in Portuguese as *Seguro Escolar*

claims are payable in full' (Sadler, 2012: 1/2). This is different from an excess which is always deducted from all claims.

The main exclusions on standard Hospital Cash policies are as follows:

- Injury or illness as a result of participating in any criminal or illegal act
- Pre-existing illnesses and accidents
- Suffering from insanity or any psychiatric, psychological or emotional condition
- Suicide, attempted suicide or any self-inflicted injury
- Work-related accidents and occupational illnesses
- Infectious diseases in cases where health authorities have declared a state of an epidemic outbreak
- Any illnesses or complications arising from HIV/AIDS
- Mental illness
- Illness or injury caused by alcohol or drug abuse
- Riots, strikes, civil commotion, war or revolution
- Cosmetic surgery or procedures
- Active participation in professional sports or contact sports
- Underground mining or shaft sinking

- High risk activities such as mountaineering or horse riding

Furthermore, insurance types such as Hospital Cash as well as Health insurance may be subject to what is known as a **waiting period** (Associação Portuguesa de Seguradores, 2003: 19). This means that the insured might not enjoy full benefits with effect from the first day after arranging insurance. This is intended to reduce the risk of selection where a person that is aware of an impending health problem might attempt to place insurance for a risk situation that has already occurred. This would be contrary to the objective of insurance which is intended to cover future unforeseen events. A waiting period is another form of a deductible that is intended to reduce nuisance minor claims or abuse of insurance (Mehr and Cammack, 1972: 234).

Finally, we should note that this product appears to have a high demand. Currently, it is one of the key products sold through bancassurance besides funeral and credit life business, which are presented in the following chapter. It is also vital to note that this policy should not be seen as a substitute for a normal health insurance. In fact, some consumers see this as some form of income replacement type of indemnity. As such they could arrange a Hospital Cash plan as a supplementary cover to arrangements that they may have for their health.

7.3. Health

Health insurance is one of the classes of business with the broadest range of types of policies in Mozambique. The key types of health policies available in our market can be grouped into the following three categories:

- Hospitalization cover—This is a intended to cover costs for treatment only for patients admitted in hospital as a result of injury or illness. It is not intended to cover medical consultations and any other health-related services that may be provided whilst you are not admitted in hospital.

- Emergency health evacuation cover—This policy is intended to cover costs of emergency evacuation in the event of an injury or illness. The means of transport may be by road or air, as may be stipulated in the respective policy.

- Comprehensive health cover—This policy is intended to cover the insured person whether in hospital or not. It may offer many extended forms of cover including evacuation. Some of the benefits such as expenses outside of hospital may be capped.

The different types of products sold in our market are developed from the basic types of policies, as outlined above. The key differences between the options relate to mainly the limits of benefits, restrictions that may apply on clinics that may be consulted, additional services offered with the policy and whether the service provider covers expenses upfront or on reimbursement basis. Currently, the key types of operators involved in the area of health are as outlined in Table 20.

Table 20–Health Insurance Services in Mozambique

	PROVIDER	TYPES OF COVER	CRITICAL ISSUES
1	Employer managed **self-funded health schemes**	Usually in the form of expense reimbursement schemes with defined limits per member per annum	• Limited amount of cover and lack of back-up mechanisms • Lack of administration systems • Lack of focus by company on core business
2	Local insurer schemes	Mainly hospitalization policies with options for evacuation	• Products perceived to be too expensive relative to cover • Very low penetration
3	Local insurer & global health operator as reinsurer	Comprehensive medical or health insurance with global scope of cover	This tends not to be affordable for most entities besides very large multi-national projects
4	Foreign service providers without a local insurer	Broad range of products from hospitalization to comprehensive	• Service provider and product not locally registered
5	Local private clinics	Basic health covers which may include some level of outpatient benefits	• Service restricted to specific clinics • Limited cover and lack of supervision of provider

6	Unauthorised financial service providers	Basic health covers which may include some level of outpatient benefits	• Operator is 'registered' with Ministry of Health but there is no appropriate financial oversight • Unregistered financial service
7	Unregistered local service providers	Basic health covers which may include some level of outpatient benefits	• Unlicensed operator • No legal protection for consumer • Limited service

Furthermore, we should also note that there have also been debates in the insurance sector about how to classify health. Whilst in Mozambique health has been classified as general non-life business; in other markets in our region, it is classified as part of life business. In South Africa, health is treated separately from life and non-life. It is viewed as a different line of business in the financial services area and there is appropriate legislation[4] covering this business. In that market, medical schemes are supposed to be structured in the form of mutual companies.

Finally, we should also note that some of the self-funded schemes have developed a fair amount of internal capacity to handle health requirements of their employees. It may be viable for them to consider upgrading these schemes into more structured autonomous entities in the form of mutual insurance licenses. As such, they could also be able to identify

---

4. Medical Schemes Act no. 131 of 1998

like-minded entities in order to pool resources for a stronger entity that could better serve the target groups. This would also help to separate funds and management of the health schemes from that of the underlying companies.

7.4. Travel

Travel insurance is one of the new types of insurance policies that has grown rapidly in Mozambique. It is mainly sold in the Bancassurance channel and via travel agents. Some insurers in our market have developed systems which allow agents to issue the policies directly from their offices through internet. In this way, new technology has been used to increase efficiency of the insurer and to allow agents to have the flexibility to run as many simulations as the client may want and to issue a policy any time of day, as may be required.

Furthermore, we should note that demand for this policy is driven by the fact that it is a requirement in the process of applying for visas for a number of countries in Europe and America. The need for one to purchase a travel insurance policy is as a result of the following two key problems:

- Most local health insurance schemes tend to have limited type of cover which may be restricted to only Mozambique, as the territory of permanent residence.

- Most people in markets such as ours do not have any form of health or medical cover.

As a result of these two reasons, when a person is intending to travel to territories such as the European Union, they are required to arrange Travel Insurance. This is supposed to provide temporary protection for the while travelling abroad (Associação Portuguesa de Seguradores, 2000: 22). Although many of the countries that demand travel insurance have public health systems, such public facilities are supposed to cover only residents in their territories that contribute to the tax system financing such schemes. As such, a travel policy is supposed to cover costs for unexpected medical expenses that may be incurred by non-residents whilst travelling there. However, it should be noted that a travel policy is not intended to cover treatment of known or existing health conditions. Travel insurance policies may also be extended to include loss of baggage, flight delays, missed connections and other unexpected expenses.

CONCLUSION

We have looked at basic types of general insurance available in the private commercial insurance market. We have discussed key features of Fire, Motor, General Liability, Miscellaneous Accident and basic policies aimed at covering people against accidental injury and health. We have noted that for some of the key policies, the insurance market needs to define basic guidelines. For types of business such as Fire, insurers could form a Fire Committee to develop underwriting of

Fire insurance and support the vital public service of the Fire Brigade.

Furthermore, we have also noted that there is room for improvement of the situation in the area of health. There are unregulated operators providing cover to the public. There is a need to bring order and ensure that there is no overlap between the Ministry of Finance and the Ministry of Health. After looking at the different types of general insurance policies available in our market, we shall now discuss life and pensions in the next Chapter.

REFERENCES

- Associação Portuguesa de Seguradores (2001). *Seguro Automóvel*. Lisboa: Associação Portuguesa de Seguradores

- Associação Portuguesa de Seguradores (2003). *Seguros de Saúde*. Lisboa: Associação Portuguesa de Seguradores

- Mehr, Robet, I. and Cammack, Emerson (1972). Principles of Insurance. 5th Edition. Illinois: Richard D. Irwin, Inc.

- Sadler, John (ed.) (2012). The Insurance Manual. West Midlands: Insurance Publishing & Printing Co.

CHAPTER 11

LIFE AND COMPLEMENTARY PENSIONS BUSINESS

Life insurance and pension funds constitute a fundamental segment in the insurance sector. According to figures in the report of the insurance regulator, in 2012, life and pensions represented approximately 14% of the total revenue of the insurance sector (ISSM, 2012: 13). Although life business is currently much smaller than general insurance business, it has far more growth potential. If we look at other markets in our region such as Botswana, South Africa and Zimbabwe, life insurance business is much bigger than general insurance. From the current market reports of the ISSM, it is not possible to determine the contribution of pensions and different classes of life products to the revenue generated in this segment. In our market reports up to 2013, life insurance and pensions are presented as a one-line item. This is not doing justice to one of the most dynamic areas in the insurance sector.

Besides protecting the livelihood of people; life and pensions are a powerful mechanism for mobilising long term domestic savings (Associação Portuguesa de Seguradores,

1997: 5 and Das et al, 2003:3). While most national development strategies in Africa are focussed on attracting aid and foreign direct investment (FDI), local savings can also play a crucial role in stimulating and supporting local development. Local investments are also an essential way of ensuring that the local population is a key stakeholder in the development of the economy. As private individuals, most of the citizens do not have financial means, knowledge and appropriate networks to play a meaningful role as investors in any of the emerging mega-projects. Life insurance and pensions offer an effective route for raising large sums of money that could also be involved in local shareholding in such large investment projects. Domestic investors will tend to be more stable than some of the cut-throat foreign investors such as hedge funds that tend to be fickle and are usually focused on extracting short term gains.

Furthermore, funds generated by life and pension business are better suited than general insurance for the purposes of long term investments such as property development (ABI, 2014: 15). Given the need to meet their obligations in the long term, life insurers tend to prefer to also match such portfolios of business with appropriate long term types of investments. Many of the buildings providing essential office rental space in some of the thriving cities in our region including Gaborone, Harare, Johannesburg and Sandton are as a result of investments from this area. With the growth of this segment in Mozambique, there will be more exploration of long term investment options than is currently the case. We shall now define key categories of life business and describe some of the basic types of life insurance policies.

1. BASIC TYPES OF LIFE INSURANCE

As we have already discussed in this book, there is a need for a review of the classification and definition of insurance classes in our Insurance Law. For the purposes of explaining life insurance in a coherent manner, we have relied on references from a manual on Principles of Life Insurance from the Insurance Institute of South Africa (2011 e). We have also verified with other references including the following websites which provide useful information on life insurance:

http://money.howstuffworks.com/personal-finance/
financial-planning/life-insurance.htm

http://www.mylifeinsurancequotes123.com/

http://www.investopedia.com/university/insurance/
insurance8.asp

The different types of life insurance products can be grouped into two basic types: temporary and permanent, as illustrated in Figure 8.

Figure 8–Basic categories of Life Insurance

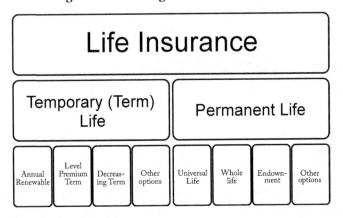

2. TEMPORARY LIFE

Temporary life insurance or term life insurance is a simple life insurance which provides cover for a defined period of time. In its basic form, it is a 'pure' life risk cover without any payout besides the claim payable in the event of death or any other covered event during the period of cover (Vaughan, 2009: 185). It tends to be a cheaper form of life insurance than the permanent type of life insurance. A term or temporary life is usually used for covering debts in the form of consumer loans, micro-credit or mortgage. At the moment, most of the insurance policies being offered in our market fall in this category. We shall now discuss some of the key term life insurance policies.

2.1. Funeral Expenses Insurance

Funeral Expenses Insurance is the most common type of simple term life insurance policy sold in our market. It is available mainly through either employer-based groups or individual funeral schemes. Employer-based Group Funeral schemes are sold either directly by the insurer or through insurance intermediaries to companies and organisations. In such policies, the employer is responsible for payment of premium. They have an option of covering only their workers or the entire family of each covered worker. In most cases, the employer offers to cover the cost of the insurance. We do not yet have voluntary types of schemes where employees of a covered company could choose different levels of cover or opt out completely.

Then, we also have individual monthly funeral policies that are sold mainly through banks and micro-finance institutions (MFI). Insurers in our market avoid issuing individual policies. This is due to a concern about high transactional costs which do not make it economically viable to set up mechanisms to collect small amounts of premium from each covered individual. However, with the growth of distribution of insurance though banks and MFIs, funeral expenses insurance has been one of the preferred types of insurance. It tends to have low levels of premium and the policies do not require complex administration. It is also not a difficult product to market because of the simplicity of type of cover. In the distribution of such low-price products with high volumes of customers across the country, banks also have major competitive advantages compared to insurers. They tend to have more extensive infrastructure than insurers and they already have access to bank accounts of their customers from which a small agreed portion can be deducted to pay for insurance premium.

2.2. Credit Life and related policies

Besides holding deposits and facilitating local and international trade, banks are also supposed to provide access to money to business and people in the form of loans. There are many reasons why people may need to borrow money. They may be planning to buy property, to cover costs of a start-up or ongoing business, to cover expenses for unexpected contingencies and any other item for which they might not have adequate money. In addition to assessing if the borrower can be trusted and will be able to pay back the money borrowed, financial institutions are also worried about the fact that the borrower could fail to pay back due to unforeseen situations such as an accident or illness. In order to protect themselves from these specific risks which threaten the lives of their clients, they can arrange Credit Life insurance. This policy is intended to cover the debtor for a period of up to 5 years. Premium can be charged on a once-off basis for the entire period of cover or in agreed instalments.

With the recent development of microinsurance, there is also what is known as micro-credit life. This type of policy was developed from traditional credit life. It is intended to cover small loans or micro-loans which are granted by MFIs. MFIs have developed as a result of the concern of providing financial services for low-income people. The amounts of loans tend to be small. The period of loans also tends to be short. In some cases, micro-loans are provided to a group of people that are collectively responsible for the loan. Some Micro-Credit Life policies may also include in one package other types of basic covers such as Funeral or simple property damage insurance.

2.3. Mortgage Life

Mortgage Life insurance is intended to cover loans of periods longer than what is covered on Credit Life. In our market, loans for a period longer than 5 years are covered as Mortgage Life. Such types of loans are usually intended for purchases of assets such as houses. Given the length of time of exposure and high sums insured, Mortgage Life policies are usually subject to stricter underwriting conditions than Credit Life. The following are some of the key conditions relevant for this policy:

- There is a detailed level of assessment of each applicant. The terms of insurance are influenced by factors such as age, gender, smoking status and state of health.

- Applicants may be required to undergo a range of medical examinations in order to determine their state of health. Following such an examination, an insurer can refuse to provide cover or may apply additional charges for any individual that might not have satisfactory results from the examination

There is a growing demand for this type of insurance in our market as an increasing number of banks have started granting loans for longer time periods than in the past. With the growth of this portfolio, there will be a need for more life underwriters than what we have at the moment. Mortgage Insurance has potential to be a key growth area in the future with a growing demand for finance for construction, rehabilitation or acquisition of residential properties.

2.4. Group Risk life

This is a form of an annually renewable term life insurance that is usually arranged by an employer to cover its employees. The key events which are covered on standard policies are death or permanent disability as a result of an accident or illness of the covered persons. The benefits on this type of insurance are usually expressed as a multiple of the annual salaries of the covered persons.

At the moment, very few entities in Mozambique arrange Group Risk Life insurance. There is a perception that the obligatory Workmen's Compensation Act (WCA) insurance is adequate. It is understandable that as part of rationalisation of costs, many employers tend to focus on bare minimum obligatory covers. We are of the view that, as the economy will develop and as companies will seek to attract and retain high quality staff, there will be an increasing demand for financial services that enhance packages offered to employees. The protection of bread-winners through Group Risk Life insurance is part of the value-adding financial services that will become an essential element of conditions of employment in the future.

2.5. Key Man

Key Man insurance or Key Person insurance is a type of policy which is usually arranged by a partnership or a business in order to provide financial protection in the event of death or disability of an identified key individual. The benefits of the policy are supposed to be payable to the entity that arranges the cover. The key individual is supposed to be a person that represents critical value to the business or has a significant financial interest or debt owed to the business. It may be difficult or costly to find a replacement for such a person or it could be someone that could affect the performance of the business (IISA, 2011F: 264). In the event of death or disability of the key person, the agreed indemnity is paid to the business in question.

This is still a rare type of policy in our market. There are signs that with the growth of the economy and the increasing number of small and medium-sized enterprises (SMEs), there will be a growing demand for such types of insurance. It is a type of product that may be used to protect the financial interest of SMEs. In markets such as South Africa, there are also more complex types of products that are used as an option for creating tax-efficient incentives for key personnel. We shall not cover these options in this book.

2.6. Credit Default

This is not a common type of insurance in our market. It is also not clear if it belongs to life or non-life insurance category. This is a type of insurance where the insurer agrees to pay a lender losses suffered as a result of bad debts. The lender could be a bank or a micro-finance institution. The covered risk is not that of a typical life policy relating to death or injury of the covered person. This policy covers the risk of borrowers failing to honour their agreement to pay their debts. Given that this is part of the business risk of financial institutions, most of the operators in this sector tend to self-insure or absorb this risk in their business transactions. We have already discussed some of these financial risk control options in Chapter 4.

3. PERMANENT LIFE

Permanent life insurance is a type of life policy that is intended to cover the entire life of the insured person or up to a defined period of cover, known as the maturity date (Mehr and Cammack, 1972: 448). The life insurer is not supposed to cancel the policy unless the insured fails to pay agreed premium or in the event of discovery of fraud. A normal permanent life policy is supposed to build up a cash value from the contributions of premium by the insured as well as provide benefits from the investment of the build-up of funds. Besides the cover amount which is payable in the event of death of the covered person, an insured can also access the cash value of premium and return on investment by cancelling (surrendering) the policy or using the cash value of the policy as collateral to borrow money. We shall now review some of the key permanent types of life insurance.

3.1. Whole Life

Whole life insurance policy is a permanent type of life insurance for the full life of the covered person (Vaughan, 2009: 185). This policy provides a death benefit as well as a cash value which usually guarantees a certain fixed rate of return. The cash value is a deduction from premium contributions. Premium payable is usually fixed for the period of contract. The cash value can be accessed by the insured through a policy loan. It usually costs more than a term life insurance in the beginning. It can be used for long term financial goals such as retirement.

3.2. Universal Life

The Universal Life is one of the most exciting types of innovations in life insurance. It is a type of policy that is intended to maintain an appropriate form of financial protection throughout the different stages of life of the covered individual (Vaughan, 2009: 190). Through a combination of risk protection from term insurance and a component of savings or investment contracts, it provides flexibility for covered persons to adapt insurance cover in alignment with key changes in their life (Associação Portuguesa de Seguradores, 1997: 34).

Furthermore, insured persons are able to define level of life risk cover they require which affects levels of cost to be deducted from total premium paid leaving a balance for investment. The insured person can choose lower levels of risk cover and have more money going into the savings account. Young people may require high levels of risk cover at the stage in their lives when they have large debts at the beginning of their careers. As they grow older, their risk of death increases and as such the cost of life becomes higher. If they would have been building up amounts of savings, they could have a reduced dependence on risk life insurance or they could allow earnings from their savings account to cover the increasing costs of risk life protection (IISA, 2011F: 104).

3.3. Endowment

The endowment policy is a type of life insurance in which the insured is paid out a lump sum if the insured attains what is known as the 'endowment age' or date of 'maturity' of the policy (Vaughan, 2009: 185). The standard maturity dates can be ten, fifteen or twenty years. In this way the insured chooses how much they want to save and the period for which they want to do this saving. The insured does not have to pass away to receive the benefit of this cover. Endowment policies cost much more than Whole Life and Universal Life due to the fact that premium contributions are made during a shorter time period.

The endowment policy is often packaged as an 'educational policy' or 'college savings plan'. It allows the insured to start building up a savings plan for the education of their children. If the insured were to die before achieving the agreed savings plan, the family would receive a death benefit and the agreed target cash value. There are alternative policies that include critical illnesses as part of the events that can trigger a pay-out like death (ABI: 2014).

3.4. Other options of permanent life

Besides the 3 principal types of permanent life policies described above, there are a number of other optional policies sold in more sophisticated life markets. The following are some of the other types of products:

-   Variable Life—This is a permanent life policy where the policyholder has control over where the funds in the savings account are invested. In this way, the performance of the fund is influenced by choices of the policyholder.

-   Universal Variable—This is a policy which combines qualities of the Universal Life and the Variable Life. Firstly, like in a Universal Life policy, the client is able to determine allocation between the life insurance risk and the savings portion. Secondly, like in a Variable Life policy, the policyholder is also able to control the investment options.

We would like to conclude our review of permanent life insurance business by noting that it is the least developed area in our market. Part of the explanation for the lack of interest could be due to the fact that there are very limited options for investment in Mozambique besides bank deposits. Without a broad enough range of investment options, most insurers prefer to focus only on pure risk business. This lack of investment options also affects the area of pension funds, as we shall discuss later.

4. KEY LIFE UNDERWRITING PRACTICES

Following our review of the key types of life insurance offered in Mozambique, we should now discuss two additional features of life insurance.

4.1. Medical Examination

For mainly Mortgage Life insurance, insurers tend to demand medical examinations before confirming terms and conditions of cover. The Insurance Law provides clear guidelines to be followed for cases where medical examinations may be required by an insurer, as defined in Articles 222 and 223. Before such examinations are carried out, the insurer is required to disclose full information of:

- All the types of examinations and analysis that will be done

- The establishment where such procedures can or should be done

- Clarification on who should pay expenses for such examinations. If the insurer provides an option to reimburse expenses, it should disclose circumstances under which it may elect not to reimburse such expenses

- Entity to which the examination results should be sent

In addition to the rules specified above, the law also provides guidelines on who is qualified to present the results to the insured if the results are such that the insurer may decline to insure or may apply additional loading factors to standard conditions. All the conditions noted above are very critical for insurers, banks and other intermediaries that may be involved in marketing and issuing of life policies where such examinations may be required.

4.2. Mortality Tables

The next important practice of life insurance underwriting is the application of mortality tables, as we discussed in Chapter 1. This table is one of the key components used in order to calculate prices of cover and projections of settlements in life and pensions business (Hafeman, 2009: 3 and Chiejina, 2004: 172). The table is constructed by measuring the average probability rates of death of people in different age groups for each gender depending on key life style factors such as smoking status.

Unfortunately, we are not aware of the existence of any current local mortality table in Mozambique. Without such a key element required for underwriting, according to Garand and Wipf (2008: 255), the market could be exposed to 'significant pricing risk'. This means that our pricing could be completely wrong. It could be too cheap to cover future liabilities or it could be ridiculously too high to be affordable and to represent true cost of risk.

For pension claims of WCA insurance, the market uses a national mortality table that was adopted from Portugal in the colonial period. Some of the companies have used in Mozambique mortality tables from areas such as the Province of KwaZulu-Natal (KZN) in South Africa, with major loadings. Due to problems of AIDS in that area of South Africa, they have the highest probability of death. On this basis they are charged higher rates than the rest of South Africa. It is assumed that the whole of Mozambique has the same level of risk as the KZN Province. There is no scientific proof that what is obtainable in KZN is applicable throughout Mozambique. There is a need for the market to develop updated local mortality tables for the different regions. Given the lack of local actuarial skills with capacity to carry out such an exercise, it is a major challenge for us to achieve this goal.

5. COMPLEMENTARY PENSION FUNDS

As we discussed in Chapter 5, the national security system makes provision for the setting up of complementary funds to the compulsory pension fund. At the time of writing of this book, there were five registered pension fund administration companies as follows:

- Global Alliance Seguros- Insurance, SA
- Nico Moçambique Vida Companhia de Seguros, SA
- Kuhanha Sociedade Gestora de Fundo de Pensões, SA

- Sociedade Gestora do Fundo de Pensões, SA (Standard Bank)
- Moçambique Previdente- Sociedade Gestora de Fundos de Pensões, SA

From our research with key pension fund administrators in this sector, it appears that their greatest challenge is the fact that private pension funds are only supposed to be complementary. Most employers and employees are reluctant to put aside more funds for a private pension fund after making the obligatory contributions to the National Scheme. The contributions of 7% made to INSS are not adequate for purposes of building up adequate savings for retirement. Based on global standards, the average employee should aim to save at least 20% of their current salary for savings. There is a lot of work required to encourage more people and companies to raise levels of savings.

Furthermore, we also believe that pension fund companies are the most appropriate entities to handle pensions under the obligatory Workman's Compensation Act Insurance, as we discussed in Chapter 9. It is not advisable that the pensions resulting from this class of business are retained under normal insurance licenses that are intended to handle short-term annually renewable contracts. While the underlying WCA policy could have been classified as a short-term contract, the pension payments are clearly long term.

Moreover, as we have already discussed, the area of administration of pension funds should also be subject to a certain type of a highly recommended insurance policy. All pension fund administrators should be covered by appropriate Directors and Officers Liability insurance. This is intended to protect the funds in case if mishandling by the administration managers.

Finally, we would like to state that the greatest threat for pension funds and social security in our market is that of the funds becoming financially unsustainable. It is critical for authorities to monitor financial performance and ensure that today's contributions are not used to cover liabilities from the past. If there would be no funds in the future to honour obligations assumed today, then the fund would be operating like a **pyramid scheme**. The financial obligations could continue growing until current contributions fail to cover them. We believe that the regulators can only carry out the required supervisory work with appropriate support of actuaries. We have already discussed the need for actuarial support for the insurance regulator. It is also our view that pension fund administration companies should also be subject to review by actuaries. This requirement should be specified in the Insurance Law.

CONCLUSION

As we discussed in this Chapter, life insurance and pensions business have substantial capacity to grow. If this segment grows, it has potential of making a significant contribution to one of the key goals of the government of mobilising domestic savings. It is important that life business already has the advantages of having the lowest premium tax compared to general insurance business, as we discussed in Chapter 5. There are a number of additional measures that could be considered by the policy-makers and the insurance association in order to stimulate growth of life and pensions business in the future.

Firstly, there is a need for a review of the parts of legislation relating to life business. The classification of life insurance in our legislation is not in alignment with traditional models. Secondly, private sector pensions could be boosted by permitting them to be an option to the national fund. By permitting private schemes, there would also be increased opportunities for group risk life insurance policies which private pension funds usually have to arrange to protect their members. The national social security does not apply such types of financial risk transfer processes.

Thirdly, the insurance association will need to develop an initiative aimed at developing and promoting supply of a broader range of life products. Besides basic term life insurance, there are a number of other types that can be found in more sophisticated life insurance markets. In Mozambique, insurers have focused more on pure risk types of products. There has been a very limited amount of research and development on investment and savings types of products. We also do not yet have creative packaging of insurance policies such as linking of life insurance to things that people value like education.

REFERENCES

- ABI (2014). UK Insurance: Key Facts. London: Association of British Insurers (ABI)

- Associação Portuguesa de Seguradores (1997). *Seguros de Vida*. Lisboa: Associação Portuguesa de Seguradores

- Chiejina, Ezekiel, O. (2004). *Foundations of Insurance: Law, Agency and Salesmanship*. Lagos: Mbeyi & Associates Ltd.

- Das, U.S., Davies, N., and Podpiera, R. (2003). *Insurance and Issues in Financial Soundness*: IMF Working Paper, WP/03/138, IMF: Washington.

- Garand, Denis and Wipf, John. (2008). 'Risk and financial management' in Churchill, Craig (ed.) Protecting the poor: a microinsurance compendium. Geneva: Internationational Labour Office and the Munich Re Foundation: Munich. Pp. 254-269.

- Hafeman, Michael (2009). *The Role of the Actuary in Insurance*. Primer Series on Insurance, Issue 4, May 2009. Washington: The World Bank.

- Mehr, Robet, I. and Cammack, Emerson (1972). Principles of Insurance. 5th Edition. Illinois: Richard D. Irwin, Inc.

CHAPTER 12

SPECIALIST TYPES OF INSURANCE

We shall now look at key specialist types of insurance which are provided in our market besides the basic general types of insurance, as we discussed in Chapter 10. This grouping consists mainly of unique types of insurance that tend to require specialised risk assessment and underwriting. Local insurance companies tend to have limited capacity and knowledge to underwrite such policies. Given that there is still a very low volume of demand from a small number of prospective clients for such types of insurance policies, there are limited economic benefits for a local insurer to try to arrange full local underwriting capacity for such types of insurance.

Furthermore, these specialist types of insurance are usually written with support of major reinsurance companies or global insurance companies that have scope to achieve appropriate volumes of business on a global scale. This is a vital condition in order to ensure efficacy of the concept of insurance which is underpinned by the key condition of 'law of large numbers', as we discussed in Chapter 4. As a result of this situation, for the majority of specialist types of insurance described below, our insurance market tends to require a significant amount of financial and technical support from international markets in order to underwrite them appropriately. We shall now discuss some of the key specialist types of insurance.

1. ENGINEERING INSURANCE

This is one of the most essential types of insurance that is required at this stage of development of the economy of Mozambique. A number of major construction and rehabilitation projects have been planned for the next two decades. One of the key areas of growth of construction business will be the exploration and development of oil and gas extraction projects in the central and northern parts of Mozambique. There has already been a notable growth of construction insurance following public and private construction projects in the last ten years. Engineering insurance can be broken down into the following types:

1.1. Contractors All Risks

The Contractors All Risks (CAR) is a policy which is intended to provide cover for mainly civil engineering projects involving construction of items such as buildings, roads, bridges and dams. It is supposed to cover such projects from the beginning to the end including the period when the contractor is required to provide engineering maintenance work after completion of the construction phase. Construction insurance is normally specified as a requirement in the project contract between a principal party or employer that is the owner of the item under construction and the contractors doing the construction. Engineering insurance is usually arranged by the contractor. The principal could opt to arrange insurance on behalf of the contractors. This is what is described as **'Principal-Controlled Insurance'** or **'Owner-Controlled Insurance'**.

Standard local market policy wordings for construction provide cover for material damage to the works and for third party liability. Given that it is an 'all risks' type of policy, it is intended to cover all sudden and unforeseen events with the exception of exclusions specified in the policy. It is also possible for the engineering insurance policy to be extended to include consequential losses following an insured material damage claim. The types of cover that can be arranged for this purpose are

- **'Advance Loss of Profits'** (ALoP)
- **'Delay in Start-Up'** (DSU) Insurance or
- **'Delayed Completion Coverage'**.

We shall not discuss the terms and conditions of these policies in this book. We should now look at another project type of insurance which is similar to the CAR.

1.2. Erection All Risks

The Erection All Risks (EAR) policy is intended to provide insurance for projects involving engineering installation. These projects include activities such as the setting up of electricity distribution lines, erection of telecommunication towers, installation of machinery, plant and steel structures. While the main focus of CAR projects is construction of buildings and other civil engineering projects, the EAR policy is intended to cover projects involving mainly erection or installation as well as testing and commissioning. It also has third party liability cover. Like the CAR policy, it is also possible to extend the cover to include consequential losses following material damage to the covered project.

1.3. Plant All Risks

We should note that standard CAR or EAR policies do not cover loss or damage of plant, machinery and equipment belonging to or hired by the contractor. The Plant All Risks (PAR) policy is intended to cover these items in engineering projects. The policy is supposed to cover any loss or damage as a result of sudden and unforeseen events besides the exclusions specified in the policy. As defined in the Insurance Manual (Sadler, 2012: 4/14), there are two types of standard cover for plant as follows:

- Cover for loss or damage to construction plant or equipment owned by the insured.

- 'Legal liability for loss or damage to plant and temporary buildings which are hired-in plus continuing hire charges following loss or damage'

The cover for owned plant can either be in the form of a 'Plant All Risks' policy or on a Specified Perils policy basis. It may cover plant at the premises of the insured, while being transported and while at work at the location of construction.

1.4. Machinery Breakdown

Machinery Breakdown (MBD) Insurance is a highly recommended type of cover for mainly manufacturing and printing industries that use machinery and plant in their production processes. It is intended to provide cover for any sudden and unforeseen damages arising from mechanical and electrical breakdowns. The standard MBD policy does not cover the following loss situations:

- 'Exchangeable tools' and replaceable parts and things like lubricants, fuel and catalysts

- Fire and allied perils because these are supposed to be covered on a Fire policy

- Political risks and nuclear exposure, as per standard exclusion on all commercial policies

- Pre-existing defects

- Wilful act or gross negligence of the Insured

- Wear and tear, erosion, corrosion, rust and other loss or damage caused by gradually operating perils

- Loss or damage for which a supplier, contractor or repairer is responsible

- Consequential losses which can be covered as an extension or on a separate Machinery Breakdown Loss of Profits policy

The Machinery Breakdown policy is one of those types of insurance which is often misunderstood by some of the clients. It should not be confused with a warranty for parts or for a maintenance programme. The exclusions of the policy are designed to ensure that there is no cover for worn or damaged parts that should be replaced through an appropriate regular maintenance plan. The key factors which insurers use to assess such risks are as follows:

- Age and conditions of upkeep of the machines

- Maintenance plans

- Claims experience from the past

- Intensity of use of the machinery depending on length of seasons, number of shifts and hours of operation.

1.5. Electronic Equipment All Risks

The Electronic Equipment All Risks insurance policy is intended to cover electronic equipment such as computers, scanners, printers and electronic data processing machines. Most modern office and home appliances such as televisions, radios, air conditioners and washing machines are also electronic. Such equipment is sensitive to fluctuation of electrical currents and require protection from electrical power surges. Electronic equipment insurance takes into account these characteristics. The standard Electronics policy is done on the basis of an 'All Risks' cover. As such it does not specify covered perils but defines what is not covered. It is not intended to cover the following events:

- Political risks and nuclear perils
- Wilful act or gross negligence
- Faults or defect for which the supplier/manufacturer/ maintenance contractor is responsible
- Wear and tear or gradual deterioration due to atmospheric conditions
- Aesthetic defects
- Consequential losses which can be covered as an extension of the policy

1.6. Completed Civil Engineering Works Insurance

During the construction stage of civil engineering projects, as we discussed above, there is usually a Contractors All Risks insurance. After the completion of the construction of civil engineering structures such as roads and bridges, it is noted that a normal fire and allied perils property insurance might not be the most suitable form of cover for such structures. Fire perils are perceived not to be the most critical exposure. However, it has been observed that these structures can still be exposed to natural perils as well as hazards relating to their operations and use. In order to cover this specific requirement for such structures, there is what is known as Completed Civil Engineering Works Insurance. This policy is designed to provide cover for completed civil engineering structures against any unforeseen and sudden physical loss or damage caused by:

- Fire, lightning, explosion, impact of land borne or waterborne vehicles

- Impact of aircraft and other aerial devices or articles dropped there from

- Earthquake, volcanism, tsunami

- Storms above a defined category

- Flood or inundation, wave action or water

- Subsidence, landslide, rockslide or any other earth movement

- Frost, avalanche, ice

- Vandalism by individuals

Given the exposure of the infrastructure in Mozambique to cyclones and flooding, this should be one of the key types of insurance for consideration by authorities in the future. At this stage, there is no evidence that any of the public infrastructure has any form of insurance. Cover is usually arranged at construction stage when the project is in the hands of the contractor. After the hand-over, it appears that there is no continuation of cover on most infrastructure with the exception of that which is part of concessions administered by private companies.

2. BONDS INSURANCE

Bonds are unique types of financial products which can be issued by either an insurance company or a bank. They are usually required as a form of a guarantee to cover an entity that has signed an agreement with another party to execute activities such as construction projects. On one hand, the party that is supposed to be the future owner of the building is known as the **Principal** or **Employer**. On the other hand, the party that has agreed to execute the agreed task (construction of the building in this case) is known as the **Contractor**. In order to protect their interests and ensure that the identified contractor will execute the agreed task, the employer will require a demonstration of commitment from the contractor that they will execute the task as required. Entities such as governments, municipal authorities and public companies tend to demand submission of appropriate guarantees issued by approved entities and in accordance with an approved format.

The entity issuing the guarantee on behalf of the contractor is known as the **Guarantor**. There are numerous types of guarantees required for different types of contracts. From the different types of bonds presented by Luís Portugal (2007: 77-78), the following are some of the more common types of guarantees issued in our market.

- **Bid bonds** or **Tender bonds**—These are types of bonds that are supposed to be part of the submission at the stage where contractors are still competing to be appointed in public tender processes, as is usually required for public projects

- **Advance payment bonds**—They are usually required by the principal parties before payment of funds that a contractor may require in order to execute an agreed contract. They are intended to protect the principal from the risk of the contractor failing to perform required duties after receiving advance payments.

- **Performance bonds**—These are bonds aimed at ensuring that the contractor will execute the agreed task as per the defined specifications and ensure the right quality of service.

- **Retention bonds**—These are required after completion of the agreed project. They are intended to guarantee the principal that the contractor will provide required maintenance work after delivery of covered works and payment of agreed contract price.

- **Customs bonds**—These types of bonds are issued as one of the options to satisfy the requirements of Customs officials, as defined in Ministerial Decree number 116/2013 of 8 August 2013, which contain regulations for customs of transit shipments. In this law there is reference to options of cash deposit, bank guarantee, counter indemnity with appropriate collateral or an insurance customs bond.

- **Court bonds**—These are types of guarantees required by courts in order to ensure that there is due performance by persons or entities appointed by courts to execute certain tasks on behalf of the court. These tasks can include activities such as administration of accounts of insolvent business entities or overseeing the handling of property of a deceased person.

Furthermore, it should be noted that, unlike other types of traditional insurance, the insured of bonds and guarantees has control of the covered event, which is performance in the agreed project. As a result of this situation, bonds do not fall within the strict technical definition of insurance (Vaughan, 2009: 58). This is one of the reasons why most insurers and reinsurers tend to avoid issuing bonds. The few markets which issue them also tend to handle such risks differently compared to conventional insurable risks. As a result of this situation, the 'underwriting' of such risks tends to involve a higher level of rigour than in other classes of insurance. Some of the key requirements include the following:

- The underwriters will usually want to closely assess the financial soundness of the contractor in order to assess their capacity to perform.

- The contractor might be requested to pledge an asset of some sort to the underwriter to cover the value of the issued guarantee.

- The underwriters may also require the contractor to sign **counter-indemnity** agreements which give them a legal right to recover from the contractor for any claims paid.

Furthermore, we should note that, FIDIC, the international construction standards organisation, as we discussed in Chapter 9, provides useful guidelines on the issue of guarantees. In general, there are two ways that an employer could 'call up' a guarantee or trigger the process of indemnification, depending on the applicable conditions which could be worded as follows:

- The guarantee could have a requirement for the employer to demonstrate that the contractor has failed to perform or

- It could be formulated in such a way that the employer does not have to demonstrate failure to perform by the contractor. The employer would simply only need to demand compensation. This type of a bond is known as an **on-demand bond**. Most insurance underwriters tend to avoid this type of bond.

Finally, we should also note that the unique nature of bonds and the very high financial value that the documents can represent has created a situation where this class of business is one of the key targets of some forms of **white-collar crime**. This is one of the classes of business that has a major problem of fake policy documents. The demand for fake documents is as a result of the unique way that such documents are issued and the very high value that the document can represent. After failing to obtain guarantees from the financial market, desperate contractors in our market have resorted to buying fake guarantees. Fortunately, some of the authorities in our market do not assume that all contractors will present genuine documents. They will also take the initiative of verifying directly with the concerned financial institutions.

However, there have been reported cases where the principal parties did not verify the bonds and they only found out at the time of a claim that they had fake documents. We believe that the Insurance Association needs to find more effective ways of combating this problem. There could be a system of a centralised registration of all approved bonds that can be accessed by interested parties without too much bureaucracy. There can also be a system of blacklisting of any delinquent contractors in order to prevent them from causing further damage to the financial market and disrupting the environment for more serious contactors that want to do proper business.

3. AGRICULTURE

This is one of the key specialist classes of insurance business which is poorly developed notwithstanding the fact that agriculture is traditionally one of the most critical economic activities in Mozambique. It is vital to distinguish between general insurance requirements for operators in this sector and the more specific types of insurance aimed at covering the business activity. Like any other economic entity, an agricultural concern can be insured under normal types of insurance, as we have discussed in this book. As such, items such as buildings, plant, machinery, equipment and stock can be insured under standard property insurance policies such as the Fire policy. However, standard property insurance policies are not intended to cover livestock, trees and plants in the field. This is where it is vital for the farmer to obtain appropriate crop or livestock insurance.

There has been virtually no agricultural insurance especially for small-scale rural farmers that represent the bulk of producers in this sector. There are a number of reasons why agricultural insurance has not developed at the same level as other classes of insurance:

- Isolated rural communities were affected the most in both wars of independence and the highly destructive civil war after independence

- Weather-related disasters have also been causing havoc for the remaining farmers

- The traditional insurance market, which tends to focus on formal business in urban areas, does not have appropriate means and resources to cover rural areas where most of such operators are located.

- Given the predominant obsession of post-colonial governments in most African countries with indus-trialization, there have not been adequate efforts to develop and support the agricultural sector. As a result of this situation, there is limited support for farmers for most services that they require. Critical support required by the agricultural sector includes veteri-nary services to assist in upkeep of health of livestock and agricultural extension services to assist in effec-tive farming. These same services would also help to improve quality of risk management in this sector.

However, there is some hope that there could now be an emerging interest in exploring development of agricultural insurance for the majority small-scale producers in rural areas. We have noted that the government of Mozambique is looking for appropriate risk management solutions for key areas such as cotton. The local insurance market has participated in small-scale pilot projects aimed at exploring the concept of Weather Index Insurance, as part of local microinsurance initiatives with support of the respective authority in the area of cotton production[1]. We shall provide more information on this emerging development in Chapter 14.

4. MARINE

As we discussed in Chapter 1, Marine insurance is one of the oldest types of insurance covering the risks of transportation. This class of insurance can be divided roughly into 3 broad categories: marine hull (the transportation vessels), marine cargo (the transported goods) and marine liability for ship-owners and other operators in the sector. Conventional liability policies for marine hull offer limited cover for liability (Sharp, 2009: 97). As part of international norms in insurance of ocean-going vessels, in particular, the owners are supposed to arrange additional liability insurance known as **Protection and Indemnity Insurance** (**P&I Insurance**) from mutual insurance clubs owned by ship-owners and other business

---

1. Known as Instituto do Algodão de Moçambique (IAM)

entities in marine transportation business (Benjamin, 1977: 13). We should note that this is one of the areas where it remains highly recommended for the local market to reinsure such exposure in full.

Notwithstanding key port facilities located here that serve a number of neighbouring territories in southern and eastern Africa, Marine Insurance has remained one of the specialist classes of insurance with very limited growth. Part of the reason for the low performance in the local market may be connected to the fact that there is still a very low number of locally registered ships.

Furthermore, although there is a growing volume of cargo passing through the ports of Mozambique, most of it consists of transhipment to other territories such as Malawi, South Africa, Swaziland, Zambia and Zimbabwe. In such instances, the respective cargo insurance is handled either at origin or destination outside of Mozambique. Even in cases of imports ending in Mozambique or exports originating from here, there are no legal restrictions preventing shippers from insuring such cargo in international marine markets which tend to have far more competitive pricing.

Given that the insurable item in a marine shipment is moving from one point to another, there are no strong legal grounds to insist that insurance should be placed locally for either imports or exports. Parties on both sides could have legal insurable interest depending on the type of marine shipment agreement in place. The emerging oil and gas extractive industries also have potential to stimulate massive growth in the local marine market depending on how exploration agreements are going to be structured for that emerging sector.

5. OIL AND GAS

At the time of writing of this book, this was an area generating a lot of interest, as major oil and gas operators started focusing on explorations and development of facilities in Mozambique. We shall not discuss too many details on this specialist area which deserves a separate dedicated book. We have noted that the national insurance market is lobbying for national policy-makers to consider adopting a **local content** development policy. This is a development policy where the authorities try to leverage on growth in one area to support development of other economic sectors and ancillary services (Chambeze, 2014: 15).

Through such a policy, it is expected that the new oil and gas companies would be required by law to support local development by giving priority to local suppliers for any services that they need including insurance. At the same time, some of the investors in this sector have been trying to avoid working with the local insurance market which they see as being interested only in extracting commissions, without adding any value.

Furthermore, one of the key challenges for the local insurance market is that most oil and gas companies as well as other major businesses tend to insist that they can only work with insurers with appropriate financial strength. For assessment of this financial strength, they tend to refer to international credit rating agencies. Key international rating agencies include Standard & Poor's, Moody's, AM Best and Fitch. At the time of writing this book, none of the insurers in our market were rated by such international rating agencies. The costs involved for such exercises are viewed as being too high.

Furthermore, it has been noted that their assessment of financial strength takes into account the sovereign rating or rating of the country. Given low rating of most countries in our region, by default, the insurance companies located here cannot expect to have a better grading. There is also a new regional rating agency in South Africa. However, it is still viewed as not operating at the same level as the global agencies. As a result of this, some international investors do not use it as a reference.

In order to ensure the involvement of the local insurance market in this key emerging sector, the Insurance Association is planning to push for enforcement of the local content policy. It will also be vital for the local market to seek support from the African Oil and Energy Pool which has development goals aligned with that of our market (Aghoghovbia, 2014: 7). In addition to the regional initiative, the insurance market should also look at case studies of successful national pool initiatives such as the Norwegian Oil Risk Pool, the Oil

Insurance Ltd (OIL) and the Oil Casualty Insurance Ltd (OCIL) in Bermuda (Sharp, 2009: 199, 514 & 547). It also appears that Tanzania might be on the verge of forming a national oil and gas pool.

6. AVIATION

This is another specialist insurance area that has continued to have low growth. Like in the case of marine business, there is a very small fleet of locally owned aircraft. The few aeroplanes and helicopters owned or leased for use by Mozambican companies are all significantly reinsured in international markets. There is also a very limited local capacity to underwrite and retain this business locally.

Furthermore, the high sums insured of aircraft and the very large limits of passenger and general third party liability required for aviation risks are beyond the financial capacity of the local market. The limits of liability in aviation tend to be very high because of the very high financial impact of aviation accidents. The national airline experienced in November 2013 one of the deadliest accidents in the history of the country. The crash of the Embraer 190 aircraft flight number 470 en route to Angola caused death of all 33 passengers and 6 crew that were on board. There was limited damage in the area of impact between Namibia and Angola because it was a remote uninhabited area. However, the disaster could have been worse if it had crashed in a residential area. The World also witnessed some of the high levels of destruction that can be caused by aircraft with the terrorist attack in the USA of 9 September 2011. The coordinated terrorist attacks (also known as the **September 11 Attacks** or simply as the **9/11 Attacks**) caused death of nearly 3,000 people and damage to property worth at least $10 billion.

7. OTHERS TYPES OF SPECIALIST POLICIES

The outline of specialised types of insurance policies presented above is not exhaustive. There are many other types of specialised insurance policies available in international insurance markets including: Bankers Blanket Bond (BBB); Environmental (Impairment) Liability; Trade Credit Insurance; Political risks, riots and civil commotion insurance. It is not our goal in this book to discuss all the different types of specialist insurance policies.

CONCLUSION

In this Chapter, we discussed the different types of specialist insurance. We have noted that the local market has little or no underwriting capacity for these types of insurance. Therefore, the local insurance market tends to rely significantly on reinsurance from international markets. Given that the concept of insurance is based on the 'law of large numbers', it is appropriate that a significant portion of exposure on mega-projects, large business activities and highly sophisticated insurance policies is reinsured into international markets.

However, in areas such as oil and gas, it is also advisable for the policy-makers to create a conducive environment for the development of local financial and technical capacity. This is part of what is known as a 'local content policy'.

With this discussion on specialist insurance types, we have now completed our review of the different types of insurance provided in our market. In the next chapter, we shall now discuss the question of how insurance provides after-sales service for the clients that may be unfortunate to experience a loss of someone or something. We shall also discuss the state of affairs regarding conflict resolution.

REFERENCES

- Aghoghovbia, Ken (2014). African Oil and Energy Pool in the African Insurance Bulletin. Issue no. 0005 of May 2014. Doala: The African Insurance Organisation. Pp. 7-8.

- Benjamin, Bernard (1977). *General Insurance*. London: William Heinemann Ltd.

- Chambeze, Isaias (2014) in a Conference Paper that was presented at the ISSM Insurance Seminar with title–*Colocação de Seguro no Exterior e Desafios para as Seguradoras Nacionais*

- Portugal, Luís (2007). Gestão de Seguros Não-vida. Lisbon: Instituto de Formação Actuarial

- Sadler, John (ed.) (2012). The Insurance Manual. West Midlands: Insurance Publishing & Printing Co.

- Sharp, David (2009). *Upstream and Offshore Energy Insurance*. Livingston: Witherbys Insurance

CHAPTER 13

CLAIMS AND RESOLUTION OF DISPUTES

We believe that one of the greatest challenges in the insurance sector is that, in general, insurance companies should not make the mistake of focussing more on selling of promises to deliver service than on the actual delivery of service when claims occur. We shall review the key elements involved in the delivery of service in connection with insurance claims and highlight some of the critical gaps that contribute to some of the major problems experienced in this area. We shall also briefly review some of the efforts of our policy-makers to address some of the key issues in insurance claims, as reflected in our current Insurance Law. We shall also consider certain types of policies and institutions which are not in place and which could create a conducive environment for resolution of some of the key problems afflicting insurance business.

We should begin by noting that the main goals of the claims function in insurance should be to ensure that:

- The **correct claims** are settled for
- The **right amount** at
- The **right time**.

The settlement of correct claims means that the insurer will check if the client presenting a claim has a valid policy and that the event in question is covered, as per the insurance policy. Then, for all valid claims, there is a need to define the right amount of settlement depending on values covered and amounts of damage or loss suffered by the insured. All this needs to be done at the right time. This means that it has to be settled as promptly as possible so that the insured does not unnecessarily suffer any further prejudice besides the claim.

1. MAJOR CLAIM EVENTS

1.1. Global Claims Experience

The largest claims experienced worldwide have been caused by both man-made disasters and natural phenomena. Please look at Appendix IX which outlines the largest insured claims since 1970. From this outline, we can see that natural perils have caused the most devastation. According to a presentation by Hain (2015), from all insured claims in the last decade caused by natural catastrophes, windstorms and flooding account for 75% of the total. The breakdown of claims impact of natural catastrophes is as outlined in Figure 9.

Figure 9–Impact of natural catastrophes

Natural Catastrophes

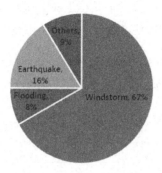

1.2. Exposure to Natural Catastrophes in Mozambique

We should now look at exposure of Mozambique to key natural catastrophes.

a. Windstorms and flooding

We should note that Mozambique is located in a region with high exposure to cyclones in the southern Indian Ocean. This is one of six global regions where tropical cyclones occur (Meyer, 1997: 14). The problem of flooding is closely connected to perils of cyclones and other forms of storms affecting mainly the low-lying coastal zones and areas close to key rivers as they flow into the Indian Ocean. Given the geography of Mozambique with an extensive coastline of 2

740 km, most of the key economic zones have tended to be affected. In the last 10 years, cyclone storms have been one of the most destructive natural perils affecting both insured and uninsured properties. The list of cyclones that have had the highest impact on Mozambique since 1994 is as per Table 21.

Table 21–Cyclones in Mozambique since 1994

YEAR	MONTH	NAME	ZONES MOST AFFECTED
1994	March	Nadia	Nampula
1996	January	Bonita	Zambezia
2000	February	Eline	Gaza
	April	Hudah	Zambezia and Nampula
2001	March	Dera	Central parts of Mozambique
2003	January	Delfina	Nampula
	March	Japhet	Inhambane, Manica, Sofala and Gaza
2007	February	Fávio	Vilankulo
2008	March	Jókwè	Nampula
2012	January	Funso	Zambezia

b. Earthquake

As we noted in the presentation of natural catastrophes on a global scale, earthquakes have also had a major impact. However, Mozambique does not have a major exposure to this peril. It appears that the key areas of exposure are in the North-West of Mozambique, which is on the bottom end of the East African Rift Valley. This valley is considered as having a high earthquake risk exposure in Africa.

    c.   Drought

Droughts are also one of the most critical natural perils to which Mozambique is exposed. They have the highest impact on the majority rural population that is highly dependent on subsistence farming. However, this peril is completely uninsured given a lack of financial inclusion of the majority of people in this segment. At this stage, there is exploration of some basic forms of agricultural insurance which cover, amongst other things, lack of rainfall. We shall discuss further the local pilot project covering cotton in Chapter 14. We should now discuss key features of the insurance claims area.

2. KEY ELEMENTS IN THE CLAIMS AREA

There is a broad range of types of service that can be involved in a claims process depending on nature and type of claim as well as amounts involved. For simpler types of policies with low limits of exposure, most of the required procedures for settlement can involve only the claims team of the insurer that may have authority to settle valid claims straightaway. However, for more complex types of claims, there might be a need for referral to other entities for the handling of services that may be required. The types of entities that may be involved in processing of insurance claims are as described below.

2.1. Role of Intermediary in Claims

Firstly, we should note that the role of an insurance intermediary is not limited to introducing clients to insurers and collecting commission after settlement of premium. Intermediaries are also supposed to support their clients from the beginning to the end when there is a claim. Such an involvement at the claims stage should not be limited to post office type of service of simply passing on messages and documents from one end to the other. In order to play a more meaningful role in relation to claims, professional intermediaries will tend to do the following:

- Assist their clients by assessing areas of exposures.

- Guide the client in designing and arranging of appropriate insurance. There should be a report to the clients showing them what is covered and what is not covered.

- Establish an appropriate claims guideline with procedures to be followed by all insured people or all people using insured property which may be affected by claims.

- Advise the clients in the handling of claims in accordance with the insurance contract. Not all clients have a thorough understanding of their rights and responsibilities in insurance contracts.

- Assist the client in the claims assessment process and any negotiations that may be required at claim settlement stage.

- Guide the clients in applying any recommended measures after occurrence of a claim.

2.2. Buyers of Insurance and Covered Persons

Whether a buyer of insurance has an intermediary or not, it is vital for them to be aware of their responsibilities if a claim occurs. Here is a basic outline of the key responsibilities of an insured entity:

- Notify your insurance intermediary or insurer immediately of all claims that may occur. It is critical to receive an acknowledgement of the notification and a claim reference number.

- Follow procedures as defined by the insurer and ensure that all statements and declarations are accurate and true. Insurers can use failure to disclose true facts as a basis to reject claims.

- Take measures to prevent further damage, as per the principle of loss mitigation discussed in Chapter 3.

- Allow insurers to act on your behalf in relation to other parties that may be responsible. This is in alignment with the principle of subrogation, as we discussed in Chapter 3.

2.3. Insurance Claims Department

The claims department of an insurance company is a key element in the handling of claims and ensuring a timely and appropriate settlement. It is the principal link between the parties expecting a claim settlement and the specialists that may be required to determine what is covered, how much should be the settlement and how it should be settled. The principal duties of the claims department are as follows:

- Receive claim notifications and register them, in accordance with the Insurance Law

- Check the policy file and advise any co-insurers or reinsurers that may be involved on the account

- Assess the claim and decide if the policy is valid, if the event is covered and what is expected settlement

- Verify if there are interested parties with a financial interest to be notified and that may have a right to a portion of settlement

- Define which claims may be settled directly or may be referred to internal/external assessors

- Refer to an appropriate assessor, if required

- Settle the claim as soon as possible after following all recommended procedures

- Make recoveries from reinsurers and other parties from which the insurer has a right to make good their loss.

2.4. Claims Assessment

After the occurrence of a claim, an insurer may appoint a claims specialist that will review the claim in question and determine whether the event is covered and quantify how much is the indemnity and how it should be settled (Vaughan, 2009: 121). Such a person is known as a loss assessor or loss adjuster. For minor claims in basic types of policies such as motor insurance, it may be adequate for an insurer to appoint an **internal assessor**. For larger claims or more complex policies, it is highly recommended for the insurer and the client or intermediary to agree on the appointment of an **independent assessor** (Mehr and Cammack, 1972: 721). The principal motivation for appointment of an autonomous firm is to ensure access to certain types of expertise which may not exist within the insurance company and in order to reduce conflicts about fairness over the assessment process (Terblanche, 2010: 76). An employee of an insurer may be perceived to be biased in favour of his/her employer. Although assessors are appointed and paid by an insurer, their profession requires them to be independent and impartial. This is an important condition because, after the assessment, it is still up to the insurer and insured to reach an agreement on the indemnity based on the recommendations of the assessors.

Besides the assessor that may be appointed by an insurer, it is possible for insured entities to also nominate their own claim adjustor. Such types of claims adjustors appointed by the clients are known as **'public adjustors'** (Thomas and Reed: 4). There are no firms set up specifically as public adjustors in our market. However, there have been some large claims where the affected clients appointed firms that normally work as independent adjustors to act as some form of a public adjustor assisting them.

2.5. Other Service Providers

There are many other types of service providers that may be involved in the handling of claims, including the following:

- Panel beaters and other types of repairers of plant, machinery and equipment
- Salvage buyers
- Mediation and Courts

The role of most of the entities described above is self-explanatory. It may be useful to review the concept of salvage buyers. **Salvage** is the name used to refer to any remaining material with some form of residual economic value after an insured item is affected by loss or damage in an insurance policy (Waty, 2007: 93). Insurance companies try to reduce financial impact of claims by seeing if there are any parts of damaged property that can be reused or recycled or repaired. This is a very important function especially for types of insurance such as motor insurance where, even after a major loss, there is usually some residual material such as scrap metal that can be re-used. Besides reducing costs of claims, this is also one of the ways that insurance contributes to environmentally friendly practices by not allowing people to simply dump damaged items when it is economically viable to repair them.

3. TREATMENT OF CLAIMS IN THE INSURANCE LAW

The subject of how claims should be handled, in general, is covered in the section of the Insurance Law from Articles 136 to 147. The law also provides specific conditions that are relevant for claims in the different sections of the law including those covering the areas of reinsurance and different types of insurance contracts. Here is a brief review of some of the key conditions covered in the law:

3.1. Notification of a claim

According to Article 136, the insurer should be notified of any situation where the insured is aware of a reasonable probability that a claim may have occurred. Such notification should be done within the time period specified in the policy. If the policy does not specify a time-limit, the law provides a limit of 8 days after occurrence of the event or after the insured is aware of occurrence of a claim. This is a fairly limited time period. Most of the insurers in our market tend to offer a limit of up to 30 days or even more.

3.2. Mitigation of loss

According to Article 138, if a claim occurs, the insured should take all reasonable measures to reduce the loss or prevent it from worsening. This means that the insured should act 'as if uninsured'. This condition is aligned with principles of insurance, as we discussed in Chapter 3.

3.3. Cause of claim

In Article 142, there is a rule regarding cause of a claim. It appears to contain some elements of the traditional insurance principle of Proximate Cause, as we discussed in Chapter 3. However, this condition needs to be reviewed so that there is a clearer legal definition of the key elements of this principle. The definition in our Insurance Law suggests that, unless defined otherwise in the insurance policy, any claim arising from an insured peril is covered regardless of what may be the cause of the event. This legal rule is not completely in accordance with the conditions of proximate cause, as per the traditional practice of insurance.

Furthermore, in the second item covered in the same legal clause, it is also noted that if there is disagreement on causes or circumstances surrounding a claim, the insurer and insured should appoint a loss assess or to determine if the claim is covered. This legal rule appears to be at variance with standard practice of insurance business. A loss assessor is not appointed after dispute over a claim. The standard approach is to refer all sensitive or large claims to a loss assessor before there is any premature pronouncement whether the claim is covered or not. If there are disagreements about the decision of the insurers after the loss assessment process, the next step should be for the concerned parties to have access to some form of dispute resolution mechanisms. We shall discuss the different options that are available for dispute resolution later in this Chapter.

3.4. Malicious acts

According to Article 143, insurance does not cover any claim intentionally caused by the policyholder or insured entity or covered persons. This is in alignment with traditional principles of insurance. Standard insurance policies in our market also have clauses which clearly exclude such events.

3.5. Settlement of claims

Articles 144 to 147 define rules regarding settlement of claims. One of the key rules defined is that after there is an agreement on settlement of a loss, the insurer should settle the claim within a time period of 30 days. Although the intention of this rule is understandable, there is a need for it to be reviewed. Standard insurance policy wordings in our market specify that, as part of the claim settlement process, the insurer reserves the right to define the most appropriate way to indemnify the insured. It should be noted that, in alignment with the principles of insurance, the objective of the insurer is to avoid unjust enrichment and to put the insured back in the position where he/she was before the claim (Silva 1963: 49). In order to achieve this objective, the insurer may consider the following methods, as outlined in the manual on Principles of Short Term Insurance of the IISA (2011A: 103):

- **Replace** the damaged insured item with a similar item. This option is applied for such items as Glass, Windscreens, Car Radios and Jewellery.

- **Repair** the same damaged insured item. This method is used mainly in the Motor class of insurance in cases where it makes economic sense to repair the vehicle. In our market, on average 70% is viewed as the threshold above which a claim is viewed as a Total Loss.

- **Reinstatement** is the method used for settling claims for property such as buildings. After damage from a Fire, the insurer could try to rebuild the property at either the same location or an alternative site.

- Make **cash settlements** to cover the loss. This is also known as **cash-in-lieu**.

In the case where an insurer may elect to reinstate a damaged item such as a building, it is important to note that after the signing of the loss agreement, the required processes of re-building of properties such as factories can take as much as one year. Therefore, it is vital to ensure that there are no unrealistic expectations of swift cash settlements in all cases.

Moreover, when insurers apply the method of replacement, sometimes the insured may benefit in the sense that he/she could end up receiving something new when the damaged item was not new. In order to prevent problems of unjust enrichment, the insurer can apply what is known as **betterment**. This means that the insurer may instruct the insured to contribute to the payment of the replacement item. However, in cases where the items are insured on a **new replacement value basis**, betterment would not be applicable.

3.6. Provisional settlement

According to the third clause of Article 146, after 90 days from the date of submission of a valid claim, the insured can request for a **provisional loss settlement** of up to 50% of estimated total settlement amount provided that the claim has been appropriately validated by the insurer. It is important to note that the law has left the insurer to agree or not to such a request for partial payments. For minor claims within the financial capacity of the local market, it is feasible for the local market to achieve this objective.

However, for any large loss on a complex risk, it is highly unlikely that the insurance market would be in a position to make an interim settlement within such a short time. The first problem, as we have already discussed in this chapter, is that there is very limited capacity for local loss assessment.

The second issue is that some claims may require complex investigations before settlements are done. Major accidents such as the November 2013 LAM airline accident, as discussed in the previous Chapter, can take many years before there is any settlement. Thirdly, in cases where there is significant reinsurance involved, the local insurers do not have financial capacity to make any interim payments before receiving respective settlement from concerned reinsurers.

3.7. Delays of loss settlement

According to Article 147, an insurer could be held liable for delays in settlement of claims. For such a situation, interest could be charged at the legal rate plus an additional 2%. We believe that this condition needs also to be reviewed. There are numerous questions that need to be noted in order for such a condition to be more meaningful. This is one of the areas that can be left for courts to determine depending on circumstances of each situation.

4. CLAIMS PROCEDURES

Besides the conditions defined in the Insurance Law as described above, we must also note key procedures in insurance claims. There are no uniform approaches in our market in the handling of claims. For areas of common interest such as obligatory insurance policies, it may be beneficial for the insurance association to consider taking initiatives to develop guidelines in order to ensure that certain minimum standards are observed by the market. This can be useful for purposes of eliminating ambiguities. We shall review some of the key procedures below

4.1. Claim forms

There are no specific rules and regulations in the Insurance Law concerning completion of claim forms and their presentation. This is a critical omission given that this procedure is a key element of fulfilment of the principle of Good Faith, as discussed in Chapter 3. In the same way that there are clear duties and obligations of the insurer and insured at the beginning of the insurance contract, it is also essential to clearly define rules on disclosure after occurrence of a claim. This is also crucial given that a significant number of claims are rejected as a result of issues arising from how claims are presented.

4.2. Excess

One of the standard conditions of insurance which causes a lot of distress among most insurance buyers at the time of lodging claims is the oncept of excesses or deductibles. An excess or deductible refers to the portion of an insured claim that should be for the account of the insured. Not many people understand the logic of an excess or deductible. There tends to be an assumption that if you are 'fully' insured for certain perils and have paid your premium, the insurer should settle the claim in full after occurrence of a claim.

Unfortunately, that is not how insurance works. One of the main preoccupations of insurance, as defined in the traditional principle relating to loss mitigation, is that the insured must always behave 'as if uninsured'. In alignment with this principle, the insured should take all measures possible to prevent losses and to reduce impact of those that they may fail to prevent. As part of the mechanisms to ensure that the insured takes measures to mitigate losses, most types of insurance of property and liability may have a form of contribution in eventual claims by the insured.

Furthermore, as we discussed in Chapter 4 in relation to the concept of risk management, in cases where there is a high degree of certainty of a loss, it is usually not the objective of insurance to cover such losses. This is part of the reason why insurers apply excesses or deductibles for types of insurances with a high likelihood of repetitive losses.

As we have already discussed when we were reviewing the Hospital Cash Product, excesses are intended to reduce bureaucracy of handling numerous minor claims that can be easily handled by the insured client. They are also intended to prevent the abuse of insurance.

4.3. Knock-for-knock

In our market we do not have any formalised **knock-for-knock agreements**. This is a type of agreement usually applied for Motor class of business. In such an agreement, two insurers may agree that when their policyholders have an accident, each insurer would process the claim for their respective clients. This is intended to achieve efficiency by avoiding a situation where insurers spend money and time trying to make recoveries against each other (Cannar, 1979: 227). It is believed that over time there is a fair allocation of claims costs. The main concern about it is that those clients that might not have caused an accident end up with a claim on their records with their insurers and this can affect the assessment by underwriters of the same client in future negotiations for renewal of insurance.

Given the lack of knock-for-knock agreements in our market, some insurers do not even want to process claims of their clients or assist them in recovering from the insurer that might have caused an accident. The moment such insurers have an impression that their client was not at fault, they instruct their client to go and sort out his/her claim with the insurer of the third party. Given that the other insurer does not have any pre-existing agreements with the client from the other insurer, the contact between the two parties tends to have a lot of friction. In some cases, the other insurer has very limited knowledge of the insured item . In most cases there is not a lot of trust between the two parties on a number of things including the basis of valuation of the claimed item since the other insurer often does not have that information.

We believe that our market could explore opportunities of setting up knock-for-knock agreements. There is an even more sophisticated model of this type of agreement in Portugal. The model used in Portugal is known as *Indemnização Directa ao Segurado* (*IDS*), as noted in the Motor Insurance manual of the Associação Portuguesa de Seguradores (2001: 34). It is more elaborate and has a broader scope of cover than knock-for-knock. It is restricted to motor accidents where there are no disputes about who caused the accident, a situation defined in Portuguese as *Declaração Amigável de Acidente Automóvel* (*DAAA*)[1].

4.4. Fast-track claims handling

One of the key challenges we have noted in our market is that insurers expect all clients to follow the same procedures regardless of size and nature of claims. In other markets in our region such as Botswana, Namibia and South Africa, some insurers have adopted the concept of 'fast-track claims handling'. This procedure is intended to speed up the processing of minor uncomplicated claims which normally have a high frequency of occurrence (Thomas and Reed, 1977: 3). A good example of such types of small claims is damage of motor windscreens. Such damages tend to have a low cost of repair or replacement but tend to occur more frequently than all other types of claims. They do not require complex loss assessing. It is possible for an insurer to reduce turnaround time of processing of such claims from many

1   Please see more information on this other items on the website of ISP as consulted on 24/04/14: http://www.isp.pt/NR/rdonlyres/95A10CFE-C814-4B73-B0E9-CBBFD3D46B34/0/Guiawebuv.pdf

weeks to less than 48 hours by reducing bureaucracy in the claim settlement process through a fast-track procedure.

4.5. Ex gratia

In some cases, after establishing that a claim can be rejected, it is possible for an insurer to consider the option of *ex gratia*. This is a situation where an insurer may agree to settle a claim that is believed not to be covered. This is usually done as some form of gesture of good will or in consideration of the business relationship between parties involved (Chiejina, 2004: 170). In most instances, the option of granting *ex gratia* is not automatically available for risks that are subject to reinsurance. As part of conditions of reinsurance, such offers are usually subject to specific authorisation by the reinsurer. Furthermore, as part of underwriting rules of most insurers, all requests for *ex gratia* are supposed to be referred to appropriate senior management for review.

4.6. Claims ratio

The **claims ratio** or **loss ratio** is one of the key items that insurers and insurance intermediaries tend to measure. It is an indication of the performance of an insured portfolio by comparing claims to premium. It is usually used as the basis for negotiations of annual renewal processes of insurance policies. The calculation itself is not difficult if you have all the basic required elements. If a client were to pay premium of Mt 200 at the beginning of the period of insurance and if there was a claim of Mt 150, the calculation would be as follows:

Claims Ratio = Claim ÷ Premium × 100
Claims ratio = 150 ÷ 200 × 100
Claims ratio = 75%

We should note that the major concern with calculation of loss ratios is how to define the makeup of the two key elements. The key questions to consider in this calculation are as follows:

- Should the figure for premium include taxes charged on premium? The taxes collected are not funds available for financing risk and the administration of the insurer. However, they represent part of the cost to the client.

- Should we include the commissions paid to brokers and the administration fees of the insurer in the calculation of the claims ratio? The idea behind this question is that the assessment of claims performance should be on the basis of Net Claims Ratio after deducting all expense items.

4.7. Claims rejection

We should now discuss the most contentious procedure in insurance business—claims rejection. This is the procedure which is followed when the insurer believes that the insured is not entitled to settlement for a claim lodged. Many practitioners of insurance tend to use the word 'repudiation' to refer to this procedure. From most of my research, it appears that this is not the most appropriate legal term. In this book, we are going to use the more appropriate expression— rejection of claims (Silva, 2000: 144). We shall not discuss in this book the different technical legal basis that an insurer may use to avoid or cancel a policy or reject a claim.

5. DISPUTE RESOLUTION

Following the rejection of a claim, as discussed above, often that is not the end of the story. From our experience in this market, it appears that many clients do not understand or are dissatisfied with the decisions of insurers. As noted by Pratt (2008: 43) the time of lodging of claims is a sensitive period because at that time the client could still be suffering 'stress' or worse still 'distress' from the event leading to the claim. However, this period of tension is also the time when the insurance company has a unique opportunity to deliver its services as expected and reassure the client.

In a study covered by Kuper (2006:127), he notes that, after a perceived failure in delivery, mechanisms aimed at resolving issues arising from such situations can make substantial contributions in restoring confidence in the system in question. Like in most insurance markets worldwide, our insurance sector has complaints and conflict concerning mainly insurance claims. There is a limited range of accessible mechanisms in our market for effective resolution of these issues. We believe that our market could follow examples from some of the neighbouring countries that have taken proactive measures of setting up formal dispute resolution systems as we shall discuss below.

5.1. Internal dispute settlement

As part of consumer protection initiatives, insurers are encouraged to setup 'internal dispute resolution mechanisms' (Lester, 2009: 17). This is supposed to be an accessible channel for settling consumer disputes without wasting money and time of aggrieved parties. In our current Insurance Law there is no requirement for the insurance operators to setup such a mechanism for handling of complaints by insured entities. We have not seen any evidence of any insurer in our market that has taken a voluntary initiative of following this emerging global practice. We believe that this is one of the key areas that should be addressed in the Insurance Law, or through voluntary initiatives of the Insurance Association.

5.2. Formal dispute settlement mechanisms

If the customer is not satisfied with the efforts of the internal mechanism as outlined above, there should be an optional mechanism in the insurance market. We are aware that there is a department responsible for handling of complaints in the office of the Insurance Regulator. However, there is a need to formalise this setup or to create an appropriate new structure for handling of insurance disputes. This can be in the form of an insurance ombudsman.

The word ombudsman comes from Swedish where it means 'legal representative'. The word is now used to refer to an official that has the responsibility of receiving and handling complaints and queries from the public in relation to certain critical services such as government service, pensions, insurance or banking. An ombudsman is also known as a public advocate in some countries. A similar entity is known as *'ouvidoria'* in Brazil or *'provedor do cliente'* in Portugal. In Swaziland, the same type of entity is known as the Claims Adjudicator. You may read more about Swazi entity on their website:

http://www.rirf.co.sz/2/index.php?option=com_content &view=article&id=100&Itemid=78

The main goal of such entities is to resolve disputes concerning insurance in a manner which is fair, transparent and efficient (IISA 2011B: 211). According to Judge Brian Galgut (2008: 29), the Ombudsman for Long-term Insurance in South Africa, by helping to resolve disputes, such initiatives also contribute to promoting public confidence in insurance business.

Besides attending to specific complaints in the defined areas of focus, the office of the ombudsman also aims to produce regular reports. These reports are intended to address any systematic issues that may be identified. As could be noted in the reports of the insurance ombudsman in South Africa, many of the complaints from consumers are valid cases. We believe that the insurance market does not have to wait for the government to setup such mechanisms. This is another area where, through some form of self-regulation, the insurance association with the support of the insurance regulator could take the initiative of setting up such an entity, on a voluntary basis (Lester, 2009: 18).

Furthermore, such an initiative could be improved by ensuring that all policy documents contain specific reference to a clear complaints procedure and ensure that there is an independent official with appropriate skills and authority to handle a defined range of complaints. The dispute resolution mechanism is intended to cover small claims up to a defined amount and may be used mainly by private individuals and small enterprises. It is vital to always ensure that large and complex claims should continue to rely on formal litigation mechanisms.

5.3. Labour tribunal

The obligatory WCA insurance, as described in Chapter 9, is the only class of insurance where the insurer or insured can automatically refer claims for an independent review by a specialised type of court, as defined in Articles 27 to 32 of the WCA Insurance Law. This mechanism tends to work fairly efficiently without causing major costs for both parties. The most critical challenge faced by this court has been how to interpret the new rules following the changes in the law on WCA insurance.

5.4. Arbitration

Arbitration is a formal legal system for an amicable resolution of disputes. The establishment in Mozambique of the mechanism of arbitration was formalized with the passing of Law number 11/99 of 7 July 1999. The institution which supports the arbitration process is known as the Centre for Arbitration Conciliation and Mediation (CACM)[2]. At the moment, costs are not low since both parties have to appoint lawyers and referees to take part in the process. It appears that it also takes a significant amount of time for cases to be resolved. It is not a useful option for the small claims affecting the majority of complaints regarding insurance claims.

5.5. Civil Court

If there is failure of amicable means of resolution of disputes described above, then, the only other option is to go through the formal legal system of litigation. This means that the concerned party can try to take the case to the civil court system.

---

2. You may find information on their website: http://www.cacm.org.mz/

In Mozambique, like many other countries in our region, it takes many years for most cases to be heard and be decided on. The process involves a significant amount of bureaucracy which adds complexity and high costs. Unless there are huge amounts of money involved in the dispute, most people do not even attempt to exercise their rights through this route.

6. SKILLS DEVELOPMENT IN CLAIMS

One of the key reasons for poor service delivery in claims, in general, is connected to a lack of skills and key service providers in claims. The field of loss assessment has a critical shortage of skills in our market. There are a few individuals and a handful of small local firms that handle claims assessments for mainly motor insurance and other small claims. In order to handle most of the large or complex claims, our market has tended to depend on foreign contractors from mainly South Africa, Portugal, Botswana and Zimbabwe.

Furthermore, contracts for such foreign assessors are often done in a manner that does not contribute to local skills development. Given that such services are secured on a free-lance basis, the contractors are able to fly in, execute the required task and fly out. This approach has served the purpose of ensuring some form of claims assessment service up to now. However, this approach is not sustainable and does not promote any transfer of skills. The insurance market could review the rules regarding hiring of foreign assessors and see how local assessors could be involved in cases where foreign resources may be hired.

Furthermore, existing local assessors should consider setting up an association in order to assist in the planning and implementation of development plans for their area of business. Such a body could also consider creating alliances with the Institute of Loss Adjusters of Southern Africa (ILASA), which appears to be interested in collaborating with other representative associations in the region. You may read more about ILASA on the following website: http://www.ilasa.org.za/

CONCLUSION

We have discussed key elements of insurance claims in this chapter. We have noted that there are a number of items that could be reviewed in order to improve the quality of service in the area of claims. There is a need for guidelines to clarify some of the legal conditions in our Insurance Law with regards to items such as realistic time periods for settlement of claims. As we discussed, there are also legal conditions in the Insurance Law that are not aligned with the current practices of the insurance market.

Then, we also looked at the question of resolution of claims. We noted that our market could take the initiative of formally setting up internal and external dispute resolution mechanisms. We also observed that the market relies heavily on foreign firms for loss assessment services. We have proposed initiatives aimed at promoting development of skills in loss assessment and other areas of claims.

REFERENCES

- Associação Portuguesa de Seguradores (2001). Seguro Automóvel. Lisboa: Associação Portuguesa de Seguradores

- Mehr, Robet, I. and Cammack, Emerson (1972). Principles of Insurance. 5th Edition. Illinois: Richard D. Irwin, Inc.

- Meyer, Peter (1997). *Tropical cyclones*. Zurich: Swiss Reinsurance Company.

- Terblanche, Stefan (2010). The insurance loss adjuster: a value-adding professional... at a cost in Cover. Cape Town: Cover Publications. October 2010. Pages 76-77.

- Thomas, Paul, I. and Reed, Prentice, Sr. (1977). Adjustment of Property Losses. 4th Edition. New York: McGraw-Hill, Inc.

- Vaughan, Emmet, J. (1992) *Fundamentals of risk and insurance*. 6th Edition. New York: John Wiley & Sons Inc

CHAPTER 14

EMERGING GLOBAL DEVELOPMENT TRENDS

From the beginning of this book we have focused on the history of development of insurance in the past. We started our review from the ancient origins of insurance in China in 3 000 B.C., through key historical milestones up to the time of writing of this book. As such, we have covered key developments in a period of 5 thousand years. As we have noted in the study of this period, key developments in international markets have significantly influenced developments in our market. In this chapter, we are now going to look at key emerging trends that we believe are also going to affect how we shall do insurance business in the future.

Furthermore, we shall discuss some of the key preoccupations driving some of the major changes we have started seeing in key international markets. We shall also discuss some of the recent development policies and initiatives in Mozambique that are also going to contribute to shaping the future development of our market.

1. CONSUMER PROTECTION

Protection of consumers is one of the key global trends affecting insurance and other financial services worldwide. This trend is driven mainly by an observation that, for certain types of services, business operators cannot be trusted to act in good faith and treat customers fairly. Consumer protection is also one of the key objectives of our insurance regulator, as defined in our Insurance Law and in the current strategy document of the insurance authorities (ISSM, 2014: 9).

Furthermore, according to Lester R. (2009: 1), 'weak consumer protection and a lack of financial literacy can render households vulnerable to unfair and abusive practices by financial institutions—as well as financial fraud and scams.' He further elaborates that protection is required especially for insurance contracts because of their 'opaque nature' (Ibid, 2009: 6). In insurance, the situation of insured clients is even worse because they cannot see and assess the service which may be provided in case a covered event may or may not occur. At the time of paying for the service, the consumer has no means of knowing what service he/ she may receive in the future. As a result, the consumer is not in a position to make fully informed decisions at the time of buying insurance.

As part of the efforts to resolve the issues outlined above, we have seen a number of initiatives aimed at improving the protection of consumers. Some of the key interventions include development of internal and formal dispute resolution mechanisms, establishment of principles aimed at encouraging fair treatment of consumers, setting of rules regarding disclosure and formation of financial mechanisms to protect innocent victims of abuse by financial markets. We should now discuss some of the key new efforts aimed at supporting consumer protection.

1.1. Consumer Protection Legislation

We have observed that, as one of the key global trends, policy-makers have started drafting laws that treat specifically the question of consumer protection. The Consumer Protection Law[3] of Mozambique was passed on 28 September 2009. In general, it covers the same key areas of interest in protection of consumers like similar legislation in Portugal and South Africa. After the passing of this law here, the next key measures which are still to be executed in full are the setting up of appropriate consumer protection institutions, enforcement of the law and implementation of public awareness campaigns.

1.2. Market conduct

The next important trend we should discuss is that of the growing concern with how financial institutions treat their customers. We would like to look at a specific initiative known as **Treat Customers Fairly** (TCF). It was started by regulatory authorities in the United Kingdom and has been

---

3. Referred to in Portuguese as '*Lei nº. 22/2009 de 28 de Setembro*'

followed by other countries. According to the Financial Services Authority (2006:5), the TCF approach to consumer protection is based mainly on a belief that protection of interests of consumers is not only the responsibility of the authorities. They see a critical need for business to take measures to ensure that interests of consumers are a central preoccupation of their strategy. This initiative was part of the changes implemented in 2012 following failure of existing systems to protect the economy during the global financial crisis of 2007-08. The principal aims of TCF is to achieve the following six outcomes, as has been identified by the same authorities:

- 'Consumers can be confident that they are dealing with firms where the fair treatment of customers is central to the corporate culture'

- 'Products and services marketed and sold in the retail market are designed to meet the needs of identified consumer groups and are targeted accordingly'

- 'Consumers are provided with clear information and kept appropriately informed before, during and after the point of sale'

- 'Where consumers receive advice, the advice is suitable and takes account of their circumstances'

- 'Consumers are provided with products that perform as firms have led them to expect, and the associated service is of an acceptable standard and as they have been led to expect'

- 'Consumers do not face unreasonable post-sale barriers imposed by firms to change product, switch provider, submit a claim or make a complaint'

We believe that the principles of Treating Customers Fairly could become a global benchmark for ensuring good conduct by financial markets.

1.3. Know Your Customer

There has also been a growing trend of application of the **Know Your Customer** (KYC) concept. The rules of KYC serve the interests of consumer protection and is also a vital component of the Anti-Money Laundering regulatory framework, as we discussed in Chapter 5. In accordance with KYC, the insurer is supposed to do a 'fact-finding' exercise in order to gather enough information on the 'personal and financial situation' of a customer in order to provide appropriate advice (Lester, 2009: 14). This concept is already being applied in our banking sector. It is not yet part of standard practice in the local insurance sector.

1.4. Financial Product Disclosure Conditions

In markets such as Australia and South Africa, it is now part of product compliance for insurance policies to provide certain information in the interest of the customers. This information is presented in what is referred to as a Product Disclosure Statement. The document provides information on the key features of the product as well as commission, fees and costs charged by the insurer. It is supposed to be written in plain language and is supposed to guide the client on all the terms and conditions of the policy under review. This is a useful document especially for areas of insurance business such as insurance of private individuals.

1.5. Right to withdraw

The right to withdraw is also seen as a vital mechanism for consumer protection (Lester, 2009: 14). It is required mainly for long term life insurance policies and other types of contracts that usually have punitive conditions for cancellation. As part of this right, insurance policies are supposed to offer what is known as a '**cooling off period**' or '**free look period**'. It is usually a period of 14 to 30 days in which new customers can cancel their policy, if they are not satisfied. Such a cancellation should be permitted without any punitive clauses and any deductions, provided it is within the specified period and before occurrence of a claim.

2. SHIFT OF THE SUPERVISION MODEL

The traditional model of insurance supervision relies on a 'compliance-based' approach. In this approach, regulators wait for the insurers to do their business as they see fit and then submit certain specific reports at a given time period, as defined in the Insurance Law. Insurers are expected to do their business in accordance with 'prudential rules' defined in the insurance legislation. The principal role of the supervisory authority is to establish that there is full compliance to these rules. In this model, the same rules are applied for all companies in the same way, regardless of the different business philosophies of the different entities.

There is a significant shift emerging in international financial markets on how to approach and handle supervision of banking, insurance and pensions. This new trend was started in the 1990's in the USA following problems of failures of insurance companies in the 1980s (Swiss Re, 1999: 22). In Mozambique like in other African countries, the banking sector has made a lot more progress than the insurance sector in starting to implement this new model. Insurance business in our market is still firmly rooted in the traditional model (Mutenga: 2014: 75). However, it appears that through interventions of organisations such as the International Association of Insurance Supervisors (IAIS) and the International Accounting Standards Board (IASB), our authorities are conscious of the need to develop the regulatory framework, in alignment with emerging global standards (José, 2013: 3).

The new model of supervision is known as 'risk-based supervision.' In this approach, the supervisors assess the way each company is treating risks. Instead of fixing the same rules for all insurers in the market, the regulators focus on the 'principles' of doing business in each company and assess the specific requirements for the different portfolios of risk in the business under review. Insurers assuming higher levels of risks would require higher levels of capital. This is very different from the current approach where the minimum capital requirement is a fixed amount notwithstanding the fact that insurers have different types and sizes of business.

Given that most insurers do not insure only one type of business, the risk-based model also requires an understanding of allocation of capital between the different portfolios that an insurer may want to underwrite. Furthermore, the regulators also need to assess risk at a broader level than in the traditional model. The regulator would need to look at Strategic Risk, Market Risk and Liquidity Risk. We discussed this broad spectrum of risks in Chapter 4.

Furthermore, taking into account this dynamic nature of the risk-based supervision approach, it is vital for the respective supervisory authorities to have appropriate legal authority that would enable them to define rules emerging from their assessment of risks in the companies. The insurance law and regulations would no longer contain the same rules for all operators. The minimum conditions on items such as required levels of capital are defined depending on assessment of risks to be covered in each portfolio. Furthermore, the authorities would need to develop appropriate skills and capacity to handle this new approach where there are no clear and simple rules applicable for all situations. This is one of the major reasons why we agree with the observation that insurance regulators also need to have access to actuarial skills (Hafeman, 2009: 18).

3. FINANCIAL INCLUSION

The next key trend we would like to discuss is that of financial inclusion. It has emerged following the signing in 2011 of the Maya Declaration in Riviera Maya in Mexico. Central bankers and financial regulators from several countries including Banco de Moçambique[4] made a commitment to improve access of the low-income population to financial services, as part of global initiatives aimed at reducing the widening gap between rich and poor people in the global economy. Mozambique also suffers from this problem, as was observed by the World Bank when it stated that 'the deceleration of poverty reduction in the face of robust economic growth is the defining development challenge in today's Mozambique.'[5]

Furthermore, as per the Human Development Index (HDI) of the United Nations Development Programme (UNDP), Mozambique is part of a group of countries at the bottom of the ranking (Bruna, 2013: 182). This index assesses human welfare on the basis of quality of education, health and level of income for the citizens. Financial inclusion is

---

4. The Central Bank of Mozambique
5. As noted on the following website on 22/April/2014:http://www.worldbank.org/en/results/2013/04/02/mozambique-sustaining-broad-based-and-inclusive-growth

supposed to contribute towards the resolution of this challenge of a lack of human development despite economic growth.

According to the Alliance for Financial Inclusion (2013: 31), the concept of financial inclusion consists of the following elements:

- The enabling of 'access' for the target population to affordable financial services.

- The promotion of 'usage' by the intended population of financial services on a frequent and regular basis.

- Ensuring that there is 'quality' of financial services that satisfy genuine needs of the target population.

Furthermore, according to a report by McKinsey & Company (2009), the most suitable target population for financial inclusion are the 'economically active poor' who may have adequate money to cover the costs of appropriate financial services that satisfy their needs. According to the same discussion document, traditional business models are not effective for purposes of enabling access to this untapped business opportunity. In order for business to better serve this target group, there have been the following key development trends:

- Exploration of new 'technology' to overcome challenges of access and to enable effective delivery. The market in Mozambique is seeing the same trend with use of technology such as mobile telephones. There is also an agricultural insurance project using satellite technology, although in its initial stage.

- Improved '*diversification*' of services in order to provide a broader range of relevant products.

- Growing '*commercialization*' of services for this target population. The first forms of interventions were mainly aid or charitable activities. There is a growing participation of business operators from different sectors looking for ways to enter this market segment. This is vital for purposes of ensuring sustainability.

- Increasing number of entities looking at financial inclusion. In Mozambique, there is involvement of insurers, commercial banks, mobile telephone operators, agricultural development agencies, agricultural suppliers and other entities.

- Regulators are playing a more significant role in creating an enabling environment for the development of inclusive markets. The Ministry of Finance and respective regulatory agencies have already taken initiatives aimed at promoting financial inclusion.

As part of local initiatives in Mozambique, the Central Bank and the Ministry of Finance adopted the Financial Sector Development Strategy 2013-2022, in April 2013. The main goal of this policy is to achieve financial inclusion, in alignment with global initiatives described above. The policy is still to be fully developed and implemented. However, from the presentation of preliminary documents, it appears to give a strong indication that the authorities will support business activities in the financial sector intended to achieve this development-related goal. Tentative plans under this policy also show that the policy-makers intend to address some of the key deficits in our regulatory framework.

4. MICROINSURANCE

Microinsurance is the initiative of the insurance sector aimed at contributing to the global trend of financial inclusion (José, 2013: 3). According to a conference paper by Karekezi (2014: 9), microinsurance and financial inclusion are critical factors for supporting the global economic preoccupation regarding 'inclusive growth'. Microinsurance can be defined as 'the protection of low-income people against specific perils in exchange for regular premium payments proportionate to the likelihood and cost of the risk involved' (Churchill, 2006: 12).

As we have already noted in this book, our Insurance Law has provisions for the underwriting and distribution of microinsurance. It can be handled by either traditional insurers or by specialised microinsurance companies and microinsurance agents. In the Mozambican market, the main microinsurance products that are available include the following:

- Funeral insurance, micro-credit life and credit default insurance,
- Hospital Cash insurance and
- Weather Index Insurance.

However, there are also challenges in our market for development related initiatives aimed at promoting financial inclusion. Here are examples of areas that could be improved in order to promote financial inclusion:

- As we discussed in Chapter 6, one of the key legal requirements for a valid insurance agreement, as defined in Article 103 of the Insurance Law, is that it must be reduced to writing and must have a (wet) signature and stamp of the insurer. Some of the ideas that have been explored effectively in countries like Ghana, Kenya and Zimbabwe involve the issuing of policies in a digital electronic form via the mobile telephone. It appears that with our current legislation, such approaches would not satisfy local compliance requirements

- There is a need to review the rules regarding premium taxes such as the Stamp Tax. Some of the new initiatives such as Weather Index end up being charged the highest rate of tax because they fall in a category of other business which has the highest level of tax.

5. TAKAFUL

As a further part of the process of the developments connected to financial inclusion, there has also been the recent emergence of the concept of Takaful financial services in mainly countries that observe Islamic religious law of Sharia. In this religious legal system, the following components of the Western model of financial services are considered unethical and illegal:

- The practice of charging interest.
- Gambling or business of taking of risk or speculation on uncertainty.

In order to address the concerns outlined above, there have been developments of financial systems that aim to comply with this belief system. For the area of insurance, the key changes include an approach of risk sharing instead of risk transfer. When risks are shared in a pool, then both parties are supposed to share costs of claims suffered and jointly benefit from losses or profits arising from the undertaking. At this stage, we do not yet have any Takaful financial products in Mozambique.

6. RISE IN USAGE OF TECHNOLOGY

According to Bhattad (2012: 13), one of the key global trends in the insurance sector is the growth in application of technology to 'automate the underwriting process and increase direct sales'. This development trend has been driven by increasing availability of electronic technology which allows insurers to process vast amounts of data very quickly and very accurately. Technology is also enabling effective access to many people at very low cost and prompt delivery. The use of electronic devices as well as handling of business through internet, emails, social websites and short message services (SMS) is part of an approach to marketing known as **'digital marketing'**.

Furthermore, the growing use of technology is one of the key drivers leading to another key trend referred to as **'disintermediation'**. This refers to a process where suppliers of services are able to 'cut out the middleman' by offering new and more efficient means for consumers to buy directly from them without relying on traditional distribution channels. However, we should note that insurance intermediaries will remain an essentially feature of insurance business given the vital advisory service that they provide, as we discussed in Chapter 8.

7. CODES OF CONDUCT

The drafting of codes of conduct is also one of the key trends following recent high profile cases of white collar crime and the financial crisis in international markets. As defined on the Wikipedia website, a code of conduct is 'a set of rules outlining the responsibilities of, or proper practices for, an individual, party or organization.' Many companies have their own set of codes of conduct. Insurance underwriting, insurance broking, banking and other financial services are business activities where there has been particular focus for development of codes of conduct. As part of the key emerging changes in the insurance sector, in countries such as Australia, the operators have elaborated appropriate codes of conduct as a form of self-regulation. The different types of codes tend to have the following general aims:

- To commit practitioners and professionals in the sector to higher standards of customer service.

- To provide mechanisms for receiving and appropriately handling of complaints and disputes that cause damage to the reputation of the sector.

- To improve consumer confidence in the sector.

CONCLUSION

In this Chapter, we have discussed some of the key trends that are beginning to emerge in international markets. Like in the past, future development of our insurance market will be influenced by these global trends. The key driver of the changes is a preoccupation with improving financial soundness of financial markets and improving protection of the consumer. The current insurance legislation of Mozambique already shows clear indications of support by the policy-makers of some of the key emerging trends such as microinsurance and financial inclusion.

However, we have also identified a number of areas requiring improvement. There is a need for guidelines on microinsurance in order to provide clarity required by the market. There is also a need for the market to develop dispute resolution mechanisms as part of initiatives aimed at improving consumer protection. This is one of the key areas where there are major gaps. Such an initiative would be a critical achievement in measures aimed at restoring consumer confidence.

Finally, we have also noted that there is a major shift in the regulatory framework in finance from a compliance-based approach to a risk-based regulatory framework. The banking system in Mozambique is slightly ahead of insurance in efforts to implement this new model. Part of the key conditions that will enable our regulatory authorities to be ready for this 'brave new world' is access to actuarial skills. As we have already noted in this book, such skills are very scarce in Mozambique. The market needs to find ways to start promoting the studying of actuarial sciences and for appropriately qualified people to be given a chance for training and development in order for them to become qualified professional actuaries.

REFERENCES

- Bruna, Natasha (2013). Ambiente de negócios e a competitividade da economia moçambicana in Mosca João; Abbas, Máriam and Bruna, Natasha (eds) Economia de Moçambique 2001-2010. Maputo. Escolar Editora. Pp.141-195.

- Bhattad, Mahesh (2012). *Trends in Insurance Channels.* Capgemini

- Churchill, Craig (2006). What is insurance for the poor? In Churchill (ed.). Protecting the poor—A microinsurance compendium. Geneva: International Labour Organisation

- Forichi, Lovemore (2014). Insuring resilient agriculture in the African Insurance Bulletin. Issue no. 0005 of May 2014. Doala: The African Insurance Organisation. Pp. 26-28.

- FSA (2006). *Treating customers fairly—towards fair outcomes for consumers*. London: The Financial Services Authority.

- Galgut, B. 2008. 'Promoting public confidence in the industry' in Cover, April 2008, Vol. 20, no. 11, Cover Publications: Randburg, pp. 29–30.

- IAIS (2012). Application Paper on Regulation and Supervision supporting Inclusive Insurance Markets. International Association of Insurance Supervisors

- ISSM (2014). Strategic Plan for 2014-18, as per their website: http://www.issm.gov.mz/images/Legislacao/pe.pdf

- José, Domingos, António (2013). *Legislação aplicável à actividade seguradora*. As per presentation at the 2nd Insurance Seminar of the ISSM.

- Kuper, L. 2006. *Ethics—the leadership edge*. Cape Town: Zebra Press

- Lester, R. (2009). 'Consumer Protection Insurance' in Wehrhahn, R., The Primer Series on Insurance, Washington: The World Bank, Issue 7, August 2009.

- Mutenga, S. (2014). *Enhancing Enterprise Risk Management in the African Insurance Industry*. In the African Insurance Bulletin. Issue no. 0005 of May 2014. Doala: The African Insurance Organisation. Pp. 75-77

- Pratt, K. 2008. 'The evolution of claims' in the **Journal** of the Chartered Insurance Institute: London. February 2008. pp. 43–44.

- Swiss Re (1999). From risk to capital: An insurance perspective. Zurich: Swiss Re

- The World Bank, as per their website on 22/April/2014: http://www.worldbank.org/en/results/2013/04/02/mozambique-sustaining-broad-based-and-inclusive-growth

CHAPTER 15

KEY RECOMMENDATIONS

We would like to begin this final Chapter by acknowledging that significant progress has been achieved in the development of insurance business in Mozambique since the liberalisation of the market in 1992. We have gone through further reforms of insurance legislation in 2003 and 2010. We have seen how the market has grown from a monopoly in the transition period after independence to the vibrant economic sector that we have today. However, we have also noted that there are a number of areas where further improvements can still be achieved in the future.

We have observed that there are a number of aspects of our insurance legislation that can be improved in order to provide more protection for consumers and to support the development of our market. At the same time, the business entities in the sector do not have to wait for supportive measures from the authorities. Most of the challenges facing the insurance sector can be addressed through initiatives driven by the operators. We have already observed that the Insurance Association has taken steps to address some of the issues that have been identified. We shall now discuss some of the key recommendations that have been discussed in this book in order to support further development of the insurance sector.

A. Risk-based regulatory framework

One of the most critical recommendations from this book is that our regulatory authorities need to consider shifting our regulation models from the current compliance-based traditional approach to a risk-based regulatory framework. This emerging framework tends to be focused on understanding how an insurer is managing the risks to which it is exposed. Most of the critical concerns raised in this book relating to financial soundness of our market and to areas of critical deficiencies are connected to precisely this same preoccupation of how risks are actually being handled.

Furthermore, this new approach will also require the regulatory authorities to be appropriately equipped with new types of skills and tools. As part of the new tools that will be required, there would be a need for a comprehensive review of the legal conditions for setting up and running an insurance company. We have noted that items such as minimum capital will need to be defined on a case-by-case basis depending on the risks to be underwritten by the insurer under review. We believe that the current prescribed capital might be inadequate for insurers that are interested in exploring business such as the new high risk area of oil and gas. In order for the regulator to be able to make such types of decisions and apply other proactive methodologies, as will be required in the new risk-based regulatory framework, it will become even more critical for them to have access to actuarial services, as per the recommendation discussed below.

B. Actuarial skills

We have observed that there is a requirement for actuaries in the Insurance Law. Their type of work, if it is of the right quality, can help to assure financial soundness of insurance operators and reliability of financial statements and accounts (Hafeman, 2009: 17). According to the current strategy documents of our insurance regulatory authority, they also want to achieve the same goals of financial soundness of the insurance market (ISSM, 2014: 5). As we have discussed above, actuarial expertise is required to 'interpret' and check the submissions of the insurers. An actuary could also help to develop more informative reports on the market. This requirement for the regulator to also have access to actuarial skills will be even greater in the future with increasing complexity of insurance business and the emerging regulatory models which are not based on a 'one-size-fits-all' type of approach to things such as solvency and capital requirements.

Furthermore, we have noted that there is a scarcity of actuaries worldwide. We believe that there is a need for the authorities and the insurance sector to start promoting the actuarial field of study. We also believe that students in actuarial studies should have access to necessary courses and opportunities for practical application of theory, which is part of the process of becoming a qualified actuary. Furthermore, the development of studies in statistics and actuarial sciences would enable us to have access to resources that are required in order to develop vital missing material such as Mortality Tables, as per the recommendation discussed below.

C. Mortality Tables

We have observed that our market does not have appropriate Mortality Tables. To cover this critical requirement for insurance and pensions business, the market uses an outdated 'national' table from the colonial period which has never been validated in relation to the demography of Mozambique. In other instances, some of the insurers use tables from parts of other countries. There is a need for the regulator and the insurance market to take the initiative of commissioning persons with appropriate skills to develop up-to-date mortality tables for the different regions in Mozambique.

D. Classification of insurance business

Some of the classes of insurance are not classified appropriately. The financial reports of the insurance companies as well as the market reports by the Insurance Regulator are not aligned with the classification in the Insurance Law. There should be a review of the classification of classes of insurance so that there is a consistent approach in the reports of the different key stakeholders in the market. This will also help improve capacity to compile market reports.

E. Codification of compulsory insurance types

We have observed that there are a number of compulsory types of insurance referred to in different pieces of legislation. The Insurance Law does not make reference to most of these types of insurance. In some cases, laws for areas such as security and travel agents define types of insurance contracts for which the market has no underwriting capacity.

There is also a need to develop mechanisms to ensure that the people or entities that are supposed to have such insurance are actually covered. We noted that for types of obligatory insurance such as Motor Liability, many drivers avoid purchasing insurance. There is also evidence that other people deliberately buy fake policies in order to deceive the authorities that do not have any means of verifying genuineness or validity of covers. We believe that the authorities could improve enforcement as well as consider setting up mechanisms that prevent avoidance of insurance. We saw how some of the neighbouring countries have reduced this problem by setting up mechanism such as the fuel levy system in the Southern African Customs Union.

F. Review of Workmen's Compensation Insurance

We believe that this class of insurance business poses a major threat to the insurance market. We have proposed solutions for some of the most critical issues as follows:

- The standard policy issued by the market has unlimited liability for insurers which is contradictory to the fact that the insurers are all limited liability companies. This should be reviewed.

- There is no facility to cover injured workers whose employers might not have arranged insurance or in the event of failure of the insurance market. There should be a public fund to cover victims of work-related accidents that may be exposed without any insurance

- While this class of business is defined as non-life or short term, part of the claims are paid as pensions, which is more related to life and pensions business.

We have also noted that there are a number of African countries that have the same type of problematic exposure. We believe that this is major issue which should be addressed by regional insurance organisations such as OESAI and AIO. We also believe that international organisations such as the ILO, the IFC and the IAIS should be interested in promoting discussions on this issue as well.

G. Handling of long term pension claims

As we have discussed in this book, one of the major challenges of WCA insurance is that although it is defined as Non-Life insurance, part of the claims involve payment of pensions. The authorities should consider shifting the pension claim payments to an appropriate category of insurance business in accordance with the definition of the law itself. Being part of social protection, the ideal vehicle for such pensions could be the already existing National Social Security Fund, as first priority. However, if there are continued concerns about viability or efficiency of this public fund, an option that could be considered is to transfer this pension liability to the new Complementary Private Pensions Funds. Furthermore, the calculation of pension amounts and respective reserves should be subject to an actuarial review.

H. Stamp tax review

We also believe that the Stamp Tax could be improved in order to eliminate some ambiguities and to create a tax regime more aligned with the development preoccupations of the policy-makers. The key items that could be reviewed are as follows:

- There some ambiguities in classification of some of the classes of business. There is a need to update the classification of the different types of insurance

- For some types of insurance, there are different interpretations of applicable tax categories. The insurance regulator should consider providing guidelines to the market

- New products in areas of critical need such as agriculture are falling into an inappropriate high tax category defined as others. There is a need to review the tax categories in alignment with the development plans of the policy-makers

I. Unauthorised Financial Service Providers

As we discussed in this book, there are a number of health insurance providers that have been registered through the Ministry of Health without following the rules of setting up and running of a financial service company. The Ministry of Finance should ensure that all financial service providers are appropriately capitalised and registered and that they are regulated appropriately.

J. Separation of life and non-life

There is a need to establish a level playing field between the oldest three insurance companies that have been allowed to continue operating virtually as composite companies while the new companies are now required to apply for separate licenses for life and non-life. In our view, the policy-makers should review this situation and consider measures to allow all the licenses to follow a consistent set of rules on this question. There are strategic advantages to be derived from operating as one license doing both types of business.

K. Setting up of a local branch by a foreign insurer

We have noted the recent authorisation of a local branch of an insurance company domiciled in Portugal. Although the Insurance Law refers to the option of setting up on this basis, there is a lack of appropriate guidelines on how such a company is supposed to operate in all key aspects of its business. We have noted that this is an arrangement from the colonial period when Mozambique was viewed as a province of Portugal. We believe that it does not contribute to maintaining of a level playing field for all the other insurers that have been fully incorporated in Mozambique. There is a need for the respective legal conditions to be reviewed.

L. Premium Guarantees for Insurance Intermediaries

As we discussed in Chapter 9, our Insurance Law does not make appropriate provisions for Premium Guarantees. We have clarified the difference between Premium Guarantees and Professional Indemnity. Premium Guarantees are intended for protection of premium accounts while Professional Indemnity is intended to provide protection to the buyers of insurance in relation to the professional service. The authorities could consider the following solutions for the question of protection of premium funds:

- The Insurance Regulator and/or the Insurance Association could setup a premium guarantee facility, as has been done by insurance markets in neighbouring markets.

- Bank guarantees are an optional route that the more established intermediaries could be permitted to setup

- Intermediaries that would be unable to access the two facilities outlined above, could consider the option of becoming **Cash Agents**. This means that they would have no right to receive premium. The clients would be required to make direct payments to the insurers.

We would like to state that this issue of premium protection requires urgent attention. Given that most intermediaries have been setup with little or no capitalisation, some of them could be tempted to find creative ways of financing their business in the face of ferocious competition in that sub-sector which is completely overpopulated with too many brief-case type of business entities.

M. Professional Indemnity for Insurance Intermediaries

As we have discussed in this book, there is no clear definition of this type of insurance. It is a vital type of insurance for purposes of protecting the insured customers in the event of inappropriate advice by insurance intermediaries. When intermediaries request for this cover in order to secure registration, some of the insurers are issuing liability covers with clear exclusion of risks that should be covered in this policy. In order to address the issues discussed in this book on this item, we believe that there is a need for the authorities to provide guidelines on:

- An appropriate standard insurance wording based on a correct form of cover for this type of policy with a correct definition of scope of cover

- Appropriate amounts of cover should be set depending on level of exposure to risk of the intermediaries

- Rules regarding qualifications to be an intermediary and changing sequence of procedures for issuing of licenses so that there is appropriate emphasis on licensing of persons that have appropriate qualifications.

N. Financial Advisory Regulation

We acknowledge that the current Insurance Law covers most of the basic legal requirements regarding insurance intermediation. Besides some of the recommended corrections noted above, we would like to also propose that our regulators should consider developing appropriate legislation on financial advisory services. It is a piece of law that covers many other key aspects of insurance intermediation that are not provided for in our current legislation. It would contribute to addressing some of the problems we are already seeing in our market such as abusive practices, improper conduct, hidden transactional costs and lack of professionalism.

O. Improved market report

As we discussed in Chapter 7, there is scope for improvement of our market report. The key areas for improvement are as follows:

- Timely submission by all operators to the regulator of all statutory reports in the recommended format.

- Adoption of a more systematic approach or methodology. We have provided a sample of one of the models that could be considered—the CARAMELS framework. It consists of performance indicators that are essential for the purposes of assessing financial soundness of the market.

- The report could also be actually published so that it can become a formal document of reference in our market. This would also help to raise standards of professionalism in our market.

P. Market agreements

Our insurance market already has an example of an effective market agreement relating to how to handle the obligatory insurance for foreign registered vehicles. The Insurance Association has observed that this type of insurance and other forms of obligatory social insurance which are usually covered by public funds require some form of structured approach (Oliveira, 2013: 10). Besides the area of social protection, the insurance market could also consider other forms of agreements between two or more insurers such as the knock-for-knock agreements.

Q. Dispute resolution mechanisms

There are no readily accessible formal mechanisms for resolution of insurance related disputes. Although the regulatory authorities are the best-positioned entities to handle this problem, the Insurance Association could take the initiative of forming some form of self-regulation mechanism in this area. There are a number of basic models that can be considered consisting of both internal and external mechanisms, as we discussed in this book. It is in the interest of our conflict-ridden sector to setup a mechanism that can allow affordable, fair and equitable resolution of disputes.

R. Guidelines

We have identified a number of key areas where there are gaps in our law. Besides lobbying for required changes and improvement of the legislative environment, the Insurance Association could take the initiative of drafting guidelines. Such market-led initiatives would not have the force of law to support enforcement. However, in our experience of working in this market, we have observed that most of the companies are ready and willing to collaborate in initiatives aimed at the development of the market. The following are some of the areas that could be considered:

i.   Underwriting of all compulsory insurances

ii. Underwriting of problematic classes of insurance such as Fidelity Guarantee.

iii. Intermediation and underwriting of bancassurance and microinsurance business.

In order for you to see some of the guidelines that can be drafted, please have a look at the website of the *Instituto de Seguros de Portugal*[1].

http://www.isp.pt/NR/rdonlyres/95A10CFE-C814-4B73-B0E9-CBBFD3D46B34/0/Guiawebuv.pdf

S. Loss assessing

As we discussed in Chapter 13, there is a lack of skills in the area of loss assessment. The market relies on foreign loss assessors for large or complex claims. Given the lack of appropriate development policies, when foreign assessors come to Mozambique on contracts as and when required, the market misses out on major opportunities for skills transfer. There is no entity lobbying for development of this area. The few local independent loss assessors we have in this market should form an association. Then, they could try to obtain support from regional bodies such as the Institute of Loss Adjusters of Southern Africa (ILASA). The Insurance Regulators or the Insurance Association should arrange basic training courses focusing also on loss assessment. While there have been a few courses in our market on underwriting, the area of loss assessment has been completely neglected.

---

1. As per the website of ISP consulted on 24/04/2014: http://www.isp.pt/NR/rdonlyres/95A10CFE-C814-4B73-B0E9-CBBFD3D46B34/0/Guiawebuv.pdf

T. Training and development

We should develop local courses for training and development of skills in insurance and related areas. We would like to propose the following specific solutions:

- Partnership with entities such as IFBM that are willing to assist whilst we go through the bureaucratic processes of setting up of our own structures, if required

- Development of appropriate local reference material with relevant local content and development of further material besides basic entry level courses

- Linkages with tertiary institutions in order to create space for students with potential to consider the option of doing actuarial sciences and complete appropriate professional courses.

- Encourage the Insurance Regulator to enforce requirement for basic training for people involved directly in insurance intermediation, underwriting and loss assessment

Ultimately, it will be important for our market to form an Insurance Institute of Mozambique and ensure that there is some form of standardisation of the educational material (Oliveira: 2013: 11). At this stage, the insurance market could take advantage of the offer from the local Institute of Bankers (IFBM), to start conducting a basic entry level course in order to cover the most urgent and pressing need for basic orientation at all levels.

U. Development of the Insurance Association

Up to this stage, the Insurance Association has been relying on services of a local legal firm that provides secretarial services of the association. It was a wise decision to take this approach in the first formative years of the association. However, with an increasing range of activities requiring coordination and the growing need for full-time representation of the association, it is advisable for the association to consider setting up a representative office with full-time staff. The association needs to start developing items such as a website with information for the benefit of the public. Furthermore, many of the tasks of self-regulation that we discussed above also require full-time support for the mechanisms that may be setup.

V. Technical committees

The Insurance Association will be able to handle more issues in a more systematic manner than in the past by creating committees involving personnel at different operational levels in the insurance sector. At the time of writing of this book, this had already started through ad hoc committees focused on certain specific tasks. Like other insurance markets in the region, it would be beneficial if the Association could formalise the establishment of permanent technical committees for areas such as the following:

- Fire Committee—for exchange of technical insights and collaboration on critical areas such as fire-fighting and construction standards

- Life Committee—for the development of this critical type of business which has one of the lowest levels of penetration

- Oil and gas risks committee to support training and development of local skills and increase local financial underwriting capacity in order to support the proposed Local Content Development Policy.

W. Formation of other professional associations

In addition to the Insurance Association, there is also a need for other associations and institutions to support development of our insurance market. The other other areas of insurance that should consider setting up associations are Insurance Intermediaries and Loss Assessors.

X. Pooling of risks and skills

As we have discussed in this book, we do not have underwriting pools for the handling of special risks. At the time of writing of this book, the Insurance Association was considering a business idea of creating a political risks pool in Mozambique. Furthermore, the local market could consider joining risk pools of the African continent. We also believe that the African Insurance Organisation and the African Reinsurance Corporation should also consider setting up pools for key development areas such as agricultural sector. In order to make more meaningful progress in projects like that of Weather Index Insurance, we shall need to create new forms of pools. Due to scarcity of skills at the national level, through regional pools, we would also have access to a broader base of skills to support development of such initiatives.

Y. Awareness Campaigns and financial literacy

The Insurance Association and other interested parties could also play a critical role in raising awareness of insurance. It appears that the Insurance Association has already started working on an awareness initiative. This will be a critical achievement for the market. The Insurance Regulator has also started providing information on some of the key insurance types on their website. There is a need for more material to be presented.

Furthermore, we also believe that such awareness campaigns would need to be followed up with more focussed financial literacy training sessions. There is a critical need for this financial literacy starting with the people in insurance and the financial sector. Most of the people working in the sector have not arranged for themselves even the most basic insurance covers. Financial literacy is also a key area that will help to improve levels of appreciation of highly neglected areas such as microinsurance, life insurance and pension funds.

Z. New Literature

We would like to state that from our research on material to include in this book, we noted that since independence in 1975, there have been very few published books on insurance in our market. We are also aware that some people like Fernando Baloi, Omar Karim, Momede Mucusse, Nazir Bhika and Momede Popat have written material on insurance which has not been published. We believe that the insurance association and other supporting entities could play the critical role of sponsoring publications. Some of the insurance markets in our region deliberately promote the activity of research and writing of books or publishing of articles in journals and magazines. We would like to affirm that we believe that there is a need for more publications on insurance and related activities in our market.

Finally, we believe that we also need a new type of literature. We have observed that manuals of some of the insurance institutes in the region need updating to take into account new developments in the insurance sector, as we discussed in this book. Most of the insurance books in our region do not make any reference to key contemporary preoccupations in post-colonial insurance markets and development-related initiatives in the economies where we operate. Many of the manuals remain firmly focused on traditional insurance dogma from the 20th Century when insurance was first introduced to Africa.

REFERENCES

- Hafeman, Michael (2009). *The Role of the Actuary in Insurance*. Primer Series on Insurance, Issue 4, May 2009. Washington: The World Bank.

- ISSM (2014). Strategic Plan for 2014-18, as per their website: http://www.issm.gov.mz/images/Legislacao/pe.pdf

- Oliveira, Rui (2013). *Papel da Associação Moçambicana de Seguradores* in a paper presented at the Insurance Seminar of the ISSM.

BIBLIOGRAPHY

1. ABI (2014). *UK Insurance: Key Facts*. London: Association of British Insurers (ABI)

2. Adepoyigi, Tola (2005). *Oil & gas construction insurance in Nigeria*. Lagos: Peniel Ventures.

3. Aghoghovbia, Ken (2014). African Oil and Energy Pool in the African Insurance Bulletin. Issue no. 0005 of May 2014. Doala: The African Insurance Organisation. Pp. 7-8.

4. Arnold, G., 2005. Africa—A Modern History. London: Atlantic Books.

5. Associação Portuguesa de Seguradores (1997). *Seguros de Vida*. 1ª Edição. Lisboa: Associação Portuguesa de Seguradores

6. Associação Portuguesa de Seguradores (1999). *Seguros de Responsabilidade Civil*. 1ª Edição. Lisboa: Associação Portuguesa de Seguradores

7. Associação Portuguesa de Seguradores (2000). *Seguros de Acidentes Pessoais*. 1ª Edição. Lisboa: Associação Portuguesa de Seguradores

8. Associação Portuguesa de Seguradores (2001). *Seguro Automóvel*. 1ª Edição. Lisboa: Associação Portuguesa de Seguradores

9. Associação Portuguesa de Seguradores (2003). *Seguros de Saúde*. 1º Edição. Lisboa: Associação Portuguesa de Seguradores

10. Assoumana, Hassan (2012). *Industrial Enterprise: Role of Risk Surveys in Loss Prevention* in the African Reinsurer, Vol. 026. Lagos: African Reinsurance Corporation (pages 18-21).

11. Alliance for Financial Inclusion (2013). *Defining and Measuring Financial Inclusion*. In (eds) Thouraya,Triki and Issa Faye. Financial Inclusion in Africa. Tunis: African Development Bank

12. Baloi, F. A actividade seguradora em Moçambique—an unpublished presentation

13. Benjamin, Bernard (1977). *General Insurance*. London: William Heinemann Ltd.

14. Bernstein, P. L. (1996). *Against the gods: the remarkable story of risk*. New York: John Wiley.

15. Bhattad, Mahesh (2012). *Trends in Insurance Channels*. Capgemini

16. Bhikha e Popat, 2010, *O Regime Jurídico dos Seguros*—an unpublished presentation

17. Borsheid, Peter (2013). *Global insurance networks.* James, Harold (ed.). *The value of risk: Swiss Re and the History of Reinsurance.* New York: Oxford University Press. Pp. 23-105.

18. Bruna, Natasha (2013). *Ambiente de negócios e a competitividade da economia moçambicana* in Mosca João; Abbas, Máriam and Bruna, Natasha (eds) Economia de Moçambique 2001-2010. Maputo. Escolar Editora. Pp.141-195.

19. Cadilhe, Carla and Pinto, Mário, Santos (2007). *Do Regime Jurídico do Pagamento dos Prémios de Seguro.* Lisbon: DisLivro

20. Casanova, Manuel, (1964) *Princípios Básicos de Seguros* in Seguros, Série Técnica. No. 106. Sindicatos de Seguros de Lisboa e Porto. Pages 140-152.

21. Chambeze, Isaias (2014) Paper presented at the ISSM Insurance Seminar with title–*Colocação de Seguro no Exterior e Desafios para as Seguradoras Nacionais*

22. Ciecka, James, E. (2008). *Edmond's Life Table and Its uses* in the Journal of Legal Economics. Volume 15, Number 1: pp. 65-74.

23. Das, U.S., Davies, N., and Podpiera, R. (2003). *Insurance and Issues in Financial Soundness.* IMF Working Paper, WP/03/138. Washington: IMF.

24. Davis, Steven. I. (2007). Bancassurance: *The Lessons of Global Experience in Banking and Insurance Collaboration*. London: VRL Knowledge Bank Ltd

25. Cannar, Kenneth (1979). *Motor Insurance Theory and Practice*. London: Witherby & Co. Ltd

26. Carter, Robert, L., Lucas, Leslie, D. and Ralph, Nigel (2000). *Reinsurance*. Reactions Publishing Group in association with Guy Carpenter & Company.

27. Chiejina, Ezekiel, O. (2004). *Foundations of Insurance: Law, Agency and Salesmanship*. Lagos: Mbeyi & Associates Ltd.

28. Christiaensen, Luc; Demery, Lionel and Paternostro, Stefano (2002). *Growth, Distribution and Poverty in Africa: messages from the 1990s*. Washington: The World Bank.

29. Churchill, Craig (2006). *What is insurance for the poor?* In Churchill (ed.). Protecting the poor—A microinsurance compendium. Geneva: International Labour Organisation

30. Crouhy, Michael; Galai, Dan and Mark, Robert (2006). *The Essentials of Risk Management*. New York: McGraw-Hill

31. Das, U.S., Davies, N., and Podpiera, R. (2003). *Insurance and Issues in Financial Soundness: IMF Working Paper*, WP/03/138. Washington: IMF.

32. Escolar Editora (2011) *Código Comercial*. Maputo: Escolar Editora.

33. Ferreira, Monteiro, Rolando (1966). *Como e seguro nasceu*. Seguros: Série Técnica. No. 114, December 1966. Pp. 121-123. Lisboa: Largo do Intendente Pina Manique.

34. FinMark Trust (2009). *FinScope Mozambique 2009*. Cape Town: FinMark Trust

35. Firmino, Luisa; Saturnino, Eduardo; Neves, Alexandre and Chongo, Angelina (2011). *Colectânea de Legislação Sobre Seguros*. Maputo: Centro de Formação Jurídica e Judiciária—Ministério da Justiça

36. Forichi, Lovemore (2014). Insuring resilient agriculture in the African Insurance Bulletin. Issue no. 0005 of May 2014. Doala: The African Insurance Organisation. Pp. 26-28.

37. Francisco, António, A. Da Silva (2002). Evolução da Economia de Moçambique da Colónia à Transição para a Economia de Mercado in Rolim, Cássio; Franco, S. António; Bolnick, Bruce and Andersson, Per-Ake (eds) A Economia Moçambicana

Contemporânea—Ensaios. Maputo: Ministerio do Plano e Finanças. Pages 15-41.

38. FSA (2006). *Treating customers fairly—towards fair outcomes for consumers*. London: The Financial Services Authority

39. Galgut, B. 2008. 'Promoting public confidence in the industry' in Cover, April 2008, Vol. 20, no. 11, Cover Publications: Randburg, pp. 29–30.

40. Garand, Denis and Wipf, John. (2008). 'Risk and financial management' in Churchill, Craig (ed.) Protecting the poor: a microinsurance compendium. Geneva: Internationational Labour Office and the Munich Re Foundation: Munich. Pp. 254-269.

41. Hafeman, Michael (2009). *The Role of the Actuary in Insurance*. Primer Series on Insurance, Issue 4, May 2009. Washington: The World Bank.

42. Hafeman, Michael and Randle, Tony (2009). *On and Offsite Inspections*. Primer Series on Insurance, Issue 13, December 2009. Washington: The World Bank.

43. Holmes, Andrew (2004) *Smart risk*. West Sussex: Capstone Publishing Limited.

44. Holton, Glyn, A. (2004) *Defining Risk*. Financial Analysts Journal, Volume 60, Number 6. CFA Institute.

45. IAIS (2012). Application Paper on Regulation and Supervision supporting Inclusive Insurance Markets. International Association of Insurance Supervisors

46. IISA (2011 A). *Principles of Short Term Insurance.* Insurance Institute of South Africa

47. IISA (2011 B). *Legal Framework of Short Term Insurance.* Insurance Institute of South Africa

48. IISA (2011 C). *Risk and Insurance.* Insurance Institute of South Africa

49. IISA (2011 D). *Introduction to Risk Management.* Insurance Institute of South Africa

50. IISA (2011 E). *Insurance Broking.* Insurance Institute of South Africa

51. IISA (2011 F). *Principles of Life Insurance.* Insurance Institute of South Africa

52. Inspecção Provincial de Crédito e Seguros, 1971, *Relatório Anual.* Maputo: Inspecção Provincial de Crédito e Seguros

53. Instituto de Seguros de Portugal, *Guia de Seguros e Fundos de Pensões.* As per their website consulted on 24/4/2014: http://www.isp.pt/NR/rdonlyres/95A10CFE-C814-4B73-B0E9-CBB-FD3D46B34/0/Guiawebuv.pdf

54. Instituto de Supervisão de Seguros de Moçambique (2012). *O mercado de seguros em Moçambique.* Maputo: ISSM

55. Insurance Institute of South Africa (2011 a). *Risk and Insurance.* Insurance Institute of South Africa.

56. ISSM (2014). Strategic Plan for 2014-18, as per their website (1 March 2015): http://www.issm.gov. mz/images/Legislacao/pe.pdf

57. Irukwu, J.O. (1998). *Insurance Management in Africa.* Lagos: BIMA Publications

58. José, Domingos, António (2013). *Legislação aplicável à actividade seguradora.* As per presentation at the 2nd Insurance Seminar of the ISSM.

59. Kirkham, Sharon. (2008). Going for Broke(r). in Risk SA, February 2008, Vol. 05 Issue 04. Pages 20-24.

60. KPMG (2008). Understanding and articulating risk appetite. Sydney: KPMG

61. KPMG (2005). Risk and Capital Management: A new perspective for insurers. Netherlands: KPMG

62. Kuper, L. 2006. *Ethics—the leadership edge.* Cape Town: Zebra Press

63. Lalá, Anícia and Ostheimer, Andrea, E. (2003) *How to remove the stains on Mozambique's democratic*

track record: Challenges for the democratisation process between 1990 and 2003. Maputo: Konrad-Adenauer-Stiftung

64. Lester, Rodney (2009). *Consumer Protection Insurance.* Primer Series on Insurance, Issue 7, August 2009. Washington: The World Bank.

65. Madge, Peter (1990). *Indemnity and insurance: a guide to the aspects of building contracts.* London: RIBA Publications.

66. McCord, Michael, J. (2008). 'The partner-agent model: Challenges and opportunities' in Churchill, Craig (ed.) Protecting the poor: a microinsurance compendium. Geneva: Internationational Labour Office and the Munich Re Foundation: Munich. Pp. 357-377.

67. Mehr, Robert, I. and Cammack, Emerson (1972). *Principles of Insurance.* 5th Edition. Illinois: Richard D. Irwin, Inc.

68. Meyer, Peter (1997). *Tropical cyclones.* Zurich: Swiss Reinsurance Company.

69. McKinsey & Company (2009). *Global trends in financial inclusion.*

70. Muchena, Israel (2012). *The Mozambican insurance market.* In The African Reinsurer. Lagos: The Afri-

can Reinsurance Corporation. Volume 26. Pages 32-35

71. Muchena, Israel (2013). 'Mozambique case study on distribution and technology in weather index insurance'—unpublished presentation.

72. Mucusse, Momede, Ali (no date available) *Resenha Histórica do Seguro em Moçambique*, article on the website as consulted on 27 March 2015: http://mucusse.no.comunidades.net/index.php?pagina=1731356382

73. Mutenga, S. (2014). *Enhancing Enterprise Risk Management in the African Insurance Industry*. In the African Insurance Bulletin. Issue no. 0005 of May 2014. Doala: The African Insurance Organisation. Pp. 75-77.

74. Oliveira, Rui (2013). *Papel da Associação Moçambicana de Seguradores* in a paper presented at the Insurance Seminar of the ISSM.

75. Plural Editores and KPMG (2009). Código Civil. 3rd Edition.Maputo: Plural Editores

76. Portugal, Luís (2007). *Gestão de Seguros Não-Vida*. Lisboa: Instituto de Formação Actuarial

77. Pratt, K. 2008. 'The evolution of claims' in the **Journal** of the Chartered Insurance Institute: London. February 2008. pp. 43–44.

78. Price, H. 2008. 'The review of insurance contract law' in the Insurance Research and Practice, a research paper insert of the Journal of the Chartered Insurance Institute, London. February 2008. pp. i—viii.

79. Quive, Samuel (2009). *Sistemas formais e informais de protecção social e desenvolvimento em Moçambique.* Maputo: IESE—Instituto de Estudos Sociais e Económicos.

80. Randle, Tony (2009). *Risk based supervision.* Issue 14, December 2009. Washington: The World Bank.

81. RSA Consultores (2013). *Legislação do Sistema Financeiro de Moçambique.* Porto: Vida Económica.

82. Sadler, John (ed.) (2012). The Insurance Manual. West Midlands: Insurance Publishing & Printing Co.

83. Sakr, Gamal (2012). Political risks, riots and civil commotion Insurance: the African Dimension in The African Reinsurer, Vol. 026. Lagos: African Reinsurance Corporation (pp. 5-13)

84. Santos, Monjane, Maria, Otília, (2013). *Mensagems da Presidente do Conselho de Administração* in Insurance Market Report of 2012. ISSM.

85. Schmuck, Hanna (2013). *The Economics of Early Response and Resilience: Mozambique Country Study*

86. Sharp, David (2009). *Upstream and Offshore Energy Insurance*. Livingston: Witherbys Insurance

87. Shillington, K. 2005, History of Africa, 2nd Edition, Palgrave Macmillan: New York.

88. Swiss Re. (2009). Sigma: Scenario analysis in insurance. No. 1/2009. Zurich: Swiss Reinsurance Company Ltd

89. Sigaúke, Abílio, Feliciano (2013). *Evolução histórica e papel da entidade de supervisão de seguros em Moçambique*. Paper presented at the Insurance Seminar of the ISSM.

90. Silva, Carlos, Pereira (2000). *Da economia e da gestão nas empresas de seguros*. Porto: Vida Económica (Grupo Editorial Peixoto de Sousa.

91. Silva, Rafael, Rodriguês (1963). *Os seguros: elementos de estudos*. Lisboa: Livraria Petrony

92. Swiss Re (1999). From risk to capital: An insurance perspective. Zurich: Swiss Reinsurance Company Ltd.

93. Swiss Re (2007). *Bancassurance: emerging Trends, Opportunities and Challenges*, Sigma No. 5/2007. Zurich: Swiss Reinsurance Company Ltd.

94. Tadaro, M. P., & Smith, S.C. (2003). *Economic Development*. Essex: Pearson Addison Wesley.

95. Terblanche, Stefan (2010). The insurance loss adjuster: a value-adding professional… at a cost in Cover. Cape Town: Cover Publications. October 2010. Pages 76-77.

96. Valsamakis, Anthony, C.; Vivian, Robert, W. and du Toit, Gawie, S. (2010) *Risk management*. 4th edition. Sandton: Heinemann Publishers (Pty) Ltd

97. Vaughan, Emmet, J. (1992) *Fundamentals of risk and insurance*. 6th Edition. New York: John Wiley & Sons Inc.

98. Vivian, Robert, W. and Morgan, Jim (2001). *Morgan's History of the Insurance Institute Movement in South Africa*. Cape Town: Francolin Publishers.

99. Waty, Teodoro, A. (2007). *Direito de Seguros*. Maputo: W&W Editora Lda

100. Young, Jackie (2006). *Operational Risk Management*. Pretoria: Van Schaik Publishers.

INDEX

Appendix I List of Insurance Companies
as at 31 December 2014

	COMPANY	COM-POSITE	NON-LIFE	LIFE
1	Empresa Moçambicana de Seguros, S.A.	✓	✓	✓
2	Global Alliance–Seguros, S.A.	✓	✓	✓
3	Seguradora Internacional de Moçambique, S.A.	✓	✓	✓
4	Moçambique Companhia de Seguros, S.A.		✓	
5	Hollard Moçambique Companhia de Seguros, S.A.		✓	
6	Hollard Vida Companhia de Seguros, S.A.			✓
7	Companhia de Seguros da África Austral, SA		✓	
8	Real Companhia de Seguros, S.A.		✓	
9	Companhia de Seguros Indico, S.A.		✓	
10	Nico Vida–Moçambique de Seguros, S.A.			✓
11	Tranquilidade Moçambique Companhia de Seguros, S.A.		✓	
12	Tranquilidade Moçambique Companhia de Seguros, S.A.			✓
13	Diamond Companhia de Seguros, S.A.		✓	
14	Phoenix Companhia de Seguros de Moçambique, SA		✓	

15	Fidelidade Vida Compan-hia de Seguros S.A.			✓
16	Fidelidade Compan-hia de Seguros, S.A.		✓	
	TOTAL	3	11	7

Appendix II–Insurance penetration in 2013

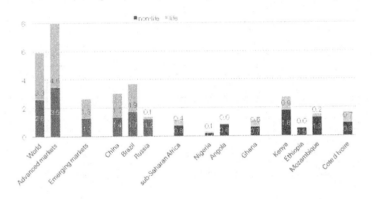

Appendix III–Flooding Risk per District (Source: INGC)

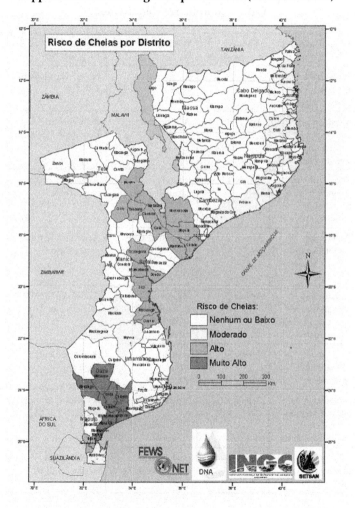

Appendix IV–Applications, Submissions and Other Compliance Requirements

What is required?	Where is it prescribed?	Who should do it?	How should it be done?
Application for new classes or types of insurance	Article 3	All operators	No specific guidelines
Monitor and report on Money Laundering activities detected	Article 6	All operators	Refer to Anti-Money Laundering Legislation
Application to open foreign branches or representation	Article 13	Insurers	As defined in the same article
Application for setting up of branches in Mozambique	Article 17	Foreign insurers	As defined in the same article
Registration of members of statutory governance structures	Article 29	Insurers, Reinsurers & Microinsurers	As defined in the same articles
Registration of shareholder agreements	Article 30	Insurers	As defined in the same article
Submission of audited financial accounts with statutory reserves	Article 52	Insurers	As defined in articles 32 to 51
Maintain adequate solvency all the time	Articles 53 & 54	Insurers & microinsurers	As defined in articles 55 to 60.

Clearance of policy wordings	Article 86	Insurers	As defined in the same article
Submission of any other information	Article 131	All operators	As may be required by the ISSM
Submission of monthly accounts of taxes	Article 132	All operators	As per model from ISSM
Publication in the press of audited and approved annual financial accounts	Article 145	Insurers	As defined in the Article

Appendix V: Solvency Margin for Non-life Insurers in Zimbabwe (Source: 2013 Second Quarter Report on Short Term Insurance by the Insurance and Pensions Commission, Zimbabwe)

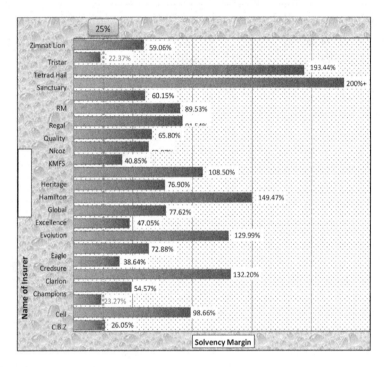

Appendix VI—Classes of Non-Life Insurance

	REPORTING GROUPS	COVERED CLASSES		REPORTING GROUPS	COVERED CLASSES
1	Health, Personal Accident & Travel	Personal Accident Group Personal Accident Health Hospital Cash Travel	8	Workman's Compensation Act (WCA) Insurance	Workman's Compensation Act (WCA) Insurance
2	Motor	Motor Own Damage Motor Liability including Road Traffic Act (RTA) Insurance	9	Rail	Rail rolling stock Rail Liability
3	Marine	Marine Cargo GIT Marine Hull Marine Liability	10	Aviation	Aviation Hull Aviation Liability
4	Liability	General Liability Professional Indemnity Other Liabilities	11	Bonds & Guarantees	Bonds Guarantees Trade Credit Bankers Blanket Bond (BBB)

5	Property	Fire Business Interruption Office Houseowners Householders	12	Engineering	Contractors All Risks (CAR) Erection All Risks (EAR) Contractors Plant Machinery Break- down (MBD
6	Liability	General Liability Professional Indemnity Other Liabilities	13	Miscellaneous & Assistance	Accidental Damage Burglary Fidelity Guarantee All Risks Legal Assistance
7	Agriculture	Crop Insurance Livestock Insurance			

Appendix VII—List of Licensed Insurance Brokers as at 31 December 2014

No.	NAME OF LICENSED INSURANCE BROKERS	No.	NAME OF LICENSED INSURANCE BROKERS
1	À Caminho do Paraíso Corretores de Seguros, Lda	24	Maleseguros Corretores de Seguros, Lda
2	Accent Corretora de Seguros, Lda	25	Mocambique Corretores de Seguros, Lda
3	Alianca Corretores de Seguros, S.A.	26	Mseguros Corretores de Seguros, Lda
4	Amani Corretores de Seguros, Lda	27	Multiseguros Corretores de Seguros, S.A
5	AON Moçambique Corretores de Seguros, Lda	28	Mundial Corretores E Consultores de Seguros, Lda
6	ARIS Corretores de Seguros, Lda	29	Nacional Brokers Corretores de Seguros, Lda
7	CARE–Corretor de Seguros, S.A	30	Optimus Mediadores de Seguros, Lda
8	ComCapital Mocambique-Corretor de Seguros, Sociedade Unipessoal	31	Poliseguros Corretores de Seguros, Lda
9	Concorse Consultoria e Corretagem de Seguros, S.A	32	Prima Corretora de Seguros, Lda
10	Confiança Corretora de Seguros, Lda	33	Proxen Corretores de Seguros, Lda
11	CTS–Corretagem Tecnica de Seguros, Lda	34	Quispos Corretores de Seguros, Lda
12	Cullen Corretora de Seguros, Lda	35	Real Risk Moçambique Corretores de Seguros, Lda
13	Fides Corretores de Seguros, Lda	36	Sabseg Mocambique Corretores de Seguros, Lda
14	Getcor–Corretores e Gestores de Seguros, Lda	37	Sandzaia Corretores de Seguros, Lda

15	GSG–Consultores e Cor-retores de Seguros, Lda	38	SCJ Corretores de Seguros, Lda
16	Hubertus Clasius–Cor-retores de Seguros, Lda	39	Shield Corretores de Seguros, Lda
17	Icon Corretores de Seguros, Lda	40	Skyddo,Corretores de Seguros, Lda
18	Interseguros–Corretores E Consultores De Seguros, Lda	41	South East Brokers Corretoras de Seguros, Lda
19	JS Corretor de Seguros, Lda	42	Tranquilidade Corretores de Seguros, Lda
20	Kican Corretores de Seguros, S.A.	43	Uniseguros Corretores d Consultores de Seguros
21	Liazi Corretores e Consultores de Seguros, Lda	44	Visão Corretores de Seguros
22	Limpopo Brokers Corretores e Consultores de Seguros, Lda	45	Yingwe Insurance Corretores de Seguros, S.A.
23	MAC Corretores e Consultores de Seguros, Lda		

Appendix VIII–Comparison of Standard Motor Insurance Covers

DESCRIPTION	TYPES OF MOTOR INSURANCE COVERS			
	THIRD PARTY ONLY (30 DAYS COVER)	THIRD PARTY ONLY (ANNUAL COVER)	THIRD PARTY FIRE & THEFT	COMPRE-HENSIVE COVER
Registration of Insurable vehicle	Foreign entering Mozambique	Locally registered vehicles but insurers can consider covering foreign registered vehicles on this basis		
Standard Period of Cover	30-day Cover	Annual	Annual	Annual
Third Party Property Damage	✓	✓	✓	✓
Third Party Bodily Injury	✓	✓	✓	✓
Cover for fire damage to your vehicle or theft of your vehicle	n.a.	n.a.	✓	✓
Own Damage	n.a.	n.a.	n.a.	✓
Windscreen damage	n.a.	n.a.	n.a.	✓
Towing, Emergency Repairs, Replacement of Keys	n.a.	n.a.	n.a.	✓
Medical Expenses	n.a.	n.a.	n.a.	✓

Legal liability cover when using a substitute vehicle	n.a.	n.a.	n.a.	✓
Car hire	n.a.	n.a.	n.a.	Optional
Motor Occupants Personal Accident	n.a.	Optional	Optional	Optional
Legal Assistance	Optional	Optional	Optional	Optional
Area of coverage	Mozambique only	Mozambique with option to cover neighbouring countries		

Appendix IX–The 10 largest insured claims worldwide from 1970 to 2013 (2013 $ millions)

Rank	Date	Country	Event	Insured loss
1	Aug. 25, 2005	U.S., Gulf of Mexico, Bahamas, North Atlantic	Hurricane Katrina, storm surge, levee failure, damage to oil rigs	$80,373
2	Mar. 11, 2011	Japan	Earthquake (Mw 9.0) triggers tsunami, aftershocks	37,665
3	Oct. 24, 2012	U.S., et al.	Hurricane Sandy, storm surge	36,890
4	Aug. 23, 1992	U.S., Bahamas	Hurricane Andrew, floods	27,594
5	Sep. 11, 2001	U.S.	Terror attacks on WTC, Pentagon and other buildings	25,664
6	Jan. 17, 1994	U.S.	Northridge earthquake (M 6.6)	22,857
7	Sep. 6, 2008	U.S., Caribbean: Gulf of Mexico, et al.	Hurricane Ike, floods, offshore damage	22,751
8	Sep. 2, 2004	U.S., Caribbean; Barbados, et al.	Hurricane Ivan, damage to oil rigs	17,218
9	Jul. 27, 2011	Thailand	Floods caused by heavy monsoon rains	16,519
10	Feb. 22, 2011	New Zealand	Earthquake (Mw 6.3), aftershocks	16,142

Source: Swiss Re, *sigma*, No. 1/2014.

CPSIA information can be obtained
at www.ICGtesting.com
Printed in the USA
FSOW03n0434300816
24342FS